80

A Memoir

Women in the Chelsea
Arts Centr oct. 1988

Pauline Bewick

80

A Memoir

ARLEN
HOUSE

80: A Memoir

is published in 2015 by
ARLEN HOUSE
42 Grange Abbey Road
Baldoyle
Dublin 13
Ireland
Phone/Fax: 353 86 8207617
Email: arlenhouse@gmail.com
arlenhouse.blogspot.com

Distributed internationally by
SYRACUSE UNIVERSITY PRESS
621 Skytop Road, Suite 110
Syracuse, NY 13244–5290
Phone: 315–443–5534/Fax: 315–443–5545
Email: supress@syr.edu

978–1–85132–191–9, paperback
978–1–85132–199–5, limited edition hardback

Typesetting by Arlen House
Printed lithographically in Ireland
Cover image: 'Spirit' by Veronica Nicholson

80: a memoir has received
financial assistance from the Arts
Council under the Publications/
Title by Title Scheme

CONTENTS

'Strange, Pauline's mother didn't want her to be educated … I suppose she wanted a real person'

Adam Mulvihill, age 12
Pauline's grandson

1

ALICE/'HARRY'

LADYS VIEW chapter –

The path through the cornfield revealed a tall, fair-haired young man.

'Are there any houses for sale around here?' he asked Alice, who was holding Hazel's hand, her first-born, aged five.

Alice knew immediately that something unusual was about to happen.

'Yes, there *is* a house. It's opposite ours'.

First they went into Alice's kitchen and, while Hazel slept, she made him a cup of tea.

'Before we finished the tea, we were embracing'.

Subsequently I found out that my mother was thirty and he was nineteen. The attraction was so strong that they made love there and then on the kitchen floor. According to my mother that is how I was conceived. I was born on 4 September 1935.

I was a teenager when I found this out. There on my mother's typewriter I read, 'I was a rose in bud with my first child Hazel, and with my second child Pauline a rose in full bloom'. She then went on to tell the story of this nineteen-year-old man called Gerald Massey Taylor.

'So my father is not my father after all?' I asked.

'No', my mother said.

'Why didn't you tell me before?'

'Because it is not important', she said, in her sing-song Geordie accent.

I had to take that short answer and not ask any more. Though my mother was a liberal, free-thinking woman, she also had an unspoken, firm strictness. I suppose we all think our mothers have a strictness about them. However, as life went on, I came to believe that Corbett Bewick was really my father.

Alice was born the youngest of a family of eight. Her eyes and hair were brown, she had a tanned, sturdy body and a lively, jokey manner; she was the pet of all her siblings. Her father was an electrical engineer and her mother a mild biddable woman who died quite young. Her father then married again, a woman who was the same age as his eldest daughter, 'and what an idiot that stepmother was'. One day she washed a feather mattress, opening up all the feathers and spreading them on the lawn to dry. When they dried, the feathers flew up into the sky all over the place and into the neighbours' gardens.

My mother was christened Alice May Graham, later to be nicknamed 'Harry'. Her sisters were especially protective of her, particularly from their strict, bossy father who would not dream of allowing Alice, at the age of 17, to go to dances full of the local Tyneside coal miners. However, Alice would sneak out and stay out till all hours knowing her sisters would cover for her.

Still in her teens, Alice met John Corbett Bewick, the manager of the family-owned Mickley Bank Colliery along with an attached pub. Corbett fell in love with Alice despite the fact that she was a born rebel. Alice was annoyed that the coalminers' pay packets went straight back into the Bewick family's pockets through this pub. Eventually Corbett won Alice over, like a lot of us females when persistently pursued. The Bewicks were Vikings from Bevic, Norway who settled in Newcastle. The famous naturalist and wood engraver Thomas Bewick was Corbett's great, great, great uncle.

Alice rarely talked of the past. However, she would tell how she enjoyed Corbett's stories of the miners, such as the miner whose toe was almost cut off as he hacked the coalface. While soaking his dangling toe under a cold tap, he simply commented, 'the bugger's hot!' and about the miner who went back for something he had forgotten in his home and found his wife in bed with another man. 'So what did you do?' Corbett asked. 'I slammed the door', the miner proudly said. Occasionally snippets of her life with Corbett slipped out like 'I once went out with another man and Corbett embarrassed me by sending a bunch of red roses to our table. My God when I think back how he dominated me'.

In a sepia photograph from 1928 I see Alice in her wedding dress, cut in the Charleston style, a white hat kept close to her head with a satin band, Corbett standing beside her; balding, self-assured and the spitting image of red-haired Hazel who was to be born to them in 1929.

Alice's sister Minnie said that Alice first denied that she was pregnant with Hazel. One day Minnie saw her holding a rope from the back of Corbett's car and running for all her might along a country road. Minnie guessed she was trying to abort her baby.

Alice must have started to loathe Corbett quite quickly in the marriage because of the venomous way she spat out, 'his mother adored him and knew bloody well he was an alcoholic, his mother even commissioned a taxi firm to pick him up after his drinking bouts'. His mother also sent taxis with hot meals that she had cooked especially for her Corbett. It drove Alice mad. Alice and Corbett owned a beautiful house called 'Bat Cottage' outside Dilston village. All I remember of that place is one day Alice discovered Hazel and me in the garage as I stood naked being painted Kelly Green by Hazel. Alice rubbed me with linseed oil and raced me in to soap off the dangerous oil-based paint.

Corbett's drunkenness finally got too much for Alice. She decided to run away in the middle of the night, taking Hazel and me and a minimum amount of things, bundling us into a taxi to go to the train station. We arrived at Letchworth Garden City in the daylight. Our mother left us in a park, paddling in a shallow cement pool. 'I am going to leave you here a minute while I go and find us a place to stay'.

I don't remember feeling insecure or upset at our situation. Perhaps my sister (who is no longer with us), would have been able to tell her feelings of the runaway. She was seven years old, I was two and a half.

'Come on, Hazel and Pauline, I have found somewhere', our mother's lovely familiar voice rang out.

A cream-coloured building comes to mind, two steps up, the front door opened and we were welcomed by the owner of the hotel, Mrs Pat Newling, nee O'Shea.

'I was going to turn ye away as the hotel is not finished', she said, 'But sure wouldn't that bring me bad luck'.

In the evening, after we were fed and tucked into bed, my mother went down to the kitchen where she and Pat

Newling sat beside the Aga cooker and laughed and talked together till the late hours.

During our short stay in that Letchworth hotel Alice accidentally broke a large dish.

'You are just like Harry, our gardener', Pat said. 'He is always breaking things. I think I will call you Harry'.

From then onwards Alice was 'Mummy Harry', later to become just 'Harry' for the rest of our lives. Alice had run away not only from her background, but from her name.

Pat Newling was from County Kerry in Ireland. She had married Jack, an Englishman. It transpired that Lucy and Michael, her niece and nephew, were living with their uncle Buttons, a postman, in a deep and beautiful valley called Gleninchaquin in Kerry. Lucy and Michael's mother and father had recently died of a disease that was rampant at the time, tuberculosis. As Buttons had to deliver post throughout the countryside, he was not there all of the time for Michael, aged seven, and Lucy aged eight. Pat Newling suggested to my mother, who was now totally footloose, that she go to Ireland and foster these two children. Alice impulsively said yes immediately, so Pat got the tickets for the boat for Ireland.

In no time we were on our way. Pat Newling came with us. Harry had no idea how mountainous Ireland was, her perception was that everything would be flat bog. By the time we got off the train in Killarney and heard the song 'Heaven Reflects Killarney', she had fallen deeply in love with Ireland.

The journey from Killarney to Kenmare was in a cab. We climbed the twisty road up the mountain, passed Ladies View which Queen Victoria had once admired. On the right we looked down into the deep Black Valley, up then to Moll's Gap, turning left through a cut in the mountains to descend through farmland to Kenmare, comfortably nested in a sunny valley.

The cabbie waited for us while we went into the Lansdowne Hotel situated at the top of Kenmare town and sat in the dining room for our lunch. The waitress was puzzled when my mother said, 'I don't eat meat, give me anything raw'. She obliged, bringing a tray full of large raw vegetables, a carrot, a parsnip, half a cabbage, a chunk of turnip and a large grater. 'This is exactly what I love', my mother said and proceeded to grate her lunch.

Hazel and I had been given little books to draw in for the journey. Mine was small and wire bound with a green cover. I first drew the waitress and then the beautiful bride who we passed on the steps of the local church. Looking back I realise that from that early age I was putting down on paper the impact and the romance that the waitress and the bride had on me, and since then throughout my life everything, good and bad, has gone down on paper, to suss out and understand the world.

After lunch Pat directed our cab driver over the Kenmare Suspension Bridge, turning westwards along the Beara Peninsula on the tarred road, the sea to our right and mountains to our left, until we came to a road leading up to the valley of Gleninchaquin and to a remote cottage.

The children's uncle, Buttons, stood as tall as a giant in the doorway with his navy blue postman's coat, a double row of shiny silver buttons travelling down his front to his feet. Lucy and Michael, on either side of him looked as fearful as little trapped mice, all waiting for the unknown woman 'from over'.

Pat Newling and her big bulldozer breasts moved forward with confidence towards Buttons.

'This is the woman over from England who is going to mind the children. She is a good woman and ye will be good for her, won't ye?' she said to Lucy and Michael, who stood silently until Buttons made them nod.

'We will', they said together.

Hazel and I stood behind Harry, staring at the two new children that we were about to share our lives with. I think I felt sorry for them; I certainly got an aura of terrible wrenching and fear emanating from them. Even Buttons looked fearful. The only one who was confident was Pat. The children were ushered into the cab which took us the back road to Pat Newling's two-storey farmhouse in Killaha East that was to be ours to live in, in return for fostering the two children.

In 1938, soon after our arrival, Harry received a telegram from England announcing that Corbett Bewick had died. I cannot remember any drama, or who looked after us while she went to the funeral in Northumbria. When she came back, all she told us was that his coffin was put onto a rowing boat to cross the river from Mickley to the graveyard, a Bewick burial tradition, and that she had rented out Bat Cottage, their marriage home, to a couple from Lever Brothers, makers of Persil Soap, for two pounds per week, which provided a living for many years.

2

KERRY CHILDHOOD

Pat Newling's house had a kitchen and sitting room downstairs and two bedrooms upstairs. Its windows looked out on a Cordyline tree, a monkey puzzle tree, down a grassy hill, over hazelnut trees, to the pebbly Kenmare Bay and across the sea inlets to The Paps, two mountains shaped like breasts.

Harry immediately made the gaunt house warm and homely, lighting a big fire from the neatly-stacked pile of turf under the stairs. A butter barrel stood by the open fire.

'That's your bath tub', said Pat.

Later, when the cab had taken Pat off to Kenmare, Harry heated water in a big black kettle that she hung on a hook over the fire. She then half-filled the barrel with the warm water and we jumped in one after the other to have our baths. It was great fun, especially when Harry put the lid on turning it into a dark steam bath. She vigorously rubbed us dry with what seemed like sandpapery towels, then she dressed us in new striped pyjamas and off we went upstairs to our beds. Lucy and Michael never said a word. I could not sleep; it was too exciting to have these two new people in beds beside us. The next morning Hazel pulled the sleeve of Lucy's pyjamas and said 'caught!' and she timidly said 'tig', and so a game of caught-and-tig started between the four of us until we were laughing and shouting. The ice was broken.

To the left of the house was a path that led to hay fields and a patch that my mother would turn into a vegetable garden. There was a stream that bubbled in and out of smooth brown stones. Michael was an expert at tickling trout from under the stones; that stream was our drinking water, bath and washing machine. Often a sock or a pair of pants got pulled from our hands by the rushing waters and later we would find them encrusted with sea shells down on the beach.

The stones on the beach had been worn by the waves into many interesting shapes. We loved to collect what we called 'dog heads', 'houses' and 'motor cars', taking them home to paint. We painted collars on the 'dog' stones, windows on the 'house' stones and wheels on the 'car' stones. They made good gifts at Christmas for our neighbours.

One day Harry stubbed her big toe on a beach stone. Her nail went dark blue and became swollen and poisonous. She became so weak she had to go to bed. Delirious, she clearly saw a leprechaun sitting on her knees. He was dressed in green with a pointed green hat and he was hammering tacks into a shoe. He paused and looked sternly at her and said, 'eat today, and you will be better tomorrow'. She took his advice and immediately felt worse.

On another occasion we were surprised to see two white naked men appear out of the sea. They sat on a rock in the sun to dry off and after a while they dressed themselves in their black suits and white priest collars.

Harry started to acquire various animals and fowl, the first being two donkeys, Patta and Mara. There was no holding the donkeys; they constantly got out onto the roads and wandered for miles. John Gaines, a young friend of Pat Newling, did odd jobs for us. Many times John brought back the wandering donkeys, and it was John who brought us Lassie, a sheep dog. Lassie developed alarming fits. One day, during one of these fits, she was violently frothing at the mouth and yelping so John grabbed her by the neck and held her head under the stream water. Harry thought he was trying to drown Lassie and with all her strength she pulled at his strong arms to release the dog. After that, Lassie lay breathless on the stream's bank, recovering.

On Kenmare fair day we bought ten hens that refused to go into the hen house; they perched up a whitethorn tree each night and laid their eggs in random places, under hedges in bunches of reeds and way off into Mrs Keogh's fields. Mrs Keogh was very puzzled one day to see Harry completely covered in a green oilskin mac. She was pretending to be a rock, stalking after a hen. It paid off because she found that the hen was sitting on a nest of 25 eggs, all hidden in a clump of green reeds.

Next to Mrs Keogh lived a bachelor called Jim Gloss. One day in 1939 Jim was clearing large rocks from the centre of his field and there underneath he found a treasure hoard of bronze axeheads, as well as a small beautiful gold frog with brown onyx eyes. Many years later I took this frog to the National Museum of Ireland who said that while the axes were 2000 BC, the frog had no stamp and was not datable, but it was sophisticated. Later I was told by a museum curator that this frog was from Peru. How amazing to think of a Peruvian frog lying under stones in the mountains of Kerry. Jim got two hundred pounds for the axes and he gave my mother the gold frog. I now wear it almost everyday, hanging from a gold chain.

We got two black shiny Kerry cows with white horns, and a strong black Dexter bull. The bull was driven mad when one of the cows was ready to mate but the poor bull's legs were too short for him to mount the big cow. So Harry and John placed him on the high path around the dung heap in order for him to mount the cow. Unfortunately the bull's over-anxious speed made him fall head first into the dung heap covering his beautiful black face in old cow dung.

One day to our delight, John brought us a cat; we there and then named him Big Cat. He was heavy, independent, dignified and black. One morning he came back with his paw mangled from a rabbit trap. He smelt of rotting flesh. When he died a few days later we buried him with a huge flat rock headstone, writing on the stone in green paint, 'Big Cat Lies Here', and planted wild flowers around the grave.

Squawker was a thin, unhappy ginger tabby cat who ran around outside the house, endlessly squawking, looking through the window pane, opening wide his pink pointy-toothed mouth and staring into our eyes in the hope of being let indoors. But Harry wasn't giving into this poor stray. I cannot remember what happened to him.

We owned a radio which ran on two glass bottle batteries filled with acid that looked just like water; these were attached at the back of the radio. I was instructed by Harry never, ever, to lick the batteries. 'Don't lick the batteries, don't lick the batteries', echoed in my mind until one day I could no longer resist. I crept behind the large brown radio and slowly licked one of the batteries from the bottom to the top. Soon, to my amazement, my tongue started to sizzle with the acid. I ran terrified to my sister Hazel with my sizzling tongue sticking out, screaming, 'I've licked the batteries!' Hazel grabbed my hand and raced me down the hill to Harry, shouting 'Pauline's licked the batteries! Pauline's licked the batteries!' 'What? You licked the batteries!' Harry shouted. I was then wrenched on either side by Hazel and Harry back up the hill where Harry poured diluted vinegar on my tongue.

Harry used to read aloud books from the library. I absolutely loved the smell of these books and the blue date stamp on the first page was like an exciting announcement of a new adventure; my favourite being *Alice in Wonderland*. To this day I appreciate the significance of some of the philosophical thoughts Lewis Carroll wrote. She also read from the *Irish Independent* newspaper, 'Curly Wee and Gussie Goose' by Maud Budden which was illustrated by Roland Clibborn. Another book she read from that had a philosophical undercurrent was *Winnie-the-Pooh* by A.A. Milne.

A man was standing at our door. He was a political canvasser looking for Harry's vote.

'I haven't got one and I don't need one. I don't want to get to the other side', she said, to which he asked, 'which side are you on?'

This conversation lasted for some time before they both realised they were caught up in a misunderstanding. Harry thought he was talking about a boat, not a vote.

One day when I came home from school, Harry said 'look what I found!' She was holding one of those large matchboxes. She slid the box open and there I saw a stinkhorn fungus lying on a bed of cotton wool with red ink spattered on it. She said it was a German's willy that had fallen from a plane – this was my only connection with the Second World War.

School for Hazel, Lucy and Michael was in Kenmare. For me it was two miles west in the other direction, to Douris. To this day I prefer to be barefoot, due to the fact that this was the way we all went to school, whatever the weather. The sensation of walking through squishy mud or warm cow dung and then to feel the water washing your feet and see the mud or dung carried down the rippling stream, the different textures of frosty grass or gravel underfoot. We would have competitions as to how hard we could stamp on furze bushes and the like. Our feet had developed their own soles and would heat up like radiators after the frost water and mud.

The first house on the way to Douris school was Healy's. Mrs Healy wore long, sun-faded black skirts. Sometimes I would hear a loud swooshing sound and it would be Mrs Healy standing upright, having a pee. She simply opened her legs and peed without even lifting her skirt. Her black shawl was always pinned around her. Her straight shiny brown hair had never been cut, and was held in a classical bun on the back of her head. She was a loving woman to us children and had two grown-up sons, Paddy and John. Her affection and wit enveloped us. We often had a cup of tea and a slice of cake and she would tell us, 'the boys are up the mountains with their guns, firing farts and shooting shits'.

One day on my way to school I ran into the Healy's yard to witness a cow being killed. First they hit the black cow between her white horns with a heavy hammer; she thudded to the ground, jerked her legs and died a few minutes later. Steam rose from the stripping of her black skin, revealing pale pink. I watched as the knife ripped and squelched. The vividness of this death is clear to me to this day.

The next house along the back road was Downey's. They had a two-year-old baby boy who loved to dance, bending his fat little legs up and down to the rhythm of the milk separator. They were a big family of seven, two of whom joined me on the road for Douris school. Then we would meet a red-headed boy called Quinn; he was from a farm on the top of the hill that descended down to the school. He told us wild stories of how he once put a cork up a cow's backside and how the cow shot it out with a great burst. I remember he was a bully. I never got to know his family. Beside the school was a little grey church set in amongst dark pine trees. Even though Harry brought us up with no religion, the ritual that I made up for my friends was ridiculous. I felt it would be bad luck if we just walked by the church so I would instruct them, 'if the church door is open, we have to get down on our knees and cross ourselves 20 times, and if it is closed we have to go around in a circle reciting, "Hail Mary, full of Grace, the Lord is with thee", six times', and after this ritual I would allow us all to move on to the tall wooden doors of Douris school. It had just two rooms and two teachers.

I remember my teacher Miss Murphy saying 'since you have no religion, Pauline, would you like to stay with us while we do prayers, or would you like to go out into the playground?' I thought carefully, and decided on the playground, in order to build a shop for them all. My shop was on top of the wall between the pine trees and the school. I laid down rows of little pebbles as sweets, pine cones for baked potatoes and dried horse dung for buns. When religious class was over the doors burst open and they all rushed to my shop.

'How much are yer buns?'

'A pingin', I would say.

Miss Murphy would be one of my first customers; she would go away laughing with her purchase of horse dung buns.

When it was my turn to come up to the blackboard, Miss Murphy said, 'can you draw the class a picture of a bird?' She knew that spelling was difficult for me. The whole class, including my desk mate, really enjoyed my bird picture. Apart from my mother, this was my first taste of positive attention for producing a picture. A ruler was used to slap our hands. I cannot remember what for and it did not instil any fear into me. Laughter, punishment, games and lessons all seemed a natural process.

As I was soon old enough, Harry sent me with Hazel, Lucy and Michael to the convent school in Kenmare. We would all walk along the road through the dark wood where amongst the trees lived a man and woman that people called the spies. No one knew where these people came from. On one occasion, when we knew they were away, Michael and Hazel entered their kitchen. For some reason, Michael looked up their chimney and found a sock full of money. This scared them both, and placing it back they quickly ran out again. Then we had to hold our noses as we passed by the dead white horse lying rotting down by the sea.

Being smaller, I was constantly shouting, 'wait for me, wait for me'. When we got to the Suspension Bridge, the three of them would climb up and over the two-foot wide arches of this bridge with a sheer drop into the sea below. We would do a detour to the pier to look at the boats, then up Bell Height hill, down through the town and finally arrive at the convent where the nuns, looking like magpies in their black and white habits, welcomed us at the convent doors.

That first day at the convent must have scared me when the nun announced to the twenty children in the class, 'this is the new girl, Pauline'. I felt a warm trickle travelling down my legs. I was peeing myself. The pool on the shiny convent floor got bigger and bigger.

'Ah, you're a good girl, Pauline. Kitty, go and get the mop', the nun said.

As my pool was mopped up from the floor I was ushered to sit beside a little girl called Josie, so I sat there in my wet knickers until the class was over. Hazel and the others picked me up at lunchtime. We threw the vegetarian sandwiches that Harry had made for us over the wall and ran to a house where Lucy and Michael's relatives lived. They felt that being vegetarian deprived us of a healthy diet of meat so they filled us up with chunks of ham, sausages and bacon. It took a while for Harry to discover this.

Again, I enjoyed the local religious ritual of the Patterns, where young and old would circle around and around the holy statues and grottos, genuflecting, making the Sign of the Cross, and fingering their rosary beads. I would imitate their every move.

Some evenings we'd walk the five miles from Killaha into Kenmare in search of entertainment which was quite varied – the circus, plays on the Carnegie Library stage or the local cinema. Films on the menu were everything from the Marx Brothers, to Alan Ladd and the gorgeous Veronica Lake, melodramas with Bette Davis, the Pathé News and the latest Mickey Mouse and Donald Duck cartoons.

The cinema was near Arthur's sawmills. When it rained there were a few leaks from the roof which would come dripping down onto our laps as we watched the terrifying black-and-white *King Kong*, with his captured female in his black hairy hand. On one occasion during the film a man behind us shouted, 'there's a fierce smell of early York', as somebody had farted.

When Duffy's Circus came to town it inspired us to paint many pictures on the little wooden off-cut boards that Harry was given from Arthur's sawmills. We painted the piebald ponies, the little dogs that walked upright on their back legs and the trapeze artists. The day after the circus, in Mrs Arthur's shop Harry overheard a woman commenting, 'sure, wasn't there only an inch between herself and decency', referring to the beautiful trapeze artist.

On the Carnegie stage we would see deep dramatic plays such as *Oedipus Rex*, performed by Anew McMaster. Goggle-eyed, we children watched the actor pacing the stage in a white sheet, moaning and groaning as he had gouged his eyes out. He had fallen in love with his own mother and paid a terrible, self-inflicted price. I would feel quite frightened on our return from these entertainments, passing the dead horse and the spies' dark house. It felt better when we exited the wood and started climbing the rough back road towards our farmhouse.

Our garden was now rampant with lettuce and herbs. Sitting on the earth amongst her bounty, Harry would cut two slices of her brown bread for herself and fill them with this greenery. The sandwiches were so big she could hardly stretch her mouth around them. I can remember the forceful way she shovelled ridges and dug potatoes.

'Come on, get your beds. We are sleeping out tonight'.

Singing *'hey ho, hey ho, it's off to bed we go. Hey ho, hey ho, hey ho, hey ho, hey ho. Hey ho, it's off to bed we go'*, we all made up our beds on the corrugated platform that Harry had built especially for sleeping out. It was placed by the bubbling stream. We lay down and looked up to the sky, discussing the stars and listening to the nightjar. A blossoming whitethorn bush sent its honey perfume into our nostrils. When it rained, we would climb under the corrugated iron platform to the dry grassless area and make up our beds again.

What next comes into my head was the time that Lucy was upstairs sick. Harry jumped onto her bike and cycled into Kenmare for the doctor. It all concertinas together, but it seemed in no time that sixteen-year-old Lucy was being carried down the steep wooden stairs wrapped in a blanket with raging, fevered red cheeks. We never saw her again. She died of galloping meningitis. Michael kept his emotions inside. He once said 'I would love to be like a little chick, all cosy under its mother's wing'. We knew that Michael was bereft without his sister. However, he had developed a great bond with Hazel which lasted all his life. He kept in his chest pocket a small passport size photograph of Hazel all his life to the end.

Pat Newling was fearful that Michael (now 16) might get the same meningitis, so she sent him to Switzerland for the good air and to learn hotel catering, which stood to him throughout his life. Now it was just Hazel, Harry and me. Harry felt unjustified living on in the farm with Lucy and Michael both gone, so we sold the cows and donkeys and Harry put the hens to sleep with dope: since nobody could catch them and they all had to be killed.

3

NORTHERN IRELAND

We packed our few belongings, including all the childhood drawings, to take to Northern Ireland, with no other plan in Harry's mind. It was 1944; we had been in Kerry for six years.

I have no memory of saying goodbye to anyone in Kenmare. The next thing we were in Derry living in a workman's caravan parked on the roadside. We then moved on to Portrush, a seaside town. We lived there in another caravan on the clifftop. Hazel and Harry started having enormous rows. Hazel had become a teenage rebel. I swore that I would never fight with Harry in that way. Even in Kenmare, Hazel rebelled and would go for hours up the mountains leaving Harry worried as to where she was. When she got her period, she used anything and everything for her STs, making Harry furious that she should have used and thrown away blood-stained dish cloths, dusters and socks.

Hazel was now seventeen and it was discussed with Corbett's parents and Harry that she live with them in the north of England where Hazel could study to be a hospital dietician, a subject she was interested in. I remember when we took Hazel to the train station in Belfast. Just writing this now makes me feel tearful, as I remember the feeling when the bus swerved out of the station, taking my sister away to the boat that took her to the north of England. Now we were two.

Harry and I were both silent on the bus going back to our caravan. The next night there was the worst storm for many years. We feared the caravan would be blown over the cliff. 'Let's go! Never mind getting dressed', Harry said and we ran to the nearest cottage. The gate was locked so we climbed onto the wall. I was wearing a large white nightdress which filled with wind like a parachute and landed me into the middle of their garden. The owners of the house put us up in their sitting room for the night. The next morning when we returned our caravan had survived the storm.

I remember spending days walking alone on the clifftops with a sad feeling, singing: *Let me be by myself in the evening breeze. Listen to the murmur of the cottonwood trees. Send me off forever but I ask you please. Don't fence me in'.*

The Portrush cliffs dropped down to large rocks, forming oblong tanks of clear seawater. It was in one of these tanks that Harry taught me how to swim. For our shopping we would walk to Portrush town, over the short sea grass hills and onto the long Portrush beach. One day, it happened to be Harry's birthday, I had a penny taken from her purse for a birthday present. The beach that day was covered with oranges, pencils and broken-up bits of shipwreck caused by the war. We gathered up the pencils and oranges, filling up our pockets and shopping basket. 'Hey! I've found you a penny', co-incidentally that penny had Harry's date of birth on it, it was shopping of a different kind that day.

A little neighbour girl used to come to play and have tea. Harry and I were amazed that she would go to the trouble of climbing under our small caravan table just to blow her nose and reappear to drink her tea.

'I'd better send you to school', Harry said one day, so off we went to Belfast, leaving the caravan and Portrush behind. I must have been ten at that time. In Belfast we got another caravan that was situated under a black cliff called Cave Hill. The caravan was protected from the main road by a large advertisement board. The silver tram lines shone on the road. One day I jumped off the tram in the wrong direction and fell with a thump onto those lines.

The school had little impression on me. I made no friends there, but I made friends with a little girl called Mary who lived on the city dump in a barrel-top caravan across the road from us. Her father was a well-known street artist. He had no legs and had made himself a trolley with wheels. Every day he rolled himself into the centre of Belfast to draw pastel pictures on the pavement in order to make a living.

Each day when he left the caravan Mary and I would play on the dump. 'Weddings' was our favourite game. There was an area with white broken porcelain wreaths dumped from the local graveyard; they made perfect headpieces and wedding bouquets. It was there, standing on the white crunchy graveyard flowers, linking arms with my 'husband' Mary that I got my first twinge of romance/sexuality.

On the top of Cave Hill Harry watched Mary and I, while in the playground we circled around and around on a thing like a spinning top. It got faster and faster and I stupidly let go and jumped off in the middle of the spin, grazing my face and shoulder on the gravely ground.

'What's wrong with you, Pauline, you are constantly jumping off moving things, just like the tram', Harry said.

It's as if young people go through a clumsy time; their bodies have not yet been fine-tuned.

As far as I can remember Hazel and Harry didn't write to each other. I am sure I have picked up Harry's way of living in the present. Hazel may as well have not existed as far as Harry and I were now concerned. We did hear that she had made a good dietician in Newcastle hospital. She married an intelligent, handsome man called Neil Cherrette with dark-rimmed glasses, brown skin and a little shorter than her. We did go to the wedding [1960]. Harry bought a new pair of green trousers and a navy anorak, and I a black dress. We travelled from Ireland to London and up to Newcastle. Harry's sister Minnie was outraged at Harry's casual clothing. 'Here try this on!' Harry tried on several incredibly-conventional clothes which made us crease up with laughter. We had a good time, ate lots and had good chats with nice Newcastle people.

Hazel and Neil had two children, Timmy and Julia. They were well into their teens when we first visited them in 1980, the year after Harry died. Hazel backed off from my greeting kiss, I could sense she shuddered at the thought of touch. Harry was never a kiss or touch person and Hazel seemed even more shy to make any contact. Even on one of our walks together, Hazel stayed separate behind, she didn't walk with us. Maybe there was a lot of hurt in poor Hazel, hurt I hadn't experienced. Harry didn't ever refer to Hazel, just like she never mentioned Corbett, her husband. Time passed.

The next connection with Hazel was her funeral, she had died too young. The large stain from her haemorrhage was deep in their carpet. Harry hadn't lived to know of Hazel's end.

It is surprising how little I knew of Hazel. I can't understand how I didn't cry when she died. I can't understand how separate I felt from her. Could it be the six years age difference? Perhaps Harry felt Hazel belonged to her father, Corbett, and maybe I picked up the vibes that she was his, not ours?

I had not attended an English funeral before. The ceremony was very quiet and restrained. The cremation of Hazel was swift, her ashes were scattered on a communal grave. We had tea and sandwiches back at Hazel's home, then I took the train to catch the boat back to Ireland.

I feel I have never celebrated my sister's life. I am glad, however, that her two children Julia and Timmy came to visit us over the years, giving a feeling of family that washed warmly over me each time we met.

4

PROGRESSIVE SCHOOLS

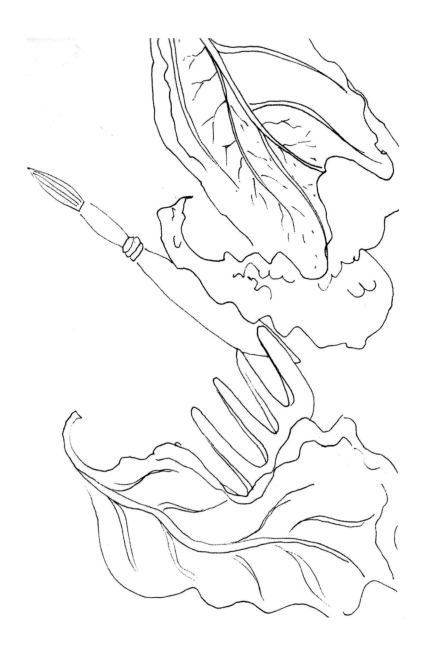

Harry was not very happy with the type of school I attended in Belfast, nor did she like the dark damp patch that our caravan was parked in, so she decided to move again. In her early marriage days she had read a book by A.S. Neill on his progressive school called Summerhill. Neill's free-thinking method of teaching became world famous, with the belief that the school should be made to fit the child rather than the other way around. In fact, before we first went to Ireland, she had investigated for Hazel and I, A.S Neill's method. On arrival she put me in the care of two young boys and went for a walk to see the playgrounds and the classrooms of the school. When she came back she found me suspended clinging on by my hands from a goalpost, nobody holding me. It seems the boys had heard that babies had a very strong, hard grip and could support their own body weight. This was one of the few stories that I would overhear Harry telling of the past.

In my twenties I often had a recurring dream that my hands were clinging on for ages to a thin wire high in the misty, grey sky. There was no sight of land and I was naked. I knew I had to eventually let go, I could not hang on to this thin wire forever, so my clammy wet hands let go and I slowly zig-zagged like a feather through the grey sky and landed on a prickly blanket. I wondered if it was the goalpost experience, and the blanket I landed on felt like the prickly green tweed coat that Harry wore at that time.

I remember doing a ginger-coloured pooh on that green coat. Harry was talking very enthusiastically to a group of teachers as I forced the pooh out. I must have been jealous. As a visitor attending Summerhill, Harry was learning and admiring A.S. Neill's philosophies. One boy was obsessed with stealing chickens. A.S. Neill said to the boy, 'let's steal chickens together tonight'. Neill had pre-warned the chicken owners that this was going to happen. For many nights Neill and the boy crept under the wiring of the hen house, capturing chicken after chicken, until the boy said, 'I am sick of it'. Another of his pupils, a young girl, ran away and jumped on a train. Neill followed the train, found the girl and offered her money. 'You won't get far without this', he said. The girl reacted by asking to go back with him to Summerhill.

After leaving Belfast, Harry enrolled me in a progressive school called St Catherine's, a boarding school in Bristol modelled on A.S. Neill's philosophy. Children that had previously been turned away from ordinary boarding schools were accepted in progressive schools, consequently the majority of the pupils were so-called problem children.

Harry got a job there as a vegetarian cook. I remember the large hall had a smell of lentil soup, the corridors were a long distance away from my mother's bedroom and mine. I shared a room with five other children. The nice man whose room was opposite my dormitory was called John Watling. He was a philosopher and a conscientious objector. He had refused to fight in the war and was signed up to work on the land as an alternative to fighting. John and Harry became good friends for life.

The classes didn't inspire or impress me. I loved the large lawn where the children and teachers relaxed in the sun. I often put on the wind-up gramophone the 'Sugar Plum Fairy' by Tchaikovsky and would dance naked, twirling, a thin veil about my head and body, feeling graceful and beautiful.

Down the fields from the lawn there was a large old dead white tree. It had a hole in its trunk big enough for two children. On Bonfire Night I crept in there with a boy, and we watched the party's blazing fire from this dark hole. At bedtime we were read aloud to by one of the teachers. The boy who fancied me would put his hand under my bedclothes and touch my body which I enjoyed. The teacher never commented; though it must have been very obvious.

All the while my mother felt it proper that she would not make the other children jealous by being around me. She and John Watling eventually both got fed up with St Catherine's; Harry felt the lessons were not as free as A.S. Neill's school and John was no longer obliged to work on the land as the war was over. So we three left together, walking down the broad, tree-lined drive, laughing, Harry saying, 'now they can burn their own spinach'.

Once again Harry and I lived in a caravan, this time on a site by a boathouse in Salford. We got to know a few of the residents; one woman reported to Harry each day how many fig seeds she found in her sons' stools. John Watling had become such a good friend he would often visit us. He was now studying psychology in University College London (1946). He giggled and joked continuously. He was wiry thin, a vegetarian and full of energy and often would bring his latest girlfriend with him. One of the first things John would do on each visit was to ask could he look at the new drawings and pictures I had done; it was good to see John and Harry laughing at these drawings of Yellow Belly and James Mason and all the strange imaginary figures I had conjured up.

Time came for more schooling, so Harry and I stowed our things, including my Kenmare violin, under the bed of our caravan and we took off for Monmouthshire in Wales, to another progressive boarding school called Blackbrook, where she enrolled me and once again became one of the school's vegetarian cooks. At meal times I felt content to see her cooking in the school kitchen and serving us vegetarian meals. Harry also painted a beautiful large mural of a hill with pine trees on the dining room wall, which I was very proud of.

This school was set in the mountains. I remember waking up one morning to deep snow drifts. The school rations had run low so one of the teachers decided that as there was nothing to eat he would waive vegetarianism. He strided out into the deep snow to see if he could catch rabbits. When he did not return we had to follow his footsteps and found that he had fallen into an eight-foot-deep snow drift and we had to dig him out. This teacher taught boat building, which I had no interest in, so he gave me plasticine to model. He was the only teacher there without a partner or mistress. He had no one to mend his woolly socks so he gathered up the holes and wound string around them creating a mushroom of wool on his toes and heels. As a result he couldn't fit on his shoes and was always to be seen walking around in his lumpy socks.

The art teacher was called Dorothy Higgins. I was her only pupil. We children were all allowed to choose our classes and what we wanted to learn. Dorothy was fascinated by trees; their twigs, branches, trunks, knots and roots. We produced drawing after drawing of trees. She became part of our lives as we introduced her to John Watling and they became partners.

At weekends we children would improvise plays to entertain the teachers. One time I dressed up as our boat builder teacher, tying a rug around my chin to represent his beard and putting socks on with the toes tied with string. I then pretended to fall asleep. The staff laughed and laughed as I had got it right. Apparently he used to nod off to sleep during staff meetings. Perhaps these plays were encouraged by the teachers to find out what psychological issues we might have?

One night Harry answered a knock on the school door. When she opened it there was a gang of threatening-looking youths from the town. I admired her method of diffusing their aggression.

'Come in and I will make you a cup of tea', she invited.

They immediately softened their attitude and shyly refused the tea and left.

Once, she told me she was asleep in a guest house when the owner man climbed up a ladder with the intention of coming in through her bedroom window. She sat up and said, 'hello, what is the time?' and somehow that sent him back down the ladder.

At Blackbrook I fell for one of the boys called Michael. He never took off his round white sailor's hat. In the snowy spell I would sit behind him on a sheet of corrugated iron and slide very fast down a steep hill, stopping by thudding into a large tree. The jolt sickened me but I suffered it over and over because I wanted to impress him. He disappointed me once by tying me up to a tree, leaving me there. One of the teachers undid the rope.

The girl next to me in our bedroom had awful nightmares which made her cry out and she would wet her bed. I asked Harry why I was here in this school.

'Am I a problem child as well?'

She assured me that I was not a problem child, but it was a place where she could work and be near me at the same time. The principal of the school was called Karl Castile. His mistress was pretty, dark skinned, with a bush of black curly hair tumbling down her back. I sensed that Karl was a womaniser and drew many pictures of him drooling over a woman that he held in his hand, like in the film *King Kong* that we saw in Kenmare, where the gorilla held the struggling white woman in his large black hand.

5

Jaunty – Our Boat

After a year in Blackbrook, Harry and I returned to our caravan in Salford. The river Avon had flooded and ruined all the things we had placed on the floor for safety. My violin was split in half and covered in dry mud; that was the end of any hope of continuing lessons. I had got as far as 'Home, Sweet Home' when we had left Kenmare. In one of the unoccupied caravans on the site I would go each day to look through the keyhole where there lived an enormous pink, yellow and green caterpillar. I was fascinated by the way it oscillated and concertinaed its ribbed body. On my way back to our caravan I picked up a young tabby cat that twirled itself around my legs asking me, I thought, to take it home. Harry allowed me to keep the young cat and we called it Salty.

There was a barrel top caravan behind ours where a gypsy man and his wife lived. One day when Harry went out shopping with his wife the man enticed me into his caravan. I climbed the steep wooden steps. On entering he gently pulled me onto his knees and started to kiss and stroke me. I wriggled from his grasp and escaped down the steps and ran to the public lavatories in the boathouse nearby, locking myself in, crying and shuddering until Harry came back from the shops. She used her minimising traumatic events technique; 'forget it, you are ok', she said, not allowing hysteria to dominate. It happened before in a park where I screeched after seeing a man exposing himself, 'don't be ridiculous, walk away slowly, just don't look', Harry said. I made friends with a little girl who told me that the gypsy man often tried to coax her into a dark shed by holding a two shilling piece in his outstretched hand. She had become very adept at grabbing the two shillings and running away quickly.

When John Watling visited us from London we often went into Bath to a café called the Hole in the Wall. It was set in a beautiful crescent of Georgian houses. We always ordered homemade scones, jam and a big bowl of clotted cream. I was told this later became a mighty famous restaurant.

Alongside the caravan site on the River Avon was a row of various sized houseboats, one of which was for sale. It wasn't long before Harry decided to sell our caravan and buy that boat. It was a 15 foot long converted landing craft, with a large 35 litre engine. It had been used in the war to cross the channel and land on the beaches of Normandy with its flat bottom. It was then further converted by Harry to be bright and airy, with windows instead of the small portholes. We named the boat 'Jaunty'.

During this purchase we met John Bailey and his wife, Beth. They lived on a long houseboat with a tiny engine moored next to ours; their boat also had a flat bottom. John Bailey told Harry of his ambition to live on the Thames, in a place called Henley. Immediately Harry offered John Bailey the use of Jaunty's high-powered engine to tow his boat up the Kennet and Avon Canal. That decided, it wasn't long before we took off on our journey with our new cat Salty. We travelled under a huge viaduct before entering the Caen Hill Locks. The canal had not been used much in years; consequently when each lock gate opened there came a rush of stagnant weed-covered filthy water. The next lock gate opened revealing white-bellied dead fish which the propeller churned, sending up a poisonous stink. When the next lock gate opened there would be a black thick mud or white soap from a nearby laundry.

One of Salty's favourite places to sleep was on Jaunty's deck walk. Each night when we moored she would jump off the boat to catch mice and birds and in cleaner water she caught tiddler fish from the shallow edge of the canal. One day I opened out a window, not knowing that Salty had settled on deck in the shade. She plopped into the weed-covered canal. We were hysterical with worry as we could not see her. The hole that she had created in the duckweed had quickly closed over. 'She's here', Harry shouted, pointing. Salty had swum all the way around the back of the boat under the dark weeds, arriving on the muddy bank. The next morning we called Salty as we were moving on; she was nowhere to be found. It broke my heart when the engine started and we had to travel on without her. As we went along I called and called her. After five miles there she was, curled up under a bridge sleeping in the shade. She stretched and arched her back and jumped onto the boat. It seemed she had been waiting for us. This cat story and our Kennet and Avon trip was written up in a large piece in the local Devizes newspaper.

Each day we would moor the two boats around six o'clock, shop at the nearest village and eat our meal. When John Watling joined us he would sometimes bring Dorothy, or another girlfriend called Lilly, and bags of exotic foods from London. I so enjoyed the way he always asked to see my latest pictures. I would show him pictures of himself and Lilly or Dorothy and a scary sailor that Lilly once brought down to meet us.

After eating dinner on the boat I would join the inevitable group of children that had come to see the boats on the canal. Immediately I made close friendships and promised to be faithful penpals for life. However once we had left they quickly faded from my memory and I never kept contact. 'Out of sight, out of mind'. I have a nugget of love held within me for friends, but it lies dormant until I meet them again.

John Bailey's son, Keith, a university student, was a soft, tall fellow who constantly sang, 'Hear my song, Violetta'. I had a mild crush on him. I wore a green wool bathing costume that Harry had crudely mended, making me ashamed to show my front to him in case he saw the knitted patch on my fanny.

The flat roof of our boat provided a discussion platform; everyone would lie in the sun laughing and talking philosophy. They talked about the philosophers and thinkers of that period, people such as A.S. Neill of Summerhill, Bertrand Russell, the importance of being a conscientious objector, D.H. Lawrence who wrote about the miners in the North of England and places such as Tuscany and his belief in free love, they talked about Isadora Duncan who danced barefoot, fully pregnant and semi-nude and of Margaret Mead, the anthropologist. Harry read George Orwell's *Animal Farm* where 'four legs good, two legs bad' was inscribed on the end wall of the barn, above the Seven Commandments of Animalism in bigger letters.

The conversations on Margaret Mead fascinated me most; her travels to the South Pacific sounded ideal – and inspired a lifelong wish to go there. All this time I would sit listening and drawing what they were talking about, subjects that were unhappy, happy, perturbed or puzzling, drawing with the art materials that Harry kept me supplied with. The fact that I was drawing excused me by Harry from many a chore. 'No, no, Pauline, you keep drawing, I'll do the washing up'. All of these drawings, from the age of two and a half onwards, were being kept by Harry in a battered leather case – strange, as she did not believe in holding onto possessions. She had thrown away her wedding ring, her name and past, not giving them a second thought.

The Kennet and Avon Canal managers provided us with as many men as were needed to open the old lock gates and to tow the boats to prevent our propeller and engine clogging up with the unclean canal water. Inevitably the weed and growth in the canal waters got too much for Jaunty, so we had to tie a rope to her front and the company sent us twenty men to pull the two boats. Their bodies leaning forward as they heaved and pulled us along the tow path, it looked like something from ancient times. There were a number of lock gates that they had to open, as before, full of various coloured water, from black thick mud to white suds to green weed. Eventually the canal brought us to clearer water and out into the blissful cleanliness of the River Thames. We had arrived at Wargrave, a small place four miles from Henley.

We rented a mooring place from Bushmills boathouse which was on a small island in the middle of the Thames. To get to the mainland you walked over a bouncy long plank, arriving amongst rows of upside-down punts, each with its own punting pole, waiting to be hired out from Bushmills for fun and games on the Thames.

Harry enrolled me into a school, a mile up the road from Bushmills. It was enjoyable but strict, with clear rules. The teachers recognised that I was good at art, and asked me to design their sunken garden. They liked my design so much that this project was carried out. At first Harry cycled with me to school until I got brave enough to go on my own. I made friends easily and they would come one at a time to play and to swim from our boat.

'You are lucky, Pauline, to live on a boat', they'd say, to which I would reply, 'you are lucky to live in a house' and I meant it.

Harry made my school sandwiches, filling them with wild herbs such as watercress, sorrel and wild garlic that she got from the river and railway banks nearby.

'Why do I have to eat all these railway bank herbs and wild things and not eat the same food as everybody else at school?' I asked.

'Because it's all so fresh and healthy', Harry said.

Eventually I persuaded her to give me five pennies a day for the cooked lunches they served at school.

One time we visited John Watling in London and were brought to a famous restaurant, The Ivy, for dinner. A waiter overheard me saying that my five penny school lunches were nicer.

It felt strange not to call the teachers by their first names, as we did in the progressive schools. Now it was 'sir' and 'miss'. It was also strange to be put standing to face the wall if my mind wandered and I drew pictures in my copybook; this happened quite often. The swimming teacher was lovely and enjoyed the fact that I was a good swimmer and the biology teacher had an intense interest in nature that was fascinating.

One of my school friends lived in a complex of houses that looked all the same. It was a thrill to open the gate and walk up a path to her front door. Her mother impressed me with her table laid out with tea for us both. The white cloth, flowery cups and saucers, it was all such a contrast to our heavy mugs on the small wooden boat table. Another friend lived in a pretty cottage in the middle of the commonage; we would walk through yellow broom bushes and green ferns. Her mother was round and affectionate. She too had a table laid for us with home-made scones, jam and a pot of delicious tea. Each house was an exciting change from life on Jaunty.

Lucy Diamont was a pale skinny girl with glasses. One day, for no reason, she waited behind a corner in the school corridor and bashed me on my head with her pencil box, all the pencils scattered along the floor. I ran to the cloakroom and started crying in the loo and made up my mind that when I grew up I would shame Lucy Diamont somehow for doing this.

A dark-haired stocky wrinkly girl whom I did not like very much volunteered to show me how boys kissed. We hid under a clump of ferns and she proceeded to kiss me on the mouth, a lesson I did not particularly enjoy.

The blue and white Thames Conservancy boat used to patrol the waters to check that we followed the rules of living on the River Thames. Limited pumping of sewage and definitely no rubbish to be thrown overboard. There was one particular patrol man who looked like Eric Portman, the film star. He wore a peaked cap and blue uniform, and said to my mother, 'Pauline is going to break many hearts one day'.

On one sunny day my friend from the council house and I lay on our tummies on the roof of Jaunty, peering through the glass, past the steering wheel to the boat moored below us where a man lived alone. He was blonde, over-muscled and over-tanned. Each day he exercised, flexing his muscles and stretching. We giggled at him, when suddenly he deliberately took off his trunks and shocked us with his dangling penis. That stopped us.

We dived and swam and often hired a punt for trips up and down the river. One day my punt pole got stuck in the muddy Thames bottom. For some reason I hung onto the pole rather than letting it go and the punt went away without me. Slowly, slowly, I slid down the pole into the water. I could feel my clothes getting heavier and heavier, finding it very difficult to swim with this sodden weight. Eventually I was able to pull myself up the slippery bank to safety, the punt was rescued later.

Not far from where Jaunty was moored on the island there was a big tree with a rope hanging from its branches. We would catch hold of the rope and swing like Tarzan across the inlet of water to the other side.

On sunny days, Harry, John Watling and I often walked along the grassy bank of the Thames to Henley. I constantly called 'wait for me!' as John and Harry were full of talk, forgetting that I'd stop every so often to peer at something like a moor hen, a flower, frog spawn or a leaf.

'Come on, Pauline, you're so slow', Harry would shout back.

One day in Henley we passed a shop selling arts and craft work where a tall beautiful red-haired young woman stood in the doorway. She wore a dress with a divided skirt tied tight around her tiny waist. The base colour was like milk chocolate, with blue and white horses galloping all over it and on her feet she wore incredibly high heel sandals and she had pink painted toenails. She had covered her lips in a vivid shiny lipstick called 'Tahiti Pink', a lipstick which Harry soon adopted.

John was fascinated, he wanted to talk to her. It was not long before Nicandra became another of his many girlfriends. John and Nicandra practically lived at this time on our boat; they made up a bed on the floor of the wheel house, far away from our beds on either side of the table in the hull. Each night I would try to get to sleep first, as Harry snored and if she got to sleep before me I would spend my waking hours thinking about things such as the two boys, named John Pricket and Michael Cox, that me and my pal had met. John Watling got a great deal of laughter out of those names.

Each day Nicandra sat in her chocolate-coloured dress reading her books and stroking her long red hair, putting the loose strands of hair between the pages of the book with the intention of making a wig one day. She had left many of our books with red hair twirled between the pages. In all the time that I knew Nicandra, she never changed that dress.

'When I find something I like, I do not change it until I am sick of it', she said.

Therefore we often got a waft of unpleasant odour emanating from the beautiful Nicandra.

Before we met Nicandra she used to live near the woods in the neighbourhood of Augustus John, the famous artist. She told us about the first day she had met him; she was walking through the woods when he spotted her and shouted 'hold it, child of nature!' Whereupon he asked her to his studio to pose for him.

He loved painting her; she became his model for years. She was married to the jazz critic Alvaro McCarthy. Despite that, Augustus John apparently wanted to procreate with Nicandra, as he did with many of his female models. However, Nicandra escaped that one. John Watling was potty about her, always laughing and pulling her towards him and patting her back and saying affectionate things like 'has my Nicandra done her ka ka today?' As a young teenager I was goggle-eyed at their behaviour.

One day Harry suddenly said, 'I would love to go back and live in Ireland, and maybe find a place in Kerry again'. There and then, that decision was made and Nicandra decided she would come with us.

6

IRELAND AGAIN

In 1949 Harry, Nicandra and I went to Ireland, ahead of Jaunty. Harry commissioned a shipping company to bring Jaunty from Wargrave to Cork on the big mail boat. It was taken out of the water and left on land to dry out. John Watling returned to University College London. No sooner had we arrived in Ireland, we found Nicandra engrossed in conversation with a tall handsome man called Frank. She seemed to have forgotten John and accepted Frank's offer to drive us in his red, rickety van to County Kerry.

As we travelled, Frank and Nicandra seemed to be getting closer so instead of Frank returning to Cork he offered to keep driving us wherever we wanted to go. We first went to Kenmare; he took us back to where we used to live, over the suspension bridge and back along the familiar rough road. We saw Big Cat's grave, the stream where Michael used to tickle trout, where the bull fell head first into the dung heap and all the familiar things from then. We passed Mrs Healy's house, the little church where I made the children pray and cross themselves on the way to Douris school, then we went on further to see Gleninchaquin, Tousist; everywhere yet nowhere a wonderful place to live.

Nicandra, Harry and I slept in the back of the van and Frank stretched out on the two front seats. Harry had promised to visit Pat Newling, who now owned the Cahernane Hotel in Killarney. We travelled through Moll's Gap that looked down into the dark depths of the Black Valley and to the left a string of incredibly silvery-blue lakes. Either Frank was tired or he was distracted, but all of a sudden we found our van with the two front wheels dangling over the cliff above the lakes.

'Move slowly out the back door', Frank instructed.

Holding our breath the three of us crawled out to safety. Frank followed on his hands and knees. The van was pulled back onto the road by three strong motor cyclists, then we continued our journey down to Ladies View, down through the thickets of rhododendrons, wild deer crossing the road at intervals, passing the gushing Torc Waterfall, making our way through black stones by the upper lake. Two miles short of Killarney, we arrived at Pat Newling's hotel. She welcomed us and offered the Gate Lodge to live in, which stood at the end of the tree-lined drive.

By this time, Frank and Nicandra's affair seemed to have dwindled, so Frank returned to Cork and it was not long before Nicandra returned to England. The dream of finding a place to live with Nicandra was over.

We settled comfortably in the Gate Lodge and started to paint Killarney scenes of mountains and lakes on wooden boards which Pat displayed at the reception desk. They were on sale, a guinea each, for the tourists.

One day, one of the workers from the hotel ran down the avenue to give us the message that Jaunty, our boat, had arrived in Cork. The next day, Harry and I took the train there. We arrived on the quay side just in time to see Jaunty being craned into the air on long chains. It swung from left to right and semi-circled in the sky and as they lowered it towards the water, one of the chains snapped and Jaunty lunged into the quay side, then plunged nose first into the River Lee. We watched as it bubbled and started to sink. At that, several men got into small boats and rushed to rescue it. Harry yelled at the top of her voice, 'let it sink, let it sink'. They took no notice, or did not hear her and pulled the lopsided Jaunty to shore. There was a large gaping hole in the bottom of the hull. The chains had snapped due to the uncalculated weight of the ballast which had got wet and heavy after Jaunty had been weighed.

Leaving the boat at a local shipyard to be mended, it was suggested that we take Jaunty to moor in Passage West, eight miles east of Cork, after the repairs were done. The harbour was surrounded by green fields and a few pretty houses and it would cost us nothing to moor there.

Once again we packed our bags to leave Cahernane Gate Lodge and, saying goodbye to Pat Newling, we went to our new mooring place in Passage West. Each day, the tide would go out, leaving Jaunty sitting on her flat bottom on the harbour pebbles. She would float again when the tide came in.

One day Harry and I were sitting opposite each other. She was teaching me how to knit when we heard bubbling at our feet. The tide was coming in through the canvas patch. Obviously the repair had failed.

'Come on, let's go', she said. We quickly packed our bags and there and then left the boat forever, making our way to Dublin, where Harry hoped to enrol me in art school. Many years later, after I had met Pat my future husband, we went looking for Jaunty on his scooter and learnt that a young couple salvaged it, keeping her in a field where they lived happily ever after.

7

ART SCHOOL DAYS

I was fifteen at this stage and Harry wanted to enrol me at art school. During our Passage West stay she had gone to meet the principal of the Cork art school, but she returned disappointed, as the life class models there had to be draped.

'That's no good. How can Pauline learn anatomy from a draped figure?' she asked.

We had been given, by a friend of Nicandra, the address of a well-known puppet-maker in Dublin called Desmond MacNamara. We were told he would be an excellent person to write an introduction for the Dublin art school, which at that time was one of the requirements for admission.

Desmond MacNamara lived in a laneway of small artisan houses in the Baggot Street area. He opened the door and behind him was a room full of incredibly-arty-looking people. Far more unusual than any of the progressive school teachers, the men had long hair and bushy beards and the women wore full dresses and coloured beads and sandals. They all gathered around the leather suitcase full of my childhood drawings and paintings that Harry had brought. As they lifted pictures of Lilly, Karl Castile or the frightening sailor, they commented, 'surely you must have been exposed to the work of Picasso?'

'No', Harry said. 'Pauline has not seen anyone else's art. That was something I did not want to expose her to'.

'This is incredible. How could she have done these without seeing such works as Miro, Beardsley, Braque and the like?' they asked.

They could not believe that one could paint pictures without seeing and being influenced by other artists.

As far as I was concerned my pictures came from a need to suss out life. All the people in the room looked at me intensely. Under their stare my eyes welled up and I started to cry. When Harry saw me she could not help but cry also, so we both quickly left, choking with tears, unable to explain why. As we staggered up the puppet-maker's lane, Harry asked, 'why on earth did you start crying?'

I blurted out, 'if the art school is going to be anything like that, I don't want to go!'

In those days the important thing was to show a portfolio of work alongside an endorsement from a well-known person. MacNamara did write the letter of introduction, raving about my talent, and with the suitcase full of my paintings these got me enrolled in the National College of Art in 1950.

We looked around Dublin for a place to live and once more found a caravan. This time it was placed on a small patch of black cinders behind another advertisement board in Kilmainham. The advertisement board was for Heinz Baked Beans, the entrance was a cut-out hinged door through the big bean tin.

On the first day of art school, Harry accompanied me to Kildare Street. The school was tucked into a corner, in between the National Library and Leinster House. Wide granite steps led into a large skylight-lit hall. We students were greeted by Paddy, a friendly porter. I nervously went into the cloakroom to put on my artist's smock, leaving my coat and bag on a coat hook, along with all the other nervous-looking students and their coats and bags.

The first class was sculpture study, starting with Michelangelo's David, then the Venus de Milo, and the Discus Thrower. We each had an easel and a large piece of newsprint paper pinned to a plywood backing board. The teacher was bearded Seán Keating who instructed us to start with David's nose. After a while Mr Keating went around correcting the general shapes that we had drawn, pointing out that David's nose was perfectly straight with its internal bone structure to support it.

Seán Keating never shaved off his ageing beard which grew from his hollow cheek bones. He had a collection of Aran Islands' costumes in which he would dress students to pose for his men and women in his iconic Aran Islands' paintings. The women wore heavy-fringed shawls, a full red flannel skirt with black bands around the hem and were bare footed. The men wore knitted berets, rough tweed waistcoats, baggy tweed trousers held up with a colourful crios and on their feet animal-skinned pampooties which they stitched themselves.

The girl at the easel next to me was called 'Barry'. Barry was the daughter of the famous writer Maura Laverty, whose plays and books were in great demand. Barry had chestnut brown shiny hair tied up into a long bouncy ponytail that seemed to have a life of its own. Her lovely face with its protruding chin looked so sweet and intelligent. She wore beautiful fluffy angora sweaters from Fran Fagan's shop and tight dark green trousers. As we got more comfortable with each other we would sit on the hot pipes, discussing hops and boys.

At the end of the day we all clattered down the stairs into the cloakroom again to remove our now charcoal-smothered smocks. The atmosphere had lightened. We were more relaxed. 'See you tomorrow!' Harry looked happy to see me running towards her and back she and I went to our caravan behind the Heinz billboard in Kilmainham.

It wasn't hard to get up early each morning and leave the caravan to go to painting, pottery or sculpture classes. I thought it was all so exciting and new. Every day I made more new friends, especially in the cloakroom. It was in that cloakroom that I started swap sales. We swapped an art smock for a hat, a pen for a brush etc, so it grew from there.

I developed some kind of snobbery because I did not want to tell any of the students that I lived in a caravan. I was ashamed, in fact, when we had started going to hops. I always asked the boy that dropped me home on his crossbar or car to leave me off at the doorstep of some respectable house in Kilmainham. I would walk up the path to the doorway of this strange house and hope that the boy would drive away before I was discovered by the owner of the house. Having made sure that the boy had gone I would then run around the corner to the baked beans doorway to our cindery caravan patch where Harry always waited up for me.

Outside of art school everything that happened in my life continued to be expressed in drawings and paintings; the parties, the students, my new friend Barry and so on. I couldn't adapt to the more formal teachings of the art school on how to paint and draw, and quickly reverted back to my own familiar style.

The next class we attended was weaving. We were taught by Mrs Clarke how to make Aran Island críos. We also studied painting with Seán Keating. He would mutter such things as 'you young people running around the place with your bottoms encased in trousers'. It was unusual in the 1950s for girls to wear trousers. On Tuesdays the class door would burst open; it was Maurice MacGonigal, saying at the top of his voice with his right finger in the air, 'remember, symmetry makes design'.

The tall red-haired principal, Mr Burke, stayed in his dark office. We rarely talked to him. The classes I enjoyed most was Professor Heckner's pottery and sculpture class. He asked me every morning in his German accent, 'how is your mother?' I think he was attracted to Harry. Heckner loved to experiment with glazes and I was his favourite experimenter. We would mix lustre glaze with plain glaze, only to open the kiln door to see that our experiments had exploded into little bits or that the colour had sunk down to the bottom of the bowl. On occasions our experiments magically worked. Each time we took notes for future use. In his sculpture class we kept up the experimentation, mixing marble chippings into cement, pouring this mixture into a plaster cast. It was disappointing to find my cement figure with a head of shiny marble chips that really were supposed to be distributed all over its body. During sculpture and pottery classes Professor Heckner would tell us of his friend who had the ability to see spirits wherever he went and have conversations with these spirits from various periods in history. Then, in front of the whole class, he would come back to the subject of 'what is your mother doing today?'

One of our portrait-painting teachers, Mr Kelly, also took the opportunity to have his students pose for him.

He would often choose a pretty student and he'd mildly flirt as he painted.

'Your lips look beautiful in repose', or 'how nice the light looks on your neck', he would say, peering through his thick wire-rimmed glasses.

We students had a desire to look different and artistic. I got nicknamed 'dishcloth' because I had made myself a top out of two loosely-woven dishcloths sewn together and dyed bright orange. From my ears I hung large brass curtain rings. I made up a full skirt with sackcloth and painted pretend sandals onto my feet. I still preferred to go barefoot everywhere since the Kenmare days.

Another lifelong friend that I made in art school was Leslie MacWeeney. I would often have sleepovers in their Foxrock home. I was influenced there by the way the MacWeeney family lived. At one time Leslie insisted on wearing a studded red dog collar around her neck, with a lead attached, I would hold onto the lead as she headed down Grafton Street. Of course people would stare, that was the point.

The boys were less eccentric than the girls, but they had their mannerisms, a way of slouching down the corridors or sticking a paint brush behind their ear, mannerisms that definitely attracted us girls.

At lunchtime we sat in the sun eating our sandwiches on the granite steps of the art school and National Library, flirting with the UCD architectural students who would come for their drawing class. When it rained we went to Bewley's Café on Grafton Street where I ordered vegetable sausages and chips. Sometimes Sara, one of our life models, came with us. She always carefully wiped her spoon, fork, knife and cup with her head scarf before she used them.

In the evenings, we'd all meet up in the Swiss Chalet for hop dances and, to our delight, the architects would come as well. Another meeting place was Davy Byrne's pub where there was a beautiful mural by Cecil Salkeld depicting Joyce's *Ulysses*. Cecil Salkeld was the father of Beatrice, who later married Brendan Behan. Brendan would impulsively leave his friends to take Beatrice down a dark lane to make love to her. We'd have jazz parties in Stephen's Green. One day when Maura Laverty saw Barry and I there she asked, 'is this what Pearse died for?'

Opposite was the pub, Baileys, owned by John Ryan, editor of *In Dublin* magazine. John married Patricia, a tall beautiful dark-haired ballet dancer. She had studied ballet in Moscow. We would philosophize for hours over our drinks, mine being a tomato juice pretending it was a Bloody Mary, avoiding alcohol. If ever I should touch alcohol Harry would say, 'I hate to see Pauline drinking because her father was an alcoholic'. Did that mean that she was admitting Corbett Bewick was in fact my real father, and not the romantic nineteen-year-old youth?

Harry decided we would leave the caravan in Kilmainham. She sold Bat Cottage to the Lever Brothers couple with all the precious antiques, including a first edition of *Alice in Wonderland*. She said 'they are just possessions'. Corbett Bewick was rarely mentioned again. She felt it was necessary to make some more money, besides the sale from Bat Cottage, as fees had to be paid for the art school and I needed art materials. So she went along to the building society to borrow money to purchase a house. She found one, No 51 Frankfurt Avenue, Rathgar. It had eight rooms which would enable her to make a living by renting out six of them. She asked me to advertise these rooms to the art school students. Soon all the rooms were filled up. Typically, the first thing Harry did was open up the front garden by knocking down the restrictive-looking black railings.

Living in a large house was a new experience, a new adventure. I loved the fact that this house in Rathgar was only a short walk to Barry Laverty's house on Leinster Road, Rathmines. Maura had furnished their house with beautiful Georgian antiques and the walls were in pale blues and greys. She was an elegant woman and over-kind. If I said I liked anything, from a vase to a cushion, she would press it into my hands and say 'take it'. So I learnt not to admire things verbally. One day Maura came into the room where Barry and I were sewing our endless full skirts. I was standing in my big knickers. 'I can see you are not out to seduce', she said. She would then tell us how *Tolka Row*, her play, was doing in the Gate Theatre.

Maura often took us to plays bringing us backstage to meet the actors. One was the famous Micheál Mac Liammoir. 'Ah, the younger generation', he said pouting his lips and leaning back in his chair. The mirror in front of him was surrounded by glaring electric bulbs. He picked up a bald wig while talking to us and forced the bald wig over his own black toupee while again pouting his wet shiny lips. In fact all he really needed to do was pull off his toupee and he would have been bald for the role in the play. We would sit in deep red plush seats, in a box, to watch *Tolka Row*, Mac Liammoir in the role of the grandfather. Not only did Maura write plays and books, she also had a programme on Radio Éireann and she would teach the nation how to cook: 'you take two podatoes, dice them into a mixture of …' She always added a 'd' into potatoes.

In Frankfurt Avenue Harry allowed all us students to draw and write anything we liked on the kitchen walls. They quickly became covered from ceiling to floor in graffiti, telephone numbers, obscenities, poems and drawings scrawled alongside our designated food shelves. One student called Lettie always ate from other people's shelves and should we stop her, she'd squeak 'mean, mean, mean, mean'.

Another student called Elizabeth, known as 'Busy', was a beautiful tall femme fatale. Every male who encountered her was fascinated. This was because she tantalised. She would turn her back and not answer questions, saying 'I am not going to tell you that', resulting in various young men making fools of themselves with curiosity.

Pat Cahill, blonde with heavy-lidded eyes, had a large grin like the Cheshire cat in *Alice in Wonderland*. She used to tell our fortunes with playing cards.

'What tops you, what hangs over your head, your life, your loves, your wishes and what's bound to be true'.

We would listen in awe to what the cards were telling us. She also introduced us to a scary game, the ouija board, where the alphabet was spelt out on the table with chalk. We sat on the floor with our fingers touching the glass tumbler as it hesitatingly spelled out messages from the dead.

Pat Cahill was loving, natural and sensual. One of her suitors, Patrick, fell in love with her, but when she got sick of him he did not give up. One night he hid in her bed and, when she discovered him, she told us she was disgusted at this bony creature lying in wait for her and banished him.

We were always playing games like playing cards, chess, alma etc. Once a Spanish student asked a group of us the following questions. He said it was a test that they gave NATO soldiers to see if they were suitable to be enrolled:

Question: You are walking through a wood. What is it like? Describe it for me.

Answer: Oak trees, with dappled sun, the leaves still on the trees, it is around September time.

Question: Is there a path?

Answer: Yes, a narrow path, overlapped a little by ferns and grass.

Question: You come across a snake. It is dangerous. What do you do about it?

Answer: I circumvent it very quietly, pass it by, holding my breath.

Question: You go over a hill and there in front of you is water. Describe the water.

Answer: It's a lake with a small paddle boat.

Question: What do you do about it?

Answer: I dip my feet into the water to see if it's warm. It is. I swim in it.

Question: There is a house on the other side of the lake. It looks abandoned. What do you do about it?

Answer: As it is too far to swim I make use of the little paddle boat.

Question: And then?

Answer: I walk to the abandoned-looking house. It is a bit scary so I go around it looking in the windows.

Question: Do you go inside?

Answer: No. I find it a little too lonely and spooky.

The Spanish student analysed this. The wood is the way you perceive your life, the leaves fresh and speckled sunlight is happiness. There is a path in your life, you see the way, but it is interrupted with a few surprises like the grass and ferns overlapping the path. You come across the dangerous snake, the snake represents how you deal with problems in life. You said you circumvent the snake and hope that it goes without noticing you. That is how you deal with problems, you hope that they will go away. You then go over the hill and you see water. In your case it's a lake which you dip your feet into. Water represents your attitude to sex. You dip your feet into it, testing it. You are cautious. Having found that it is not too cold or dangerous you swim in it, therefore this is how you behave sexually. You see the house. This represents death. You are curious and go to it but are afraid to enter the house, so you have a fear of death to a degree.

Ever since that Spanish student told us how to play this test we have done it through the years. Each person describes a different scenario. Anne Rynne, sister of Christy Moore, said that she saw an inconsequential puddle to which her husband was incensed!

Franco Biggs was one of the few in 51 Frankfurt Avenue who was not an art student. She played violin in the RTÉ Symphony Orchestra.

'I only like musical jokes', she said.

We loved to hear her practicing for hours in the top room. When she was not practicing she put on Beethoven's violin concerto which was a contrast to the Bessie Smith or Jelly Roll Morton jazz that we would have on the record player.

Apparently Harry also told Franco Biggs the story about my father being Gerald Massey Taylor and not Corbett Bewick. She told Franco that when Hazel was born she didn't want to have any more to do with Corbett and that after Pauline was born she didn't want anyone to own her and didn't want her to be educated or influenced by anybody.

The sitting room was the largest room in the house and forever full of dancing students, visiting boyfriends and Harry fooling about as young as any of us. We had an indignant neighbour next door who shouted 'Mrs Bewick, conduct your house!' This made Harry laugh, so she pretended to be a conductor waving her arms about in the air.

Harry set a table by the window in the sitting room and tried to get customers for vegetarian meals by placing an advertisement in the local shop window. This brought one customer, Sheila Fitzgerald. She lived ten doors down the road. A tiny bird of a woman, she found it difficult each day to eat all the vegetarian food that Harry put on the table. Harry and she became close friends. They decided one summer to hitchhike around Ireland staying in youth hostels. In one particular hostel they had to share a bed which was very damp so they put on their mackintoshes to sleep in. Sheila wrote a letter home to Edward, her son, saying, 'Harry and I slept together in mackintoshes'. Somehow this letter turned up years later in her solicitor's office and to Sheila's embarrassment was read out when she was settling a business project.

Kate Kennedy Martin took a room in No 51. She was from Scotland and was studying in Trinity College.

'I could have gone into their room and hit them over the head with my crucifix', she complained.

She was talking about Goodall, who made a lot of noise when making love to her boyfriend, Sam. He used to show off in front of us all, saying 'Goodall, tell them how I can bull', in his broad Northern Irish accent.

'I bet I can bull better than anyone else, don't you think Goodall?' to which she would duly answer, 'Yes, Sam'.

At one of our Frankfurt Avenue parties, Peter Murray, a rather posh tall student, said to Brendan Behan, 'You are dominating the party, stop roaring', whereupon Brendan made a move to hit him. He continued roaring, standing in the centre of the floor, then he turned his face into Peter's face, 'You know bloody nothing about 1916', to which Peter then broke his wine glass over Brendan's head, creating a bleeding cut.

Brendan came tumbling over to me by the fireplace, roaring 'I'm pouring with blood!' The blood trickled down his fat face. 'Oh! You poor thing', I said. 'You poor thing?' he shouted, insulted by my comment, and slapped me hard across my face. I ran out of the house crying, with our friend Camp Teddy running after me, 'Bubsy, Bubsy, don't cry'. Camp Teddy was a sweet, blonde fellow who loved women, not men. Teddy gently calmed me down and took me back to the party, where Harry was dancing cheek to cheek with one of the Trinity students. My mother's vitality overshadowed her age. Looking back, I realise there was quite a stream of young men who were attracted to Harry.

In a flat down the road in Frankfurt Avenue lived an African student, a dumpy dull man, who regularly visited Harry to 'listen to the news'. That annoyed me as I felt that he was coming for something else. Besides, Harry had no interest in world affairs, but she was putty in his hands. Also one lazy pale student called Sebastian hung around Harry, again turning her into a silly woman. She pampered to his every need, making him cups of tea and going out to buy cigarettes for him. Again, she did not approve of cigarette smoking. In those days I noticed that some men had a jumped-up opinion of themselves. Many's the woman treated her man like some kind of a God, not to be put upon at any cost, the man considering himself an enormous bubble of a human being. Harry surprisingly had that weakness in kowtowing to these men.

I had a big crush on an architect called Brian Hogan. He was gorgeous with straight eyelashes. Any man with straight lashes was very hard for me to resist. He always took me up to dance at the hops. Then all of a sudden he left and went away to Halifax to do further architectural studies. He never told me he was leaving. I had to find out through other people. He broke my heart for a while. Once after I told a group at a dinner party how I loved straight eyelashes a witty man sent a letter saying 'I spent all day trying to straighten my eyelashes ...'

Then there was Benny and his friend Dessie, also architectural students. Benny and Dessie arrived at Frankfurt Avenue one evening to take us up the Dublin mountains.

'Jump into the car quick, we are off to see the aurora borealis'.

Up the mountains, Benny rolled me around under the aurora borealis in a hayfield. Oh, how I loved being rolled around by Benny, but he too left for England without a word of explanation.

Pat Melia was friendly with Judith D'Arcy. They were in Trinity together studying Medicine. She was one of a tribe of sisters. Margaretta, one of the sisters, gave a party in a basement flat on Stephen's Green. On entering, one's eyes had to get used to the dark candlelight room. Jazz played loudly and a rumble of Trinity students entered down the steps behind us and immediately with their arms in the air invited us females from Frankfurt Avenue to dance.

'Who is the blue tail fly?' shouted Trinity student John Latham to his friend Pat Melia, who just laughed. He was flamboyant and loose-limbed, flying me around the party floor. This was the start of my lifelong relationship with Pat.

Margaretta made it very clear to all at the party that she was in love with sculptor Frank Morris, as she held one of the candles under her forearm burning her skin, crying and wailing, 'I love Frank, I love Frank, he wouldn't come tonight, he doesn't love me'. Her friends pulled the candle from her hand, as the jazz dancing continued. From that party onwards, Pat Melia and various Trinity students would call on all us girls at Frankfurt Avenue, taking us to dine in Jammets, or to films in the Adelphi, or plays in the Gate. I remember seeing Chekhov's *The Cherry Orchard*, directed by Hilton Edwards, as well as seeing Kabuki dancers from Japan and the great Marcel Marceau in the Gaiety. These were all made into pictures by me.

Then there was Desmond. We met in art school; a tall fatherly young man with a receding chin and long hair. His intention was to become a sculptor. He smoked through a black and silver cigarette holder and wore green corduroys. He seemed as wise and comforting as my mother. He never forced himself upon me. In fact, I remained a virgin for what seemed like years with Desmond. He and Harry would talk gently about my character, my painting and my virginity. I learnt to trust him. In the summer of 1952, Desmond and I went on a holiday to Kenmare together. A friend of his lent us a large house to stay in, overlooking Kenmare's Suspension Bridge. The house was covered in ivy. We arrived late in the dark of night and fumbled our way to a large four poster bed where we shivered and shook in fear of ghosts.

The next day we went down to the conservatory and peered around the ghostly rooms of the house. I showed Desmond the place in the pine wood below the house where the dead horse used to lay, and how it stank, and how we would have to run quickly past it. I told him of Anew McMaster and of 'Oedipus', and how Harry had taken us to see such deep plays with the hero gouging out his eyes when he discovered he had fallen in love with his mother. Further along I showed him the 'spy's house', and how Michael had found a sock up their chimney full of money. These stories and walks relaxed us both, and finally we made love, which I found disappointing. I could not understand how anyone could find it a pleasure. Poor Desmond. He was so apologetic and so gentle, and, of course, when we got back to Frankfurt Avenue it was all discussed by Harry and Desmond.

After we had made love I soon went off Desmond and after a few weeks back in Frankfurt Avenue I found to my horror that my period did not come. I was pregnant. It was devastating to have conceived, so stupid and blind not to have realised the consequences. I saw it not as a baby but as a missed period.

I asked Harry to ring John Watling in London to see if I could come and stay with him in order to find someone to terminate the pregnancy. Poor Desmond. He came with me to London, begging all the time to keep 'Willbyforce'. He so much wanted that baby. I had now developed a deep aversion and had completely gone off Desmond. I asked him to stay away from me. I would look down from John Watling's flat in Park Road to see him pacing the street below, up and down in the dusk.

John and his girlfriend Lilly found an address of a kind middle-aged woman with an understanding of my situation. She prepared a white enamel bowl of warm soapy water to squirt into my womb with an enema. It could be a fatal procedure should a bubble of air get into the womb. To this day I associate Warren Street Tube Station with that experience.

I haemorrhaged and ended up in hospital in a ward with twelve other women who had various operations. One girl had her protruding lower jaw shortened. Consequently she had a pronounced lisp as her tongue was too long for her mouth. She was a witty girl who made us ache with laughter as she shouted after the ambulance men, 'come on, hop into bed beside me'.

John and Lilly looked after me during this time and Pat Melia came and visited me from Ireland. I stayed on a while living in Park Road with John and Lilly until I fully recovered. Then I got work painting huge plywood cut-outs of lions and unicorns for the street parades to celebrate the coronation of Queen Elizabeth which was to take place in June 1953. I was the only female in this commercial art factory and had great fun laughing with the lads. I took these enormous cut-outs on to the factory's flat roof to paint in the sun.

The other tenants on John's floor were a handsome blonde man and his brown-haired plain wife. They had a belief that their marriage should be open and that they should have extra marital affairs if they wanted to, and, boy, did she want to. She was having an affair with a gruff D.H. Lawrence type. There was no doubt that it upset her handsome husband. He would come over to visit us and endlessly try to justify his wife's behaviour.

'She doesn't love him, she just finds his lifestyle and the fact that he is a working class man with a Yorkshire accent fascinating'.

Apparently one Sunday she asked him, 'what would you be doing today if you were not making love with me?' to which he answered, 'oiling my cricket bat'.

This appealed to John Watling's sense of humour. He repeated over and over in a Yorkshire accent, 'I am going to oil my cricket bat'. The more he said it, the funnier it got.

Each day a sad-looking porter stood in the Victoria and Albert window opposite us, so John invented a song to the tune of *If I were a Blackbird*:

> If I were a porter, I'd whistle and sing
> and stand near the case that my true love stood in
> and on the top shelving I there laid my vest
> then I'd pillow my head on her lily-white chest.

John often put on kwela African pennywhistle music by Spokes and Kippie which Alvarez, a philosopher friend, introduced him too and we would dance around to this amazing rhythm. Eventually I was well enough to return to Ireland. After my experience of Desmond, I was afraid to make love to my subsequent boyfriends for fear of another pregnancy. In Ireland it was impossible to buy any form of contraception, the only way was *coitus interruptus*, which must have failed Desmond.

8

WORKING LIFE

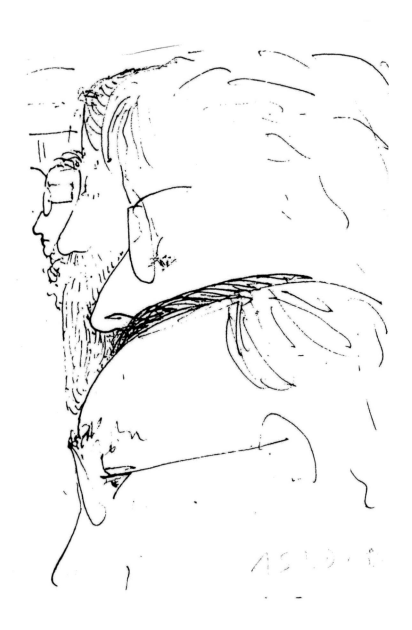

I got a job painting artificial eyes for an optician called Dr Keys in Wicklow Street. I carried out Dr Keys' new experiment. I would hold a cardboard disc, the size of the patient's iris, on the handle of a paintbrush and copy the patient's good iris in great detail, all the lines and squiggles and the exact colour of the patient's eye. Dr Keys then boiled these discs, setting them each in an orb of plastic that had been cast from the patient's eye socket, so fitted perfectly, therefore it moved with the muscles. This differed from the static glass eye of the day. The problem was that after a few months the colour that I had so carefully painted faded, so Dr Keys then sent me to London to research a paint that would not fade. This research has stood to me ever since, teaching me the awareness of light and time on fugitive colours.

Outside Dr Keys' shop was a street busker, an old lady harpist. She played beautifully her huge harp to make money. Dr Keys went into the front of the shop when the bell rang. He delighted in trying to sell his latest state of the art unbreakable sunglasses. Even when he jumped several times on them to demonstrate this the glasses just sprang back into shape and the customer would buy them. However, one day it was just too much for this pair of glasses that he used regularly and they exploded into smithereens. That was one customer that did not buy.

I found work in the Clover nightclub on O'Connell Street. Every evening at 9, I cycled in from Rathgar, parked my bike behind the Clover door, then went down steps to enter the intimate darkly-lit nightclub. They gave me dinner as part of my wages of two pounds. After dinner I sang Marlene Dietrich and Bessie Smith songs, my lips close to the microphone, *'You've got that look, that look that leaves me weak, you with that let's-get-more-than-friendly technique',* to which Paddy Burges Watson, a Trinity student, howled like a wolf, which spurred me on to an even deeper and sexier voice, *'you with your eyes-across-the-table technique'.* And Bessie Smith's *'Gime a pigs foot and a bottle of beer ... give the piano player a drink because he's bringing me down he's got a rhythm yea'.*

It was on one of these nights in the Clover that Alan Simpson and Carolyn Swift, the directors of the small Pike Theatre, asked me if I would dance and sing in their 'Follies' show, as well as paint the folly set designs. This job in the Pike was to be varied and was not daunting as I had gained some experience in Trinity College's Theatrical Society doing the sets and acting in one of Louis Lentin's productions.

The Pike became famous in Dublin for putting on plays for the first time such as Brendan Behan's *The Quare Fellow* and Ionesco's *The Orator,* and the one that almost made the Pike close down, *The Rose Tattoo* by Tennessee Williams. The main part in *The Rose Tattoo* was played by the voluptuous Anna Manahan; her performance was objected to by a woman shouting from the audience, 'the air is polluted!' Within a matter of minutes, the Guards invaded and the show had to come to a stop. The next day this was written up in the newspapers in Ireland and abroad. Alan was arrested and eventually acquitted, but the planned six-week transfer of his production to the Gate Theatre was cancelled by Lord Longford.

The Pike Theatre was located in Herbert Lane, in a converted garage. I would say 'good morning' to the man who lived opposite the theatre as he chopped boxes into kindling, making up bundles to sell in the local shop. I was given the key for the Pike door, which took me into a pitch dark foyer that held 70 seats. I had to feel my way to the light switch, and proceed to unroll a canvas for the next set design. On one of these occasions as I went to unroll my canvas I found George Desmond Hodnett, the composer and jazz pianist for the Pike, fast asleep rolled up inside the canvas. He had lost the keys to his house. 'Hoddy' also was the jazz critic for *The Irish Times*. He lived in a big beautiful old family mansion in Blackrock where we visited him one evening. In the dining room was a large glass display case full of beautiful antiques, mixed up with lots of tinned food. These tins had no labels or torn labels. Hoddy had got them from the shops for half price. He never knew what his dinner would turn out to be, it could be beans, rhubarb or dog food. There was always a yellow butt-end of a rolled cigarette stuck to his lower lip. He could talk and it never fell off.

Nearly all the Pike people subsequently became famous; Milo O'Shea, who played the comedy act, later acted in films and was twice nominated for Broadway's Tony Award. Deirdre McSharry, the Glam Girl, became the award-winning editor of *Cosmopolitan* and *Country Living* magazines. David Kelly played the carpenter in *Fawlty Towers* and Rashers in *Strumpet City* and the inimitable Donal Donnelly became one of Beckett's favourite actors. T.P. McKenna, who played the romantic act, was constantly chewing gum. One night he kissed me backstage while still chewing. He played the priest in Edna O'Brien's film, *Girl with Green Eyes*, that took place in Calary Bog, in the farmhouse that belonged to Camille Souter and Frank Morris. While T.P. was waiting for his call he said to us, 'Jesus, this fecking priest's collar is so bloody tight'.

I received a call from Mr Kiko of the Kiko Gallery in Japan asking if they could exhibit my work and we met up in London. I chose a small folder of drawings for this gallery to exhibit. He said my work had an oriental flavour. I was also commissioned to do the cover for the Trinity College magazine *Icarus* and of Michael Srigley's *Poems Opuscular* published by Hodges Figgis in 1956.

Liam Miller of the Dolmen Press seemed keen on my work and in 1955 asked me to illustrate Thomas Kinsella's *Thirty Three Triads*, a collection of proverbial Irish sayings in triad form. I used black scraperboard for these illustrations, it was a joy to intertwine these images. The slim publication turned out to be very successful. It was signed by Kinsella and myself in a limited edition of 75 hardbacks, with 200 paperback copies also.

I had my first Dublin exhibition in 1957 at the Clog Gallery and Café, exhibiting all the drawings and paintings of my life. 'Quidnunc' of *The Irish Times* opened it. The Solomons family were well-known art collectors. 'I'm not going to buy', Bethal Solomons announced as he entered, and left having bought four. In the visitors' book was the signature of the writer J.D. Salinger. I loved his *The Catcher in the Rye*. A few months later [4 February 1958] I posted him a sketch I did called 'Catcher in the Rye', but heard nothing back

from him. The Clog exhibition was exciting, the paintings and drawings looked good on the white wooden walls.

Pat and Harry got on very well together. I felt there was more to my relationship with Pat than just fun and flirting. Once I had flu and he came regularly to read aloud to me from James Joyce's *Ulysses*. I felt so at home and comfortable with Pat.

In 1958 Pat and I took off on his Peugeot scooter during his TCD midterm break. We first went to Paris. We found a small hotel in Saint Germain des Prés, called Hotel du Dragon. There we saw a poster of Sidney Bechet, he was playing in a nightclub, 'Vieux Colombia' nearby. 'Dépouiller' [undress] everyone shouted, clapping in a circle around Pat and me. We had taken to the floor and jived with abandon. Bechet played *Petite Fleur*, his beautiful woman stirring the bubbles out of his champagne. Later that night I did one of my best paintings, called 'Bechet Bubbles'.

Each day we brought a picnic of cheeses, cherries and wine and ate this on the walkways beside the River Seine. Pat delighted in introducing me to various wines. He was a perfect Paris guide for jazz, opera, exhibitions and restaurants like La Polidor. One night Pat ordered, to my horror, a skewer of sheep's testicules. The waiter presented it with a flourish.

'I dread to think what you are going to have for dessert', I said to Pat in disgust.

We then continued on Pat's scooter to Saint-Tropez. Each day Pat and I went swimming on the closest beach. One day a woman in her forties stopped us. She was called Bianca Gilchrist.

'I could not help but notice you both walk the same path to the sea every day, you both swim out the same distance. You seem very much in love'.

She told us she was a jewellery designer using gold and diamonds.

'I never left one man unless I had another lined up', she advised.

We ate dinner with Bianca, listening to her litany of sad love affairs. On an evening stroll looking at the yachts and quay-side restaurants, me in my high-heeled clogs and shorts, everyone looking at everyone else, suddenly my ankle went sideways and I fell into the harbour water, receiving a loud cheer.

After a week in Saint-Tropez we continued on down through the coast of Italy, laughing at the strange places we could afford to stay in. It amused one guesthouse woman when we asked for a double bed. 'Ah! Un letto matrimoniale!' – making her whole family laugh. They could tell that we were not married.

9

HARRY AND LARAGH, COUNTY WICKLOW

The artist Pat Hickey had found a cottage in County Wicklow for a pound a week, and upon leaving he asked Harry if she would like to take it. This eventually became her permanent home. I had by this time left Dublin and moved to London with Pat, for me to find a job and for Pat to continue his medical studies at Tooting Bec Hospital.

Harry loved living in the cottage in County Wicklow. However it was rather dark inside and damp so she put up a wood-framed glasshouse in the field above the cottage and moved in all her possessions, which consisted of hot water bottles, sleeping bags, a golf umbrella, two long benches with a row of tins containing oats, lentils and various foods. She had an oil stove and a gas stove. There was one camp bed inside the glasshouse and another two beds outside, set in the long grass. These beds were made out of six Boland's bread trays that had fallen off the bread van one day. Harry dragged all six bread trays over to her field where she slept outdoors on them, in all weathers.

Harry grew a patch of herbs and vegetables with a mountain of compost at one end. There was a community of rats that lived off that compost heap.

'They are just like squirrels without the fluffy tails', she crossly said to Bea Brown, one of her Dublin visitors, who screeched hysterically at the sight of those rats that were happily eating the compost with their two front paws. After Bea Brown's hysteria Harry decided she had better do something about the rats, so she set up a basket with a string attached to the lid holding it open. Inside the basket she placed a tempting morsel to interest the rats. The first rat entered, Harry captured and carried it down to the bridge with the intention of throwing it on the bank of the river, far away from her glasshouse. The closer she got to the bridge, the further out of the crack in the basket the rat had squeezed. It was almost out, its hind legs nearly through the hole. She just managed to send it hurtling down onto the riverbank and see it run free.

Bea Brown was a large old lady, always in an old tweed coat. She had a broad Dublin accent, full of intellect and interest in plays and books. Her job was looking after the lavatories in the Royal Irish Automobile Club on Dawson Street. We'd sit, beside us a pink glass of powder with an ostrich feather puff, and talk and talk. To my surprise, Bea was instrumental in my meeting BBC's Libby Purves who did a long interview about my work.

It was in January and it was snowing. I was on the camp bed in the glasshouse and Harry had tucked herself into her bed outside on the six bread trays. The snow gathered on her golf umbrella and on her bed cover.

'Come in', I shouted.

'No, I'm all cosy', was her reply.

She stayed on in her bed with her two hot water bottles and several sleeping bags and on top of all that was an oil sheet, plus her golf umbrella over her head. I awoke to see the snow had gotten deeper. When I next woke up she was almost buried in the white snow.

'Harry, wake up, you must come in', I kept on calling her, until she sat up.

'Blast!' she shouted, as all of the snow avalanched from her umbrella down into her sleeping bag. I had ruined her night.

At first when she lived in the glasshouse she would put a kettle on the oil stove to steam up the windows so that people could not see her undressing from the road. Eventually she did not give a damn who saw her.

It was around this time that Pat and I bought a gypsy caravan. We called it the wagon and placed it on a grassy hill two miles from Harry's glasshouse. It had a sweet little wood-burning stove with a chimney that went out through the curved roof. A double bed for Pat and I and under the bed a large basket to accommodate babies.

On sunny days, Harry would lie naked on her Boland's Bread trays, getting more and more wrinkly and browner and browner. Her hair getting whiter and whiter. She looked like her hero, Krishnamurti, the philosopher.

She was obsessed with Krishnamurti.

'What does he say?' I asked her, to which she answered.

'Nothing, absolutely nothing. He is marvellous'.

Harry's beliefs must have rubbed off without my knowing it, as she never preached to me any of these philosophies.

One day when she was reading in the sun, she did not hear the tinker tailor man climbing up the stepping stones in the wall, through the grass, towards her. He was obviously shocked when she sat up, and he said:

'Oh my God, Mrs. I did not see you there with your titties hanging down like a young girl'.

She thought it was a funny contrast; 'hanging down' and 'young girl'. She was well known in the small village of Laragh. 'The woman that lives in the glasshouse'.

She had several visitors, mostly young students from Dublin. They worshiped at her feet. She would advise them such things as 'for goodness sake, sleep together, it would be awful if you married to discover that you were not compatible'. This was unusual in the 1950s when it was considered a sin to live with anyone outside of marriage. She was like their guru. She would rave about her latest young friend.

'Sammy is going to the middle earth, he is marvellous'.

'Jennifer does not give a damn. She smokes hash and is wild'.

But there was one thing I knew. Should I smoke hash or go to the middle earth, Harry would definitely not like it!

Up the road from Harry's glasshouse there was a sweet little cottage that Peter Murray bought. He lived there with Nuala O'Faolain cultivating a garden and honey bees. Unlike Peter, Nuala lived in her world of radio, university and writing. Many years passed until their relationship broke up and Peter married again. Nuala went to America. Her story would fill another book besides her own *Are You Somebody*.

Harry was now living off the invested money that was left over from the sale of 51 Frankfurt Avenue after the building society was paid off. She invested this money into Portuguese telephones, cardboard and black molasses. She chose these because she felt that they were morally ok, not realising that she had hit the jackpot, and her investments increased hugely. So from something like £20,000 she was making quite a bit of money.

For her shopping she would go up on the Wicklow bus at 11am and get off at Stephen's Green in Dublin, returning on the same bus at 4pm. She often came to visit us in our mews house in Heytesbury Lane, with a full navy blue roly-poly shopping bag of health foods, garlic, nut butters, ointments and homeopathic remedies.

How things have catapulted forward. The change in Ireland from then is explosive. Now there are health food shelves in all the supermarkets, then there was just one shop, on the quays, that catered for vegetarians with these nut butters, black molasses etc. They sold Harry's favourite vegetarian magazine, *Here's Health*, the editor being Stanley Leaf. That name Leaf used to make John Watling laugh.

In Laragh the fruit man dropped off boxes of rotten bananas and out of date vegetables for Harry. She would find lots to eat from this free supply. Black bananas were her favourite.

Just down her grassy pathway was Eugene Smith who owned a tiny shop and post office on the main road. They had a number of small children. One fellow, Sean, age five was shown a home film of himself as a tiny baby.

'Look Sean that's you, look your first swim in the sea, that's you on the swing, there you are Sean on your bike', to which Sean said when the film ended.

'Who am I anyway?'

Harry filled the dark cottage with boxes of trouvé art [the French word for found art]. She bought Evo-Stik glue, assembling her found pieces into really wonderful works of art. She called this work 'scavenger art'. She was given an exhibition by Bruce Arnold, receiving good reviews and good sales. Being a bit of a rebel Harry started to grumble about the length of time her pieces took to make and felt unimpressed by praise and sales. This did not make her career as an artist progress which was a great shame. If she had had that type of ambition she would have found a more permanent glue and her works would be collectibles. The pieces that I have kept are still so beautiful. One is of a horses stable with a brass horses head, old stirrups and leathers, all assembled on an old piece of wood which really did feel like the sum up of a stable. She found a dried dead rat and placed the rat on an old clock face and with various additions she called this work 'rat race'. Her works were truly original, but she lacked the humility to accept that she was just starting in the world of art.

When she was young, and still called Alice, she went to art school in Newcastle, where she worked painting Wedgwood cabbage plates. However, in Kerry she completely put herself aside as an artist and she identified with each of us children, encouraging Hazel, Lucy, Michael and myself to do painting. This went on for all our young years.

One evening Luke Kelly, Mary Black and Leslie MacWeeney all came to visit Harry. A huge singing session went on way into the night. Harry loved to cook huge curries for everyone. The craic was mighty.

One morning in 1963 I left Harry making her lapsang souchong tea in the glasshouse and travelled over the Wicklow Mountains to Dublin. I was to appear on *The*

Late Late Show with Gay Byrne. As I entered Dublin a strange atmosphere hung over the streets. It puzzled me all the way to our pad in Heytesbury Lane. While airing my sleeping bag the phone rang. It was June Levine, *The Late Late Show* researcher.

'I'm sure you will understand we are not doing *The Late Late Show* tonight'.

She said it with such conviction that I would know what she was talking about, I just said, 'yes, of course'.

'We will ring you again in time', she said.

I put the phone down and decided to get some food shopping.

Still puzzled at the odd atmosphere that hung about the streets, it was at the checkout in Williams' shop that I found out that John F. Kennedy had been shot.

'He fell into Jackie's lap', said the checkout girl. 'Awful isn't it?'

10

LONDON LIFE AND TRAVELS

Dean St
London

The
French
Soho -

Gaston.
and St Smith
I nes full of French
but I round kissing
& fighting at about 76 77 yrs old

Beards

26 Jan 88
Book 8.

Pat was offered a job in St Ebba's Hospital, London after his studies were completed so I decided to return there with him. We moved in with John Watling for a while before Pat went to live in the hospital.

Pat used to ask me to their hospital parties. They were mad. One psychiatrist sat on top of the door throughout the party, another psychiatrist threw a rope out the window pretending to fish, hauling and tugging at his rope. I was asked to dance by another psychiatrist. Not once did he answer any of my questions but asked me questions in return.

It felt good to be in an exciting city where there were new attractions and new people to meet. I moved in with Sally Travers, the Irish actress. She had a room to rent in her mews house in a lovely quiet lane in Hampstead and I set about looking for work from there.

One day, by chance, I met Desmond on a London bus.

'Oh Pauline', he said in a pity-me voice, 'I feel so cold!' as if he wanted me to take him in my arms and warm him up. Poor Desmond. It was the shock of the 'Willbyforce' experience that turned me off him so drastically.

After Pat and I lived apart, we didn't seem to need to meet up. Life was new for us both. Sally was a niece of the actor Micheál Mac Liammoir. I loved when he used to visit Sally. He'd lie on her old red velvet food-stained chaise longue, telling us stories in his famous theatrical voice. Sally was attracted to black men. They used to pop in and out of the mews, often disturbing the flow of one of Michael's stories, whereupon he commented, 'my dear, this place is like a game of chess … with the whites losing'.

When Sally lived in Dublin with her uncle and Hilton Edwards she found an abandoned script on a pile on the floor. It was written by Brendan Behan. She subsequently gave it the title *The Quare Fellow* and showed it to the director Joan Littlewood. It was put on in the Pike Theatre with Alan Simpson, then Joan Littlewood brought it to the West End in London. Sally and I attended the first night. Brendan was in the audience and took a notion to go up onto the stage and proceed to take over the whole performance with drunken shouting, delighting the London audience.

One of Sally's black boyfriends, Joe, from Trinidad, had an inflated idea of his powers.

'I brought the sun out today, Sal', he claimed.

Sally collected two shilling pieces for her television set, the television was the only thing that kept Joe from rushing off on some mad delusion. When all the two shilling pieces were used, the television screen went down to a small white spot, then off. Sally would rush back to the kitchen where she was cooking a spaghetti bolognaise for him. When the spaghetti bolognaise was cooked, she'd swing from the kitchen, wiggling her hips, with a plate full for Joe. Bits of it would slop onto the pink carpet and the chaise longue. None of this bothered her. Her only interest was to enjoy her darling Joe.

Another one of her boyfriends called when she was out one day.

'I have always been attracted to you, Pauline', whereupon he pushed me into my room and proceeded to pull at my clothes. I knew he was going to rape me and I tried to diffuse the situation by going utterly limp, but he continued. So then I said.

'I have something to tell you'.

'What is that?' he asked.

'I have got a disease'.

'What disease?' he said with alarm.

'I did not want to tell anyone, but I have got VD'.

'No', he said, holding me at arm's length. To my relief he was about to leave but then he stopped and said, 'how could a girl like you have VD?' and proceeded to attack me again, with renewed energy.

'Stop. I want to go to the lavatory', I said, fleeing from his hold. I locked myself into the small lavatory room and proceeded to force my body out of the tiny window that led to the mews roof. I was terrified that I would get trapped in this window and he would catch me, but I pushed and pulled and escaped onto the roof where I stayed, scared and shaking, waiting there for ages until I heard him bang the door and finally leave.

I watched his back walking up the lane from the roof. Sally came home and just laughed as she pulled me back in through the small window.

'Typical of him, don't you worry about it, girl'.

Mac Prane, from Scotland, with his huge purple pockmarked nose, called around to show me his new red MG sports car.

'Come Pauline, let's take a drive to Suffolk to visit Sally and John Seymour, famous for their book collaboration *The Fat of the Land*'.

I jumped in beside him and enjoyed the open top red MG journey. They lived in a beautiful old farmhouse set amongst wild broom. Mac and I immediately set to work and helped gather the broom blossoms for wine making. They also had a studio where they made pottery. I was to sleep on a camp bed amongst the clay pots strewn around the floor drying for the kiln. Before dinner Mac took me around their property and assured me that though he would like to he was not going to 'take off my breeks'. On our return John Seymour was standing on the doorstep looking at the sunset, having kicked something into the far distance and shouted, 'who shat on the doorstep?' It could have been a number of the children or animals that were milling around the place. The next day Mac and I drove back to London, my breeks untouched.

Harry would love to have met them as she was avidly reading a book called *Ploughing in Prejudice* where the author believed one should not disturb the earth, but build with compost on top of it in order to plant.

Back at Sally's I met her new boyfriend, but this one was very white. He had very blonde/white tight-curled hair and full lips. He was for all the world like a white negro. He was a budding writer, one of those people who thought being a writer justified stealing. He stole books, clothes and food, triumphantly placing his spoils on Sally's table. She accepted his every move. Indeed, he did become a famous writer. He thought it perfectly ok to bed several women other than Sally. I thought it quietly ate Sally up. Sally was slim, very agile, a herbalist and she seemed very fit, but she developed bowel cancer. Throughout Sally's illness, he continued to play around, yet he loved her and consistently stayed by her bedside. He would tell her every detail of these affairs. Throughout all this pain Sally put on a brave front, not showing that she was deeply hurt. She died, never expressing her inner torment.

I believe it is in the nature of the male species, and less so in the female, to love someone yet want to play around. Perhaps society should face up to this propensity in humans and not sweep it under the carpet and not pretend or hope it doesn't exist. I think the answer is acceptance. It is an on-going treacherous breaker-up of true love. It is a pity to break up deep love over a fling! When you look at nature and see the behaviour of male species, it is obvious that one female is not enough for their sex drive. He needs to spread his seed to carry his DNA. It is a drive that is over-powering and can override cultural and moral taboos.

In London I made my living in many ways. I was commissioned by the famous harpsichordist and composer Thurston Dart to do line drawings for his music sheets, which were published by Stainer and Bell. I loved meeting him for coffee to discuss ideas for these drawings. My next job was painting biscotware beads for necklaces, commissioned by two eccentric old ladies in Shepherd's Bush. Then, Troy Kennedy Martin, our pal from Trinity who wrote *Beat on a Damask Drum* and *Z Cars*, introduced me to Osith Leeson of John Murray publishers. She was a strong bushy-haired woman who promptly hired me to illustrate Shirley Deane's *The Road to Andorra* and Noni Jabavu's *Drawn in Colour* and then Deane's *The Expectant Mariner* and several other publications. It's funny to see these books up on eBay today. Throughout my career publishers have used my work to illustrate such people as Nadine Gordimer, Fay Weldon, Doris Lessing etc. On each of these occasions when I was given a commission or asked to illustrate a book, I would celebrate by buying myself a miniature cactus plant. I soon gathered quite a long row for my window sill.

In 1960 Mr Kesbe of Shell Chemicals asked me to do a children's colouring book.

'We will talk over lunch', he said.

He had booked a table where we sat opposite a huge advertisement for Durex condoms, distracting me from the children's colouring book.

'I want you to place one of our sacks of Shell fertilizer subtly in each drawing', which I did, young fool that I was. After lunch he escorted me to the 14 Bus to Beaufort Street, the new cactus tucked into my bag. I was happily sitting on the back of the bus, when a tall, dark-suited young gentleman with a bowler hat and newspaper primly sat down right beside me, put his hat on his knee, turned his head toward me, and said:

'Your mother was sick when you were two years old'.

'I don't know', I answered.

'And your father is Australian'.

'I don't know', I answered.

'You used to live in a place called Frankfurt Avenue'.

'Yes, that is true'.

'You are going to marry Barry, and you have a very good friend called Pat'.

'It is the other way round', I answered, 'I am going to marry Pat, and my very good friend is called Barry'.

It ran through my mind that this man was making a pass at me.

'I am not making a pass at you or trying to pick you up, but if you would like to talk more we could get off the bus and have a coffee'.

Being young and nervous I refused, but looking back I wish I had listened more to him. Subsequently Harry told me that she had been sick when Hazel was two, not me. Later the chef Albert Roux said he had a racehorse being looked after in Australia by a man called Bewick.

It was Mac Prane who encouraged me to show BBC TV in 1960 my drawings and stories of *Little Jimmy*, stories about a little wood mouse who had a hedgehog friend called Prickly Ginger. I had started writing these stories back in Frankfurt Avenue, primarily to amuse myself, but friends like Mac, Troy and John Watling had become big fans of them. Many stories still sit in my bottom drawer. Taking Mac's advice, I took some stories along to the BBC. I was asked to bring back a full finished story of *Little Jimmy* with 60 illustrations. Barry's boyfriend, Philip Castle, helped me make an 8mm film of it. Ursula Eason of the BBC saw this. They commissioned a series of 6 ten-minute stories. Later it got to 24 stories as it received high ratings. It was an experience working for the BBC. I met interesting people like Ewan McColl, the traditional singer. I rubbed shoulders with producers, directors, performers and technicians. Studio Five was designated for the *Little Jimmy* programmes. They had set up seven easels and seven cameras that tilted, zoomed and panned, which would give the illusion of animation. For example, camera one would move over the large line drawings, along the woodland path, passing Little Jimmy's nose, panning along his body, passing his tail, giving the impression of movement, then camera two takes you up to the school, where Little Jimmy meets a centipede called Sid.

The story went: Sid the Centipede told Jimmy that he was an artist and that he was able to paint with every one of his 100 legs, all at the same time. Jimmy invited him into his school desk to join the art class. Jimmy handed Sid down paints and brushes to use. When art class was over, Sid had painted enough work for a full exhibition. The following week Sid invited Jimmy and Ginger to attend the opening, so they dressed up, sticking little berries on Prickly Ginger's spines, and Jimmy wore fancy boots and a fancy hat. They met another centipede at Sid's exhibition. She turned out to be Sid's sister.

Jimmy asked her, 'Do you paint as well?'

'Oh, no!' she replied, 'Sid is the clever one – I just knit'.

If ever there was an example of being unconscious of our society's rules and sentiments, this was one example. I can't believe now in 2015 that I should have said such a thing as 'Sid is the clever one – I just knit'. There are many things in society that we are blind to when we are living right in it. It is hard to stand back and hear what we are saying. The *Little Jimmy* programmes were aired weekly at six o'clock in the evening.

A Swiss television company sent a man, Mr Suter, to purchase the *Little Jimmy* programmes. During a coffee break in the television canteen he sat between me and the secretary. On the table were scripts, scissors, folders and a metal de-stapler. The Swiss man was most embarrassed as he thought the de-stapler was a sugar tongs. The secretary looked over her shoulder and coolly said, 'you will find it easier to pick up the sugar lumps with your fingers'. She was so belittling to the poor man.

From the newsroom I met Jeffrey Martin who asked me to lunch, and then to a party held amongst a park full of statues the BBC used as props for various programmes. As darkness fell Jeffrey and I sat around a bonfire while two Irish men created a hilarious scene.

One was the set designer who went around the world in a yacht, Michael O'Herlihy. He climbed up a tree with Kevin McClory and sang loudly to everyone, 'you're drunk, you're drunk, you silly old fool'. None of the English were as outrageous as the Irish. Jeffrey Martin and I took a walk, we sat down, he on a marble lion, while I dangled my feet into a marble pool.

A beautiful Maltese woman called Rosalind Mayer commissioned me to do a portrait of her young daughter. We became friends and one Sunday she asked me to go swimming with her. I packed two bathing costumes and a bikini. High black gates opened slowly to a mass of naked men and women. Rosalind and I disrobed. She kept her high heel snake-skin shoes on, when from behind a bush came a fat man with a huge camera on his belly. Rosalind loved the attention and posed this way and that for him.

'Hey Pauline, would you get us some lunch?'

The queue was very long. I decided then that an all-over-even tan forgives fatness. In fact, it looks pretty gorgeous. The queue consisted of all shapes and sizes, belly to back and back to belly, too close. The chefs kept jumping as the sausages were spattering hot oil on their naked skin.

Meanwhile, Barry and Philip bought a beautiful boat, it had sails and an engine. They called it the 'Carn Ingli'. They wanted to travel the Mediterranean. I was invited to join them, and as there was a pause in the *Little Jimmy* series, I accepted with joy. Six more programmes had been commissioned for the autumn. I took off to join Barry and Philip. We travelled down the Mediterranean coast from France, where Pat joined us for a couple of weeks, re-uniting us again. Nuala O'Faolain joined us in Villefranche, where I met an interesting plumber. We travelled all the way to the heel of Italy. Each evening when we moored a small crowd would gather to stare or beg a cigarette from us. A gang of youths in Santa Maria di Leuca played on a wind-up gramophone the record 'Think of Me Diana'. They played 'Think of Me Diana' all through the night. It stayed in my brain for ages afterwards.

After Pat left, we travelled over to the Greek island of Corfu. We anchored in a blue cove, a wide low boat went by us filled with rocks, on top of the rocks sat sun bronzed men and women in pale blue bleached clothes. They were singing together. It was so beautiful, Philip and I cried. The background of the pale olive trees and the thin turquoise water seemed to be steeped in history. Each of the Greek islands has their own unique atmosphere and their own stories. We stopped at many on our way down to Athens.

After Athens we went to Hydra where I met wiry-haired, beady-eyed energetic Costos Legacus. We had an affair. I stayed on with him on this island. As there was a ferry to Athens each day I would be able to take it for my return to London, so Barry and Philip left me behind with him. I had about a month left before I had to work on the *Little Jimmy* series again.

Costos taught me Greek dancing to bazuka music. He did the traditional thing of throwing wine glasses and plates that shattered around my feet as I danced. Later I met the famous bazooka composer Mikis Theodorakis, he was sitting in a white marquee looking incredibly depressed. Apparently he was wanted by the police as his music was banned by the government. He was involved in the resistance.

Costos bought me gifts of turquoise earrings and sandals with the same turquoise beads stitched onto them made by an old friend of his. Costos had that wildness about him that I loved.

When I parted to return to London it felt so sad. Costos planned to reunite in Paris. Meanwhile we wrote to each other. His letters were in Greek so I found a Greek café in Soho and asked one of the waiters to translate Costos' letters. The waiter put his heart and energy into the translating, exclaiming 'oh, he love you *sooo* much, this letter break my heart'. I would leave the café elated. However one day I went into a Greek travel agency and asked a serious looking young woman to translate the same letters.

'Do not trust this man', she advised. 'He is saying too much about love to you. He is lying'.

I hated the way Costos counted the change when I bought some food. When we reunited in Paris we stayed in a flat that belonged to a friend of his, near the Arc de Triomphe. The second time Costos asked to count the change I splattered the coins all over the floor in temper. It was half-sad, half a relief to say goodbye to Costos. I didn't cry when I sat into the Paris/Le Havre train for London. Years later, I got a letter from Costos telling me that he had a serious operation. I do not know whether he is still alive.

Pat was aware of my affair with Costos. We were not living together, but we often would see each other. The comfort of his presence, his intellectual mind and his humour made me realise he was the easiest to be with. He was calm and never possessive.

By this time, Pat was living in Chelsea and I in Edward Fitzgerald's house in Chalcot Crescent by Primrose Hill. Edward gave me this tiny room with no windows, just a hatch door that opened to the kitchen. The little room was filled with the strong smells of cooking, so most days I would go and sit on Primrose Hill to relax and sunbathe after my *Little Jimmy* work.

On one of those days an old man sat down next to me, practically on my knee. He opened his Oxo tin of sandwiches and proceeded to eat. I said, 'I beg your pardon', to which he said, 'this is my spot, I've been coming here all my life. You are sitting on my spot'.

Another day on Primrose Hill a highly-tanned muscled man sat near me wearing leopard skin bathing trunks. He started chatting with me and said that he worked in the movie business making blue movies.

'Would you believe I don't find naked women in any way exciting? They have to have something covering them up for me to be interested', he said.

Another man said, 'if you give me some of your cherries, I'll give you a drink of my Tizer'.

Edward was as gay as gay could be; blonde, tall, lisping, lovely Edward. I adored him. He was one of my best friends. His work was landscape gardening and horticulture and I often helped him to do up London gardens for parties and weddings. Each day I could not wait to share with Edward all the things that were happening in my life. He was such a close friend.

Edward and I often went out together. He took me to many snobby dinner parties, many in his boyfriend's huge house.

'She's not exactly top drawer, my dear'.

He took me to balls in Oxford and Cambridge where we punted and ate strawberries. We'd also go to the lowest nightclubs in the docks of London, where huge burly dock workers would shout and clap the ageing stripper woman who danced precariously on the top of the piano. From the docks we would go to Soho and eat in a Jewish sandwich bar and then down to the bowels of the earth to our favourite club, the Rockingham. It was a Trinidadian nightclub where there were a group of steel band players, led by Russell Henderson. Edward and I danced with joy. We got to know Russell and other members of his band, who would join our table to laugh and joke along. I loved the humour of the Trinidad people. On my way to the toilet I walked by two Trinidadians. One loudly said to the other, 'do you take this girl to be your lawful wedded wife?' to which the other replied, 'I do, I do'.

There was a marvellous calypso singer. She sang along with the steel band. As she sang she moved her hips in a way that no white woman could do. Nearly all the dancers on the floor had this fluid movement. I was asked up to dance by a small Trinidadian called Nico, with a moustache, wearing a yellow-and-black striped t-shirt. Pouting his lower lip, in self-mockery, dancing eyes to the floor, he announced, 'I'm going to put sex back on its pedestal where it belongs', then he changed the subject. 'I kind of fancy myself as Nero, Call me mighty Nero. Dig that man, fiddling while Rome burned ...!', with the steel band rhythmically boing, boing in the background. Then he said 'You can call me nigger! That's how I get my kicks; they don't know they're doing me a favour, when they call me nigger'.

'Do you know Russell?' I asked him.

'Oh, that's Russ. I dissected his small brain, but I can't put it back. That's why he's walking about like this today, crazy'.

All my life I had painted black people without ever having met any. I don't know why, but I was always fascinated by their beauty. I commented to Nico on the beauty of the calypso singer and he complained wistfully.

'It's not fair. When I meet a nice girl, Russell starts playing "Worker's Playtime" and I start working on the girl. I dance with her, I take her to coffee, to dinner and Russell fucks her. How unfair! I'm falling in love with you Pauline and it hurts. See what you've done to the mighty Nero'.

I asked him what he did for a living.

'I own this nightclub', he quipped. 'Love me and love £60,000. I don't like peasant stock. I want you to paint me, not as I am but as you see me, utterly abstract'.

I complained he was dancing too close to me.

'This is my native dance', he said.

'Who's that?' I asked, about an amazingly agile dancer.

'O, he is an emperor, an emperor of the Mickey Spillane world of thieves, drug addicts and prostitutes. He owns a Rolls Royce, he doesn't keep it too clean. The Rolls Royce folk offered to clean it up, on the house. They said a Rolls Royce don't walk that way'.

'Tell me, Pauline, do you just want a black man for kicks? I'll understand'.

Later at the bar Nico was looking for a lift home. He had missed the last tube. A uniformed AA man sat at the bar. In a very loud voice Nico said, 'My mother always said, "son, when you grow up, join the AA"'. He got his lift from the amused AA man.

Edward decided to throw a party in Chalcot Crescent [1966]. His mother, Sheila, and I came over from Ireland. We helped Edward with the food and wine and organised the furniture so that we could dance. We had phoned all his friends and were looking forward to the evening. We had our party outfits on an hour before the party was to start. Sheila called Edward who was in his room. She got no answer. When she opened the door she found Edward dead on his bed. He had taken an overdose. The letter beside his bed explained to Sheila that he could not bear to live any longer as he had just discovered that Patrick Trevor-Roper, the man he loved, had been unfaithful. Then, on the hour, the guests arrived all holding bottles of wine, laughing with excitement for the party. Sheila and I had to tell each guest that Edward was dead. If only he could have told us he would have got full understanding from Sheila and myself. Perhaps he found it hard to express his unhappiness as we all perceived him as such a positive person. Maybe he could not bear to show his other side? I remember the colour of the cement on the lit doorstep, the curve of Chalcot Crescent and the cold. I can see so clearly Sheila and I standing delivering the dreadful news and the quiet reactions and how they walked away with the wine in their hands. I'll miss Edward forever. He died on 7 September 1966. Strangely he had left a will and I was included in it; for his six traditional, four Chieftain and two Chief Irish chairs, which we use daily in Kerry.

Sheila moved to Mayo to live alone in a caravan in a wild field. She adopted six stray cats and a small dog and a brown envelope full of ants that she treated as pets. They lived on the window ledge. She continued to be vegetarian and to follow Chinese medicine. She told me she could hold long conversations with Edward as if he were present. Sheila, like Harry, attracted a stream of young intellectual people. They would visit her regularly and loved her as I did. Eventually Sheila wanted to live near us in Kerry. It was such a shame that the old people's home in Glenbeigh closed down just as she was about to move down. With further research her friends found an old people's home in Wexford where she lived until she died. Dermot Bolger wrote a novel based on Sheila's family called *The Family on Paradise Pier*. She believed that Edward continued to communicate with her till her death.

11

I Knew it was Pat

Deep down I knew that it was Pat I loved most. There were no areas of mystery. Everything was said out, especially by me. Pat's a cooler person, he thinks before he talks. Our sex life was happy and uncomplicated. We were at ease, compatible, we fitted in our wit, our intellect, very different, yet complimented each other. The things that did not fit were small – like I am random and impulsive, Pat is ordered and goes by the clock. Pat waits to see if things blow over. He has to be pushed into talking of his inner thoughts. I used to be jealous when I knew Pat was attracted to someone else. I would ask him over and over, 'what do you think of her; is she more attractive than me?' Silly questions that I would not dream of asking now.

Pat and I shared a flat with Barry and Philip in a large red-bricked 1930s building in Beaufort Street, London, with England's largest mulberry tree in the back garden, where I often sat amongst the knarled roots and the dropped black mulberry fruits, painting in the shade.

One evening as I swooshed the water about in the bath Pat said to me, 'we might as well get married'.

'Why?' I never really thought it important to get married and never really wanted to have babies. I was worried about the world being full enough of people. However, marriage and babies came about as I thought it may look sad if I never wore a wedding ring. Things have changed, couples live together as partners. Pat wanted to marry because of his mother, another social symptom of the times. I met Pat's mother Edith and his father Paddy in Wrexham, Wales, in a house built with yellow bricks. Pat's father was a very quiet man. Pat told me that during the war a plane dropped five bombs over Wrexham. Their cook, Mrs Hughes, got such a shock she dropped Paddy's last bottle of whiskey. Paddy went back to bed, despite the bombs, to sulk and didn't join them under the stairs.

One day in Beaufort Street I was putting our bins out, full of pictures that I had decided to chuck out. Two girls from upstairs knocked on our door and asked could they take the drawings. I allowed them and they took them all. Now I'd tear them up and burn them as I don't like anything I am not happy with going out into the world.

It was decided we would marry in the local registry office in Chelsea. I had bought a black and white tweed suit for the occasion. It was January [1963]. Pat and I arrived at the tall Chelsea civic offices and ran up the steps.

'I do', my voice rang out, loud and clear.

Pat sounded nervous. His 'I do' quivered.

'Why were you nervous?' I later asked Pat. I have come to realise that any figures of authority make Pat nervous.

It felt no different being married, nobody seemed to notice. My wedding ring was like something out of a Christmas cracker and my engagement ring was a topaz stone set on a gold band made by a jeweller in Hampstead.

Pat took two months off from Tooting Bec Hospital for our honeymoon. First we travelled to Paris where we met up with the good-looking author Jill Neville. She had left London and was now living with Angelo Quattrocchi, the anarchist and poet. We didn't meet him but we saw their apartment, the attic bedroom was darkened with a curtain over the skylight.

'I don't like Angelo to see me in the bright morning light', she laughed.

After Paris we travelled to Nice and walked the glamorous streets where many film stars had trodden. In one of the back streets I saw a window with unusual haircuts.

'I'm going to get my hair done', I said to Pat.

Amongst the warm scented smells of hair products, I was served a coffee by a young negro wearing a gold turban. I hadn't realised that this was the salon belonging to the best hotel in Nice called the Le Negresco. They cut, puffed and curled my straight hair into a halo of curls. Pat was thrilled when I exited the salon, 'you look marvellous', he said. However, after my shower in no way could I get my hair to look like a halo of curls. It looked so awful I went back to have it cut in a shorter style. This time when I exited the salon Pat roared with laughter, 'you look like Burt Lancaster', and from then on throughout our honeymoon he called me Burt.

We travelled on to ski in St Anton, Austria, where many's the time I fell, grazing my skin on icy hard snow as Pat swung his light hips from side to side, gliding effortlessly down to the villages. One day I was waiting in the village for Pat to appear from his morning skiing, when the sirens screeched out that there had been an avalanche. I could hardly breathe with fear that Pat was caught up in this avalanche. I was in the public toilet at the time. In the next loo I heard a man's voice 'ah, I haven't had a shit for two weeks'. By now a crowd had gathered at the bottom of the ski slope. Stretchers came down with the injured. I blurted out to each stretcher bearer.

'Have you seen my husband? Is he all right?'

At last I was told that he was, and that he was busy digging out his trapped companions. The next day the church bell tolled for a young mother's death.

12

RETURN TO DUBLIN

When the BBC asked me to stay on and work on a fully animated version of the *Little Jimmy* series, I somehow wanted to stop, much as I loved the job meeting singers, actors, directors. I enjoyed how my neighbours' children used to repeat the stories back to me. It took away a lot from my own painting time. I couldn't paint *Little Jimmy* unconsciously and I didn't want it to be always a given agenda, so I turned down the offer to animate it.

Pat and I decided to leave London and move back to Dublin. He had been offered a job in St Patrick's Hospital and also in Trinity College as the Student Psychiatrist. We moved into a huge sunny Georgian room in Upper Mount Street. In the evenings I attended the Graphic Studio, opposite us, where artist Pat Hickey taught etching and lithography and Elizabeth Rivers taught wood engraving. I was interested to learn how Thomas Bewick worked. Apparently, he used cherry woods as it is very hard and can hold very fine cut lines. I learnt how he was the first engraver to press back areas of the block to achieve distance. We were an intense group, consisting of Michael Kane, Brian Bourke, Leslie MacWeeney and Anne Yeats who inked up some fine woven gauze with black ink, printing it onto etching sheets.

Next door to the Graphic Studio was Dolmen Press, run by the publisher Liam Miller. He commissioned many precious books and printed each by hand, each letter placed in a wooden holder and printed in black or Chinese red. It was a great compliment to be asked by Liam Miller to illustrate. Liam was totally dedicated to his publishing. He had a small black goatee beard and talked slowly with his head very much to one side. It was as if he did not care about earning a living, he cared about the beauty of his work. His publications have become sought after by collectors.

Liam gave me Thomas Kinsella's poem on St Patrick's Hospital, where Pat worked. It was not a very positive story and Pat felt that Dr Moore, the Head of St Patrick's would be offended, so I turned down this commission.

Lesley MacWeeney also had a flat opposite ours. She would hold life classes, and instead of hiring a model we all took turns to pose nude. '*Jaesus* Pauline, keep on those boots', Brian Bourke said, and stupidly I did! I have many nude drawings of Brian Bourke. I think he is a superb artist, he is also a puppet maker supreme. We would often have parties where he would set up his puppets and do a show for us. Brian's work was genius as far as I could judge. He worked with oils mostly, creating gaunt significant portraits of his wife. His trees and scenery gave out the very smell of the scene. Brian flirted with us women, but said one time to my disappointment, 'a woman could never paint as well as a man'. One of his paintings of me was sold in Zurich and I was recognised by a TV crew when they arrived in Dublin to make a programme.

One of the group was the handsome Michael Kane who had a dry Wicklow sense of humour. His work was strong and Germanic in atmosphere. Lesley's work consisted of strong black lines, rather like the lead lines in stain glass. She was given a big commission of the stations of the cross, woven in tapestry. These life classes came in useful for the anatomy of Christ.

In nearby Baggot Street there were two pubs, Doheny & Nesbitt and Toners, where all of us artists used to meet up. One frequent visitor to Dublin from Zurich was the artist Alex Sadkowsky. He had fallen in love with a beautiful dark-haired girl called Theresa. They would fool and joke together, he would take out of his pocket a plastic horrible-looking piece of dog shite which he would place, to everyone's horror, on the table to trick us. His etchings were dark, intense and large. In my opinion he is an original and I have many of his etchings in my exchange collection. The two pubs filled with people of that time, artists and writers such as Leland Bardwell, Camille Souter, Harry Kernoff, Brendan Behan, Patrick Kavanagh, John Jordan and Del Kolve, Chaucer scholar, the latter two I did my best portraits of. Each one behaved eccentrically. Harry Kernoff, a Jewish artist, was a short man wearing steel-rimmed glasses, he wore a large felt hat and would tout his paintings in a folder, selling them for one or two pounds. Now these works fetch thousands and hang in the National Gallery. We did nothing but mock him, it is sad that it took such a long time to realise that he was a genius.

On Saturdays, Lesley MacWeeney and I would go to the Iveagh Market and later to the Dandelion Market to find 'Treasures'. Lesley particularly liked old cracked crockery. I found a beautiful book under a pile of old clothes called *Philosophical Transactions.* I loved the handmade paper, all uneven and off white. This book turned out to be very valuable, it was the only copy missing from an important series. This was discovered when a London magazine, *Ambit,* published some of my drawings that I had done on various pages in the book. For instance, if I saw the word sheep I would draw a sheep around it. The editor begged me for the book and to please stop drawing on it. He then organised two exhibitions of my line drawings in the Parkway Gallery, London in 1959 and 1960.

I found furniture for our big room in the market, like a two-seater chair. I painted it white and covered it in old velvet, making our one room in Upper Mount Street beautiful and decorative. Best of all the sun shone over the Dublin mountains, over the Georgian rooftops and into the room. It had a very happy atmosphere.

In 1964 I wanted to have a Dublin exhibition in a real gallery. The best gallery in Ireland was called the Dawson Gallery, run by Mr Leo Smith. Rather than face him, I wrote a letter stating that I had enough work for a show. A letter came back from Leo Smith, the first page stated, 'I am afraid I can't show your work', and with a deep sense of disappointment I turned the page and read, 'until next year'. My heart rose to the ceiling, he was giving me an important exhibition in Ireland, to open in 1965.

Mr Smith framed the works in his sawdusty, rickety old workshop. I came full of excitement into the gallery when everything had been hung. Mr Smith had a cruel tongue which he thought was a sense of humour.

'Nobody is going to buy these, or tear them off the walls'.

That comment made me go down the stairs with my chin wobbling, trying to hold back the tears. Another time he said, 'women give up art for the bed'.

The opening of the exhibition brought several interested collectors. Ann Reihill, who edited magazines, collected many works. The Swiss Embassy commissioned a painting of their two dashhound 'sausage dogs'. That was a challenge – there is nothing wild or wonderful about sausage dogs! They invited me for cucumber sandwiches and tea. I looked around the Swiss Embassy for a suitable background for their two dogs. I found a manicured garden pond and painted their manicured dogs beside it. I enjoyed the humour of it. They loved the painting but wanted a little bit more 'liquid brown in Dum Dum's eyes'.

'For God's sake', said Leo Smith. 'We won't take it out of its frame. I'll tell them that you have just put a little bit of liquid brown in Dum Dum's eyes'. He reported back to me that they said, 'it was much better'.

'Miss Bewick', Leo Smith said one morning. 'Sybil Connolly has just bought seven works of yours and invited us both to tea'.

I took a long time deciding what to wear for this famous dress designer. Typically Leo Smith made me feel awful as we walked up the stairs. He muttered behind me, 'you look like a pink elephant', as I climbed the stairs in front of him, in my rust, pink velvet jumpsuit. Sybil had potted kumquat fruits and many exotic plants on each landing. We drank china tea over a conversation about my work.

That was the start of several exhibitions in the Dawson Gallery, one in 1969, 1972, 1975 and 1977. The heartthrob Mike Murphy opened one of these exhibitions. He could hardly open the door as the floor of the gallery was weighed down by the crowd. One of the best interviews was when Mike Murphy questioned me about my life. He laughed throughout the interview which made it very enjoyable to tell him more and more.

In 1976 I exhibited at the Kenny Gallery, Galway, opened by Alan Simpson from the Pike days. In 1970 and 1974 I went to the Cork Arts Society, which consisted of two rooms looking out over the River Lee, dotted with white swans. Pat and I polished the windows, cleaned out the fireplace and added pots of fresh flowers. Lord Mayor Gerald Goldberg opened the show saying 'she is my favourite artist to boot', which for a moment I took it up wrongly.

In 1972 I exhibited in the Italian Cultural Institute in Fitzwilliam's Square. Seán Mac Réamoinn opened this exhibition of my first Tuscan paintings. The sun shone into the room showing up the sculptures and line drawings to perfection. I used carnauba wax on the Owl and Cock. Line drawings of Tuscan hills, farmyards and olive trees filled the walls. Seán Mac Réamoinn, round, jovial and flirtatious, presented a religious programme for RTÉ. We frequently met up with Seán in McDaids or Jurys. He always had an amusing story to tell. He once vomited his false teeth into the Gresham Hotel lavatory and had pulled the chain before he realised it. This story was to illustrate how handy it is to have friends in all walks of life – one of these friends worked in the Dublin sewers and knew exactly which grid to go to for Sean's false teeth. Sure enough he found them in the Gresham Hotel grid. Sean's teeth glinted as he continued the story of how he gave them a good scrub and popped them back into his mouth.

Leo Smith of the Dawson Gallery was the subject of many conversations between us artists. We would share how we loved him despite his insulting comments, with Brian Bourke, Camille Souter, Norah McGuinness and Anne Yeats, daughter of William Butler Yeats. After Leo Smith died on 3 May 1977, John and Pat Taylor took over the gallery, calling it The Taylor Galleries. We were gobsmacked to hear that under his carpet, Leo had stashed, in flat bundles, hundreds of pounds. I've been exhibiting regularly with The Taylor Galleries since 1980 with John and Pat Taylor who have been incredibly supportive and have allowed me spread my imagination all over their gallery.

Camille always wore a black knitted beret, tucking her long red hair into it, creating heaviness that filled the hat. She always wore black and on her feet soft black plimsolls. She used old newspapers that she covered in coloured oil paint. She was soft spoken. Married to the sculptor Frank Morris, they lived in an old farmhouse up on the Calary Bog. Camille took up an interest in airports and aeroplanes, painting a whole series of paintings on that subject. Her first job surprisingly was as a Matron Nurse. She changed utterly from that job to an eccentric artist.

Norah McGuinness painted scenery using flat brush strokes, her colours were very vivid, she used kelly green, bright reds and yellows. Peter Davies used one of Norah's paintings on the cover of the first edition of Harry's book, *A Wild Taste* in 1958. (Harry had started writing the book in Kerry in the late 1930s and, in 1943, got advice from George Bernard Shaw staying nearby).

Anne's uncle was the artist Jack B. Yeats. 'He never allowed us to see his paintings midstream. His studio was out of bounds for us young children', said Anne. One day in 1965 when she was giving me a lift home she said, 'I must go and see how Michael Redgrave played Daddy in *Young Cassidy*'.

Pat's parents gave him £2,000 towards buying the mews house that we had found, Number 17 Heytesbury Lane, just off Baggot Street. It had a long back garden with a plum tree, two apple trees and a glasshouse. The front courtyard led out to a friendly-feeling lane, something like where Desmond MacNamara had lived making his puppets. Life was so sweet in this mews house, it seemed so sunny.

Pat and I slept downstairs in the sitting room. We always kept the garden doors wide open. A hedgehog would come in from the garden to visit on a regular basis. He always scuttled under our bed. The hedgehog fell in love with our fireside brush. After he noisily and sloppily finished drinking the milk we put out for him we would hear him rhythmically making love to that brush.

Our little wood-framed glasshouse needed some manure as I wanted to grow a crop of tomatoes. Small Bobby offered to call for me. Small Bobby married big Mike, her head would go way back as she looked up at him. Bobby knew of a worm factory – apparently it is a perfect manure. The worm factory was on the north side of Dublin under a railway bridge.

'Pick me up from the Indian fashion show', I said to Bobby. During the show we were given Indian sweet meats and rice wine. By the time I left the show, my eyes were zigzagging and I could see halos of colour. Bobby explained to me the sweet meats must have had hash in them, as they do that in India. So with my eyes zigzagging, we entered the dark arches under the railway bridge to look at barrel after barrel of worms. They were destined to be taken to Russia where the land had been overused, and worms were needed to recondition the fallow soil. In the summer our tomato plants grew with strange curled up leaves, all crooked because of the rich worm manure. However, the tomatoes tasted very good and there were lots of them.

One hot day when I got back from the shops I thought it private enough to totally strip and lie on the lawn in the beautiful sun. I thought I heard a pebble drop and opened my eyes to see, peeping over the wall, Gerry from across the way.

'I was just collecting stones Pauline', he explained in his squeaky voice.

I later heard from our neighbour Jenny Kingston that Gerry regularly climbed the walls of the mews houses to peep over into various gardens. Later, when I passed him in the lane, he repeated to me.

'I was collecting stones, Pauline, would you believe they are very hard to find'.

Artists Richard and Jenny Kingston lived on our left, they made the lane feel like a small village. They were to be seen chatting to all those who lived there. Bongo, so called, as he played the bongos, had a guttural gravelly voice.

'You can find some good stuff in these bins'.

He had found a toothbrush and an old cracked mirror. Further up the lane lived Vanessa and Victoria Mary Clarke, whose step-father was Dardis Clarke, poet Austin Clarke's son. They were the same age as Poppy and often came to play. Victoria is the partner of the Pogues singer, Shane McGowan.

There was a beautiful girl living near the top of the lane, she was the daughter of the broadcaster, novelist and mystical writer, Brian Cleeve. Someone had written on her dusty window a Shakespearian quote, 'we are such stuff that dreams are made on'.

Also up the lane lived the Perdue family. Poppy often played with their children, romping around the garden naked. They laughed at Poppy when she said to Reverend Perdue as he walked downstairs in his pyjamas:

'Have you got a willy like daddy?'

To which he answered, 'yes, I do'.

I was broken hearted when the Perdues left the lane.

In nearby Wellington Road, was a Montessori school run by Laura Burke, where Poppy got such affection and a good start to schooling.

I was going to burn three old canvases so Richard asked could he paint on the backs. Somebody, somewhere might have a canvas with a Kingston on one side and a Bewick on the other.

All us artists, writers and photographers were inspired by Bewley's, Dublin's famous coffee house. One morning I was sitting on a bentwood chair with a hot bubbly coffee. Chelita Navaro joined me with her friend, Dogfood Reg. Reg sat thin and dandy beside voluptuous Chelita, his long, painted nails dotted with smudges of cream cake, his pencilled eyebrows matching his thin smiling lips. Chelita's cyclamen-coloured mouth and huge breasts burst like pomegranates from her dress. They had been to a late night Spanish party.

My artist friend Patricia Bianchi introduced me to the brothers Ruben and Fonsie Mathews, two men that had worked all their adult lives in the stained glass studios for Harry Clarke in North Frederick Street. They knew every pane of Bewley's windows. Both small slender men in their seventies regularly visited Kerry and painted with Patricia, Helena Brunicadi and myself. Ruben and Fonsie loved to paint Killarney's lakes and falls in watercolours. They'd book into the Lake Hotel for a week or two and if they sold a watercolour to a tourist they could stay on for an extra week. One day Ruben sat back in my studio and told us this story:

I was painting in a field overlooking the sea near Bray when a young girl of about twelve came over to me and said, 'my sister says she likes you', and I don't know what came over me because I said, 'you go and tell your sister that I like her too', so she ran off and returned again and said, 'my sister says could she meet you', and

I said, 'tell your sister I'll meet her down there by that railway tunnel in ten minutes'. So I finished off my painting and when I was waiting at the tunnel I got a terrible fright when I saw a beautiful young lady walking down the field to me. I couldn't face her so I ran into the tunnel to escape. Then I heard a train coming. Because I didn't want to go back and face her, I lay down between the tracks and let the train go over me. The noise was fierce. I was in an awful daze when the train had gone and demented as to which way to turn so that I didn't have to meet her.

Regular customers at Bewley's included the actor Charlie Roberts, '*Jaesus*, Pauline, I'm dying for a cup of coffee'. Taking off his bicycle clips and laying his latest script on the table he said, 'wait till I tell you … who did I just bump into but Carolyn Swift …' Novelist James Ryan and *The Irish Times*' Caroline Walsh with their son would breakfast together, a unit of happiness in a plum-coloured snug. I put them all into my sketchbook. When I got home I did a large painting and then an even larger one, a diptych. Subsequently one of these paintings was used on the cover of *The Legendary Lofty Clattery Café: Bewley's of Ireland*.

Peggy Jordan, a vivacious fifty-year-old young woman, lived her life at night, giving endless parties and promoting wild and wonderful Irish singers. Her most famous group were The Dubliners. There was always music and singing at her parties, bearded fellows drunkenly swaying about and shouting, 'hey, Ronnie, sing *The Butcher Boy*, will ya'. 'Bugger the butcher boy!' Then Luke Kelly, left hand behind his ear, started singing, 'her eyes they shone like diamonds …' One after another wonderful songs were belted out.

I could never keep up with Peggy's energy. She would often say, 'hey Pauline, let's go on a skite'. When the party finished, Merci Madigan said I could stay over in her pub in Rathmines. Her bedroom was over the bar, with a huge bed and a black coal fireplace. Merci proceeded to tear up a shiny magazine called *Der Spiegel* and lit match after match to try and light the coals, page after page just died, till all the pages were gone.

'They called back this copy, it's got some secret printed in it, they offered money for it', she said, after burning it.

Under the large bed Merci kept her collection of bathing caps.

'I'm on BT's list when new ones come in, I have to go and get them', she said.

Dawn was breaking when Merci's brother walked into the bedroom.

'Sing Pauline a song', and without hesitation he sang a rollicking Irish ballad for me. After tea and toast in their large warm kitchen I walked home. We lived a lot of time in the Dublin pubs.

Brendan Behan had a great belly on him and he would roar his way into the pubs. One night he spotted me and he remembered the time he hit me. He bought a round of drinks for four of us paying from a big new-looking Moroccan wallet with camels burnt into it. When Brendan was in Baggot Street Hospital he'd lean out the window and shout down to people he knew.

'Howa ya Mike?' … 'Get em off ya'.

The poet Ted Hughes was doing a reading of his poems upstairs in a pub called Sinnotts opposite the Gaiety Theatre [1970]. (His sister Olwyn had been my agent in

London in 1960 – things didn't happen as she was always waiting for the stars to show the way). The place was full of artists, writers and singers; Patrick Kavanagh, chin on chest, loudly clearing his throat and grunting. In walked Hayden Murphy, a handsome, slight, pale fellow with long mousse hair. His broadsheets came out every month full of the poets of Dublin and my black and white line-drawings. He seemed to perpetually have his arms full of these broadsheets. He was selling them to all the people while they waited for Ted to read. Poets John Jordan, Pearse Hutchinson, Leland Bardwell and Micheal Srigley and many of the intellectuals of that time filled the bar. I was standing with Pat. Pearse bent over him asking Pat, 'could you lend me a few bob'. Pat looked at his hand full of change and said, 'you can have this' 'The price of contempt', Pearse growled and walked away with the money.

Ted Hughes gave off a huge cloud of depression and yet his poems were not depressive. His wife, the poet Sylvia Plath, was not present in the room. Apparently that evening she had taken a walk in the streets of Dublin and didn't stay for Ted's reading. I had an empathy for Sylvia, who later committed suicide.

At this poetry reading, I was wearing a green and white football shirt as a mini dress. Luke Kelly sought Pat and me out, as he often did.

'What's a poor fella like me to do about Pauline …?' he said to Pat, who good naturedly laughed.

Flirtations were the norm, but Luke impinged on me. He was like a faulty roguish God, a red cloud of hair and a beard like a goat, white skin and short strong limbs. He was like one of my early imaginary pictures come to life; and he became the subject of lots and lots of drawings and paintings. I put hooves on his feet and horns on his head. He seemed to have yellow slit eyes and his teeth square like Dublin's Georgian houses. I met him one day in March 1973 on his way to the Gaiety to rehearse the part of Herod in *Jesus Christ Superstar*. He had lost his two front teeth. I never realised they were false. It was like two houses had fallen from the streets of Dublin.

Luke led an unrestricted life, often separate from his wife Deirdre, who ran the small Focus Theatre in Pembroke Lane. She put on deeply serious, intelligent and intellectual plays such as Doris Lessing's *Play with a Tiger*, Sartre's *I am a Camera*, and Pirandello's *To Clothe the Naked*. Deirdre taught acting under the Stanislavski method. Luke and she seemed opposites; he witty and extrovert, yelling 'Howiya' to workmen and fans; she upright, eyes down as she walked silently, dressed in black, a black gauze scarf covering her pulled-back gold-red hair.

The first time I became aware of Luke Kelly was in the Light House Cinema. Harry and I were sitting in front of him, his knees and feet kept agitating and digging into the back of my seat. I whipped around at him and whispered loudly in temper.

'Stop kicking my seat'.

Apparently, he fell for me then.

Luke was brought up not far from the Dublin Docks. One day he showed me where he and other lads jumped into the dark waters of the River Liffey. I could picture his white youthful body and his red hair bobbing about, swimming in the dark river. It never occurred to me that it was wrong to be inspired by wonderful Luke. It never was a question of Pat *or* Luke – it was Pat *and* Luke. I found his persona mythological, the total opposite to Pat's rational and scientific mind.

'You know I sang that for you'.

He was talking about *High Germany,* 'oh Polly Love, oh Polly the rout has now begun and we must go a marching to the beating of a drum ...'

I didn't thank him, saying, 'anything about war I hate'.

One autumn evening I gave Luke a lift to Dartmouth Square. He invited me in. We went up the steps of his house. I felt so shy as he turned the key of the door into the hall. We went into the cold living room. Standing in the middle of the room was a tall skinny blind man. He said in a northern accent something to Luke about taking the last of the milk, then left, guiding himself out of the door and down the stairs.

'I gave him the basement', Luke said, with no further explanation.

Luke took my hand and walked me upstairs to his bedroom. He left me there and continued up to the attic bathroom. I took off my coat and waited, standing in the semi-dark.

A little light shone from the landing, then Luke appeared completely naked, his alabaster white body and red hair looking surreal. He came down the stairs, clutching a silvery grey glistening pigeon tight against his white chest. It had flown in through the attic window and Luke brought it down to show me. I thought the pigeon might die, he held it so tightly. My concern for the pigeon wiped out any excitement of what was about to happen between Luke and me. Then Luke poured water into its open beak from a huge beer glass. Finally I persuaded him to go up to the skylight and release it.

By this stage I had gone off the idea of making love with Luke. In a diminished form of excitement we lay on his crumpled bed. Luke had drunk so much, lovemaking hardly happened. It was not exciting. Then there was a loud explosion that boomed from the cellar.

'Sure, that's the blind fellow experimenting with his bombs', Luke said.

I switched on the bedside lamp, he lit up a cigarette and lay back on his arms as I got ready to leave. Despite our botched time, Luke still had a magic that rose out of him. I leant over to kiss him to say goodbye when out of his hair crawled a large flat yellowy-orange head louse. Luke was a wild man, and odd things such as head lice and blind men in the basement and missing front teeth was all part of him.

I never stopped loving Luke Kelly. Luke is a legend and always will be.

In 1984 he died of a brain tumour. I went to his funeral. It was massive. A huge cloud of love came from everyone there. Madeleine had rung me up to see if I would stay with her the night before the funeral. I adore her, as I do Luke.

We lived a couple of more years in Heytesbury Lane, having holidays in John Watling's summer house situated by the coral strand near Sneem in County Kerry. Each time we'd return to Dublin I'd pester poor Pat for us all to go and live in Kerry. One evening I cried during a film.

'What's wrong', Pat asked.

'I so want to live in Kerry'.

I longed for the country life that I had experienced as a child there. Happily Pat agreed, and he went off to look for a job in Killarney. We put our house up for sale for which Tom McGurk and Luke Kelly made a bid for and eventually it was sold to a couple from outside Dublin.

13

LORDS

In the way in the chemist
at Zuoz Dec '83

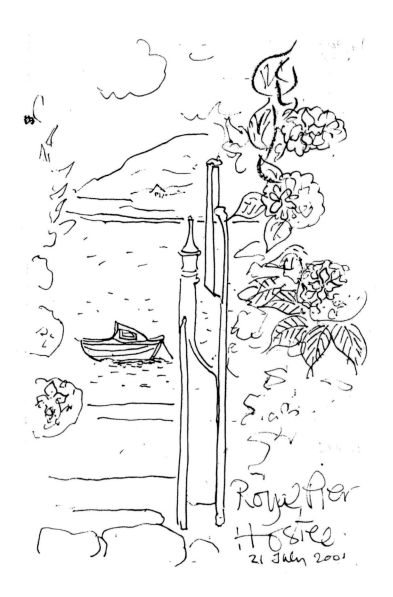

Royal Pier
Hostel.
21 July 2001

The phone rang. It was an invitation to a pyjama party in Fitzwilliam Square. Just before the party we had a visitor. It was The Honourable Desmond Leslie, so I loaned him a pair of Pat's pyjamas. He was a big man but he could just about squeeze himself into them. I wore a long white nightdress and attached a blonde ponytail to my short hair and off we went. We walked up Baggot Street to Fitzwilliam Square. On the way Desmond asked us 'would you like to hear a *bumbumbeulum*?' pulling up his sleeve and blowing strongly on his upper arm, creating an almighty explosive noise. He did this several times before we arrived at the door of the party.

The place was dark and packed with dancing people. I was asked up to dance by a small fellow I had often seen in Toners. He said, 'you remind me of somebody who often comes into Toner's pub with her mother, I would love to get to know them both'.

'And why didn't you?' I asked.

'Oh! I'd be far too shy'.

I couldn't hold back my laughter and rushed out of the room to tell Pat and Desmond who was entertaining a circle of people with his loud *bumbumbeulum* noises.

Desmond was quite famous in Ireland for many things including having a famous wife, the singer

Agnes Bernelle. They both were deep into ghosts and spirituality and were often televised talking of their out of body experiences. Desmond authored books on UFOs and also wrote a series of satirical books. Desmond was of Irish and Scottish descent and was related to Winston Churchill.

Desmond Leslie introduced us to a very handsome Lord called Mount Charles who was having a wild affair with the beautiful Elizabeth Rudd. They were constantly gazing at each other and calling each other 'darling'. One day Elizabeth rang us to say 'Darling Mount' was in hospital. They had been on a walk in the Wicklow Mountains when he climbed a barbed wire fence which split his balls so badly that he had to be hospitalised. This didn't cool Mount Charles' ardour for Elizabeth for whenever she rolled her eyes skywards, which she did quite often, Mount would hold onto his balls and say, 'oh darling, please don't roll your eyes again'.

During this time I had my hair cut and bleached by Michael Rayner who also styled the hair of Lady Mount Charles, who got prettier every day. I have noticed this happens to women who separate, they get slim and beautiful. I would sit there having my hair done staring at her and in would walk Luke Kelly who would have his hair singed instead of cut and the place became full of the smell of burning hair.

In those days we used to holiday in John Watling's cottage in Kerry at the Coral Strand, Sneem.

'We'd love to come', said Mount and Elizabeth.

They brought with them a Mount Charles crested double sleeping bag which we rolled out onto the straw matting of the cottage. On our arrival I offered a cup of lapsang souchong tea, boiling the kettle with water from a spring stream. With the first mouthful we nearly all fainted. It was strongly flavoured by a dead sheep that lay rotting upstream.

We were introduced to another lord – John Kilbracken. He was tall, bearded with gaunt cheekbones and thin long stringy hair. He spoke with a clear upper-class accent through his yellowed teeth. He pricked up his interest when meeting Pat and invited us both to Killegar to assist with his research on Van Meegeren, the master forger who copied Vermeer. He wanted Pat to give him a psychological slant on why the painter should spend his life copying another artist and he wanted me, as an artist, to give my slant on what it would be like living through the eyes of Vermeer. We arrived at Killegar to huge iron gates falling sideways off their posts. The driveway was long and full of large watery holes. Coming towards us on a bike was a young woman with her legs up in the air, spread out in order not to get splashed. When we arrived at the house it was an ivy-covered mansion. There was so much ivy we could not find the front door and to our surprise John Kilbracken stepped out of a large French window. He was wearing a loose Aran sweater with two leather patches hanging off his elbows, off one cuff hung a tangle of Aran Island wool. He took an amber-coloured pipe from his mouth.

'Welcome! Welcome!' Following him we stepped into the dining room through this window. There was a huge old mahogany dining table and above it a circle of spent wax candles with years of drips like stalactites hanging from this candelabra. He then brought us into the lounge where there was a tree stuck into the large fireplace with a minimal flame circling its enormous trunk. Every so often John would attempt to push the tree further into the fire to excite more flame.

We sat in couches that were as long as the tree trunk and slowly the dark of evening came upon us as we talked and answered his many questions. Pat offered that Van Meegeren, the fake artist, suffered from an inferiority complex and therefore enjoyed tricking the public into paying for his fake creations. My offering was that he must have been rejected for his own painting, therefore taking the mantle of another painter who was famous helped him live through the compliments that his fake paintings got from the collectors.

Seven o'clock came and it was time for our dinner. Mary, the girl on the bike, had prepared for us something in the dining room. Mine was a tin of salmon and on top was a tin opener sitting on the lazy suzy in the centre of the table. Mary had cooked Pat and John some beef in the library on a small camping stove. I opened my tin, that seeped watery juice, and poured the pieces of pale pink salmon onto my plate. As we ate John's beard was gathering little bits of beef which circled around while he was chewing and talking. He lifted his arm and pointed at one of the large windows from ceiling to floor and said, 'my mother shot herself outside that window thare'. How very spooky that window looked, the dark ivy was tapping quietly on the pane and the moon was in full circle brightly glimmering on the lake below the grass hill. I got a fit of the giggles and excused myself and went into the library/kitchen. It was terribly hard to gather composure to go back and continue listening to his extraordinary stories.

When bedtime came, around 11pm, we were brought up the very wide staircase by candlelight, huge patches of wet soaked the staircase and all along the corridor. On Pat's side of the bed a book, *La Pétomane*, who was apparently an expert farter, he could actually make a tune with his farts. He was one of Paris' darlings. On my side of the bed, an enormous long stemmed bunch of beautiful blossoms taken from his full rampant garden. My socks had got soaking wet from the leaks on the carpets. I took them off and lay in bed looking at the room in moonlight, a feeling of queasiness from my salmon dinner came over me.

'Pat, I feel I am going to be sick. Get me a bowl'.

Pat leapt out of bed, he placed a large blue and white bowl on the floor for me to vomit into. I didn't actually vomit, the slight breeze was refreshing from the open window, it helped me to get over the sick feeling. That slight breeze turned into a gust which toppled over the tall vase of flowers, smashing the blue and white bowl in two.

In the light of the morning, I could see the beautiful bowl, now in two halves. It was a precious Ming dish. I crept down the stairs with the two halves and went to the gas stove in the library. I cracked open an egg and wet the cracked surfaces with the white of the egg, with the intention of cementing the two cracks together, lighting a match, holding the flame to the wet egg, the egg bubbled, crackled and went brown, a disastrous attempt to disguise a shocking reality of breaking such a precious item.

Over breakfast I had to confess to John the breakage. Of course, I could not say that his salmon had made me feel sick.

'I know someone in Dublin who stitches ceramics together. She is an expert at securing valuable pieces with copper wiring'.

'My dear Pauline, if you could take a basket of other broken items to be stitched I will totally forgive you for that breakage'.

What a relief that was, how comfortable he made me feel, the vase must have been worth thousands and thousands.

After breakfast John took us to see his huge estate. Along muddy roads through fields and through woods enormous mushrooms grew out of the dark damp large trees.

'That is Mary Ann, she suffers from brucellosis'.

He was naming and pointing at his herd of cattle, giving us the family line of each cow. We had one more night with John, eating our cheese and slice pan from blue and white William's plates and drinking wine out of precious crystal glasses. My glass had etched initials of some visiting prince.

'I was once offered by a travelling tinker £1000 each for these glasses. I knew that meant that they were at least double that', John told us.

Later in Heytesbury Lane there was a knock on the door. It was John.

'Killegar has been burnt to the ground. Every item of clothing and all my writings gone', he announced. He stood there looking pathetic, in a red nylon sweater with a tan colour plastic suitcase. No more Aran Island wool or leather elbow patches, he looked half the man, but it wasn't long before he recovered and was living with a very beautiful young woman who wore green boots up to her thighs.

Later in the 1970s, when we had moved to Kerry, I invited John to our home in order to capture his thin long hair, his beard and Killegar in flames in a portrait, now hanging in the permanent *Seven Ages Collection* in Waterford Institute of Technology. The studio got a depressed feeling while I painted him, he looked so sad and mournful. He requested that not a chink of light should get into his bedroom. He soulfully told me about his life and living in the desert with the Kurdish tribesmen, moving over the sand on camels and putting up tents each night. I captured his likeness and spirit but was glad when it was finished.

John and his young wife Susan had a baby together and one day in 1981 they were having tea in the Shelbourne Hotel in order to meet the writer Ulick O'Connor. John went to the loo and Susan decided she would breastfeed the baby on the soft Shelbourne couch. In walked Ulick O'Connor who spotted this young lady breastfeeding. Thinking her a total stranger he went over and berated her for breastfeeding in public. At that embarrassing moment John appeared from the loo and said, 'darling, I see you have already met. This is Ulick O'Connor'.

14

BABIES AND OLD AGE

PAPPY JUDGING A PAINT

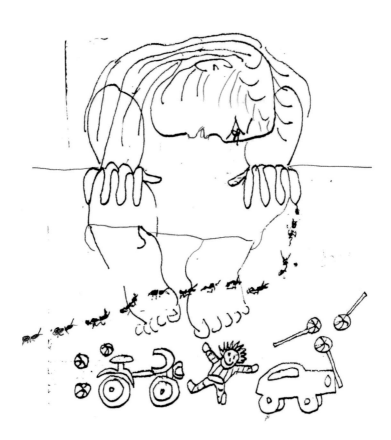

It's chance that begets us to this one or that.
It's like picking a ticket out of a hat.
It's like closing your eyes and stabbing a pin
that brings us into the world that we're in.
So now that we're in it and have brains in our heads,
let's not get too carried away in our beds.
Let's use some proven method to keep down the masses,
to stop man from building all over the passes.
To stop man from digging and rooting down pipes
and stringing long wiring through skies and down dikes.
Let's call to a halt when we've bred one or two.
Then after that make it for pleasure we'll screw.

Pat wanted us to have a baby, but I feared the threat of
an atomic war and didn't want to bring a new life into
this scary world. It wasn't fair. I thought I would love
the child so much I could not bear to see it suffer.
However, I wavered because I was thirty and child-
bearing years were coming to an end. I feared I might
regret not having a child. I also thought having a baby
might stop me painting. I would be overtaken. Society
conditioned us then that all the baby work was to be
done by women, feeding, nappies etc, so I insisted if we
did have a child that Pat would play a large role in all
this work. He quickly agreed.

I think I remember the night of conception of our
daughter Poppy, born in 1966. Somehow I knew I had

conceived. During this time I drew pictures of pregnant women, tears running down their faces, women on hands and knees on the kitchen floor, belly hanging down, their changing hormones left them feeling bewildered.

I asked Pat, 'do you want a boy or a girl?'

Pat wittily answered, 'yes'.

Harry had told me that men always flirt when their wives are bulging with pregnancy, and that when the baby comes men become jealous of the attention the new baby gets.

There was a party in Anne's Street. I was bulging with pregnancy. The composer Seán Ó Riada was there, he composed the music for the film *Mise Éire*. A young student sat on the floor leaning on Seán's knees, looking at him in awe as he played his music and sang. The party people were engrossed in themselves. I watched as if it were from outside. No one seemed to connect with me nor I with them, it was just me and my big belly. Then I saw Pat flirting with a pretty girl. I agreed with Harry and that night when we got home I had a row with Pat that it was so unfair that I should have to sit around, no one talking to me or paying me attention. I was lonely with the big belly on me, while Pat carelessly flirted with a gorgeous slim girl. I made Pat realise how hurtful this can be and he never did it again.

Poppy was born in Hatch Street, the labour pains came in waves. I held Pat's hands very tightly. My body was put into a very unnatural position. They tilted me with my bum higher than my head so gravity was ignored.

'Can I get into a crouch', I pleaded.

'No this would tear you'.

However I had to be cut to allow the head to come out and forceps had to be used. I knew gravity was the answer. Never have I felt so trapped into the wrong position. Poppy emerged a dark-haired little grown up.

I was lucky enough to have a room to myself because Pat was a doctor and we got special treatment. The gynaecologist, Dr Solomons, did not charge for his services. I repaid him with a piece of work that he had admired in the Clog exhibition. It was a sculpture of a carnauba wax coloured owl. Dr Solomons proceeded to collect several of my works. Both he and his father were huge fans.

When Poppy came into the world the nurse had to teach us mothers how to breastfeed. It was an awkward business getting the baby to suck. It took a few days before I could relax into it. Pat would walk Poppy around the room with a besotted expression on his face. He had fallen deeply in love. Later we went home to our mews house, carrying our new baby. Pat would get up in the night and bring me hot drinks, prop pillows behind me and carry Poppy over from her cot for her nightly breastfeed. I felt I had married a good man.

I found having a baby made the days roll on with great empty patches. I painted what it felt like being a mother, the dullness of going to the shops with the pram, but I think I suffered for a year from post-natal sadness. As soon as Poppy started to become a little girl, when she could walk and talk, each day became more interesting. I often asked her advice about a current painting, holding it before her eyes, and reading from her expression her answer. I felt that she was the wisest creature I had met.

One evening when Pat came home, Poppy ran into his arms and asked.

'Daddy how old are you?'

'I am 37'.

'How old is Mama?'

'34'.

'How old am I?'

'You are two'.

Poppy thought for a minute and said, 'too much'.

Sixteen-year-old Madge from Wicklow was our child minder. She was tall and pretty, and had a teenage crush on the singer Donovan. She wore a Donavan cap and chequered miniskirts and sang 'they call me Mellow Yellow'. She would spend hours playing with Poppy. Poppy loved this. Madge and Poppy often stood in the garden chatting away to the neighbours over the wall. I only had to look at Poppy's expression to see that it was so good for her. It made me realise a relaxed life was more important than having a tidy house. Poppy enjoyed being in Madge's comforting arms and being talked to by the neighbours. If it was me I would have filled Poppy with the urgent importance of folding, putting away and tidying. Madge made me realise how unimportant all this was, although I am still an obsessive tidier.

Leaving Madge to babysit, Pat and I would go out to parties and to pubs such as McDaid's and Neary's, famous for their actors, writers and artists.

Harry fell in love with Poppy, so much so that she wanted to take her down to her glasshouse in Laragh for the good air.

'You are being selfish keeping her here in the city. You are only thinking of yourself'.

She even carried her off towards the bus one day. It was around then that Harry and I started to have rows.

At first these rows were far and few between. We stayed every weekend in our tinkers' caravan and would call to Harry, having fun with Poppy crawling about on the matting of Harry's glasshouse. Harry often cooked us a vegetable curry or served up a huge crudely-prepared salad. I never wanted oil dressing on these salads because the sun shone on her olive oil tin causing a stale bitter taste.

'Don't be ridiculous. It is delicious', she would say to me crossly.

A long blonde-haired young man, Willie, Harry's special friend, was a regular visitor. As Harry was getting older, he looked after her. He would buy her provisions, even finding her clothing. They would both trudge over the mountains. They talked and talked and walked and walked onto the main road, then they jumped into the bubbling soldiers' hole. He was a wonderful companion.

I really felt Willie loved being with Harry. He would tell her all about the girl he was going to marry and his innermost feelings. They talked philosophy for days on end. They were at one.

When Poppy was four it was Pat's idea once more to have another baby.

'It's too much for a child to be the only one'.

I saw sense in that. Poppy showed interest all through my pregnancy, listening to my tummy and feeling the baby kicking. Then Holly was born in Hatch Street in 1970. Giving birth was sheer hell. Again I pleaded to sit on my honkers, again I was instructed to remain in this un-natural position, my pelvis higher than my belly. It was as difficult as trying to drink through my ear, it felt so wrong. Dr Solomons used gas to put me out, but just as I was going out, I felt an expulsion. It was Holly coming into the world. That was it, no more babies. No more populating the world. However I am very glad Pat persuaded me to have two children, good idea.

It felt so lovely kissing the top of the baby's head beside the vulnerable pulsating cranium. Such a warm round head. Her character differed from Poppy. Her cry was a loud roar, Poppy's a quiet, *ma ma*. I breastfed Poppy on the exact instructions of Dr Solomons, not a minute after or before the given feeding hours. Holly's roar to be fed was so loud and strong, it was not possible to ignore her. She created her own demand feeding. I have a theory about this. Holly had more room in the womb to kick, push and express herself and Poppy was held close and remained un-demanding.

In the 1970s Harry came down from Wicklow to Kerry many times with her friend Willy and they would swim in Caragh Lake and walk the surrounding mountains together. Whenever she came on her own, without Willy, she became critical, especially of me as a mother. She would often go into her room with her head in her hands, dramatically saying, 'I can't bear it, you are so harsh when you correct Poppy!' And when I entered my studio she muttered that I was 'fiddling while Rome burnt' and that to paint in my studio non-stop was like 'masturbation'. She felt I should be doing something for the world like reading Krishnamurti. I had become in her eyes a bossy parent, no longer her girl.

'I can't make head nor tail of it', she would say looking at one of my paintings. Previously I was used to her raving with joy about my work. When I built the little round house up the field for Harry to live in, we called it the Clochán. It hurt when she said that to come back to Kerry was 'going backwards in life'. I see that but there was no thank you for asking her to live with us. However when she got back home to Wicklow, she told everybody.

'Pauline has built me a sweet little house to live in'.

Then Harry started to write hurtful letters to me. The very sight of them in the letter box would make me shake. Pat being Pat, and a psychiatrist, had to comfort me, saying, 'Harry has turned against you, Pauline, now that you have become a parent'. She was anti-parent, anti-her father and anti-her mother. She preferred teenagers, whom she could commune with and hated the atmosphere of dictatorial parents.

In 1979, I was alone in the studio, the children at school and Pat at work. I went to my large sink with a bottle of Indian ink and suddenly it tippled out of my hand, splattering black ink all over the sink and up the wall. I had a horrible feeling of foreboding. Not long after that, the guards rang from County Wicklow with the news that Harry had been killed by a car, a Mercedes Benz, on the road at the bottom of the Sugar Loaf mountains, the drunk driver had killed a child also. Apparently, all her garlic and almond butter, things from the health food store, were scattered across the road. It was Pat who identified her, while Poppy, Holly and I waited outside the mortuary of Loughlinstown Hospital.

I believe the reason for this accident was that she had given up on life. She had refused to return for lenses after a cataract operation, therefore her sight was severely impaired. I believe she could not accept what age was doing to her. She crossed that road without full attention. She had become unhappy, maybe lonely and she couldn't accept the idea of coming to live in Kerry with us. Perhaps, she felt with this disability of sight that her adventurous life was over.

Her funeral brought all the folk that used to live in Frankfurt Avenue. Busy Hickey, Pat Cahill, all bearing gifts, like wild flowers for her grave which was in Laragh, Harry's local graveyard. She was much loved and admired by so many, especially young people. Harry had left a life-changing impression on so many people. However Willie did not turn up at her funeral. We met him in Baggot Street. He explained that Harry had hurt him deeply. She had started accusing him of taking her gas drum. I understood him as I was hurt by Harry too.

The priest knew Harry was not a Catholic, yet welcomed her to the graveyard with a beautiful poem that he had written for her. I wish I had a copy of it. I had a plain granite headstone carved, Harry Alice May Graham Bewick, 1903–1979. When they lowered her coffin, I obsessed about the fact that her head was not facing her glasshouse but I was too embarrassed to tell them to turn the coffin around and it niggles at me to this day.

For years the local children played in Harry's glasshouse until it finally deteriorated. Harry is still vivid to all who knew her.

15

TUSCANY

There was a tremendous amount of IRA activity under the surface of life in Dublin. Not only did Nelson's Pillar get blown up on the eve of Poppy's birth but also the British Embassy later on was burnt down. There was a huge explosion in the Nassau Street area and in Talbot Street, killing many innocent people and an unborn child. If only they would use battlefields. I rushed to take down my curtains because I realised they were red, white and blue, so I dipped them in a bath of purple cold water dye. I feared a bomb might be thrown through our window.

Another example of this undercurrent of fear was when the artist Brian Bourke rang up and asked could he call around with Theresa and a couple of friends after the pubs were closed. Pat was attending a conference in London at the time and I had Leslie MacWeeney staying with me. We were both in our nightdresses and ready for bed. Brian and his friends knocked on the door. I opened it to a mixed crowd of passivist artists and aggressive IRA night revellers who had tagged onto Brian. In they came to our living room. Leslie and I were shocked at the size of the crowd, and the row that broke out between a Dubliner and an Englishman when the latter said, 'I am terribly sorry for what my ancestors have done to you', whereupon the small black-bearded man stuck his beard into the Englishman's face saying, 'you fucking British!' It was so difficult for Leslie and me to keep the peace in the living room. It seemed like an eternity before they all left the house. Those sorts of tensions were under the surface of many the pub or singing venues in those days due to the troubles in the North.

In 1972 I borrowed £5,000 from Harry who had to sell her black molasses investments for this loan. The idea was I pay Harry the same percent as her investment did. So we had the money to buy an 18th century farmhouse in Tuscany. There were many abandoned farms in Tuscany going for such ridiculously low prices. We choose there because Barry and Philip Castle had sold their boat and bought part of Briccano and were painting happily in their own abandoned farmhouse attached to our house set in the Tuscan mountains. I also didn't like going through the fear of living in Dublin, especially after the bombing of the British Embassy.

We arrived in Briccano at night in March, the ground was white with snow. It was the next day we saw terracotta Tuscan mud peeping through the white snow. The large farm kitchen had a dreadful smell of damp and hen shit that wafted up through the old stone slab floor. I still carried with me from Ireland an irrational fear of the IRA. I stopped Pat putting on a fire, imagining that planes overhead might see us and drop a bomb on us if they spotted the light. After a few days my craziness lifted and the sun melted the snow and dried the mud to become raw sienna-coloured dust, wild flowers shot up covering everywhere, blue chicory, fennel, camomile and orange marigolds. The sun made me and the others relax and fall in love with Tuscany. Each day we visited the two farms up the hill from us. Gigi and Catherina lived in one with a pet goat, a dog, many hens and rabbits, the land around them cultivated and full of vines and fruits. Attached to that house was Bruna and Pierro's house, with them lived Pierro's brother Gino. They made us so welcome, hugging us close.

I loved the fat hot smell of sun-warmed Tuscan arms and the breath-catching odour of fresh underarm sweat mixed with the smell of sweet-scented soap. The way Tuscans touch each other as naturally as figs in a bowl, leaning against each other and hugging us against their big warm soft bodies. We had found a swimming place through the oak woods down from Lecci village. It was a turquoise ice-cold stream that formed deep pools. We would settle there for the day bringing with us cheese rolls, yellow melons and peaches for our picnic.

Eating the melon I dropped the salty seeds into the pale water. I was closely studying the little black living things that were attached to the stones, waving with the river's movement. The only indication that they were not plants was that every so often they turned and fought with each other. When I looked up, Poppy was making for a swim into the pool. Her foot was poised to land on a stone, her balance still on her back foot, when she spotted a viper under her raised foot, coiled asleep by the water's edge. She quickly retreated, bumping into Holly close behind.

'Mummy, I've just seen a viper. Come quick, look'.

Yes, sure enough, it was a viper, zigzag grey and black markings. It was still oblivious of us, it lay occupying the warm stone.

Earlier, five local boys had gone up to the higher pool.

'Vipera, vieni qui!' we shouted for their help, eventually, we heard their cracked youth voices coming towards us.

'Dové?'

'La'.

The five boys picked up rocks, their brown bow legs prepared and flexed for the attack. They lifted the rocks over their heads, then heaved them towards the sleeping viper. It lay there still, unmoved. Not even the shudder of the thudding stones disturbed its deaf sleep. The next stones hit the viper, not visibly injuring it. We watched as it slowly moved off into the dense growth. By four o'clock the sun had left the river. We walked with extra care and watched our every step as we climbed home up through the woods to Lecci village and made for Briccano.

At home we flopped our sun hot bodies onto our beds for an hour or so before we prepared dinner of courgettes, yellow spaghetti, pecorino cheese and strong scented basil soused in our own green olive oil. The saucepans used to get black from our gas. It needed adjusting.

Bruna cooked their own prolific rabbits, their own chickens, salami made of wild boar that hung from the huge oak beams. They ate polenta made of corn, cooked green beans, huge tomatoes, drank their own wine, lemon tea and stuffed into their Tuscan mouths yellow sweet cake. Except for the wild boar and porcupine, all was their own home produce.

'Senora, why don't you eat meat?'

Gino then would ask Poppy and Holly what we had to eat for our dinner. They would rave about how delicious it was, knowing very well that Gino thought being vegetarian was laughable. He knew nothing could be as good as the food cooked by Bruna, his sister-in-law. Every evening their television sets blared Italian pop, incredibly luscious overblown women and vain men.

'The Pope's a vagabond', Gino said as the Pontiff kissed the ground.

The night moths circled the lamps above the oilcloth-covered tables. Their dinner over, Pierro picked from the air one of the circling moths. The poor thing fluttered its wings until it was released. Gino and Pierro, in white vests, fresh from their wash after working the land.

Holly and Poppy practically lived up at the two farms of I Rossi and I Mealli. Our house sat also on a hill, lower than their hill, the view stretched over to other hills, striped with terraces and dotted with olive trees, sienna-coloured farms and villages sitting forever in the pale haze of the heat. The walk back to our house through fireflies, stars, the sounds of nightingales, owls, the distant voices and dogs barking, to our beds.

In the early morning at around six was the best moment to paint. The sun hadn't really got going. The farmers had been working since five. I would set up my easel and watercolours on the balcony under the vine laden with bunches of tiny green grapes. The heat dried up the watercolour faster than in Ireland.

'Mummy, Gigi's up our walnut tree'.

His heavy-muscled arms beating the walnuts down to us, huge and green-coated, they tasted milky and sweet, bitter if the thin yellow skin was left on. Caterina picked up a fresh water crab from beside her foot. It too fell to the ground, leaving behind one of its legs in her hand.

'Oh, poor thing', said Poppy and Holly.

'He had too many legs anyway', said Gigi.

Aprons, baskets and bags bulged with walnuts, half of them for us to take to Ireland and the other half for themselves. I was then taken to Castagnoli Vigliotti to paint Checha, a wild boar, clean and brown in a pigsty. I needed one or two of the long dark hairs on Checha's back to stick onto the painting I did of him.

'Prendi, prendi', they said enthusiastically, pulling hairs from its ridged back. There is so much to paint: porcupines, bunches of daisies, courgette flowers, the neighbours, the viper and the scorpion, not to mention the concerts in Siena.

Towards the end of our stay we had a huge dinner with all the neighbours. Long trestle tables seating thirty or more were set amongst the olive trees. Gigi cooked meat on a shovel, held over a bonfire, our laughter and shouts echoing into the night. We always went up to say goodbye to the two families.

SIENA
TUSCANY
BOOK
2

I'm not used to having emotions when parting, but Bruna set us off crying, picking up her apron, lifting it aside to fetch out a little ironed handkerchief.

'No, don't start', we left red and sniffling, saying goodbye. We cried until the next bit of fun en route to Ireland.

16

RETURN TO KERRY

Pat hired a car and drove around Kenmare, Sneem and Killarney looking for a house that should not be too far away from St Finian's Hospital, Killarney, where he was offered a job. While he travelled around, Pat stopped to pick up two hitch-hikers. When he opened the boot of the hired car to stow the girls backpacks an enormous Alsatian dog jumped out. Apparently it had been on Kerry radio that this hired car had got an Alsatian dog on board and would they please report back to the garage. Luckily it was a docile dog and spent the rest of the journey sitting between the two hitch-hikers.

At first we settled in one of the hospital houses in Gortroe, situated on a busy main road just outside the town of Killarney. I was so happy that Pat accepted the job in St Finian's Hospital. It was sad for him to leave behind his wonderful Dublin job in St Patrick's Hospital and Trinity College. I worried that I'd pushed him into this, however, it turned out to be a huge success. Pat adores nature and the countryside and the Kerry job was so different, so interesting.

His first Kerry patient was a joy, a contrast to the students of Trinity who knew from their book reading what their problems and neuroses were about. He told Pat he had been sitting outside his cottage, sunning his body, when a travelling barber asked him did he want a haircut.

'I do', he said.

After giving him his haircut, the barber suggested cutting the hair on his body into the shape of a cross like a donkey's back.

'Go ahead', he said.

However, when his two brothers came back from the bog and saw the cross on his back they bundled the poor man into the mental hospital. Pat could not find anything wrong with the man and sent him home.

We lived in one of the hospital houses, enrolling Poppy in the Presentation primary school.

'It's better to have some religion than to have none at all', said the head nun, standing under the high windows, where all you could see were the tops of trees and the sky. Poppy was very happy in this school. I had been apprehensive seeing all the nuns in their black habits. We later enrolled her for violin lessons in the Loreto Convent under Mangerton Mountain. She was taught violin by one of the nicest sisters you could meet, Sister Killian. We missed her terribly when she moved to Canada.

It was during this period I did a painting called 'Flying Over the Cathedral'. It was of a nun floating freely up in the sky without her constricting habit. This work was subsequently chosen by a female priest to celebrate her ordination in England. The English press published it and were very critical of her choice of subject. I also did a painting of a woman 'Floating in Lough Leane'. The lakes sometimes made me feel sad. They give off a gloomy atmosphere. That painting was followed by 'Small Town Lady Letting Loose', the woman was naked flying over Killarney town, beneath her the shocked faces of the town's people looking up at her freedom.

We found a Montessori School in Killarney for Holly, run by the gentle, intelligent Mrs Collier and her daughter.

'So this is your little girl', said Mrs Collier to Pat, when Holly firmly looked up and said 'big'.

Holly felt she owned the nursery trampoline and whenever she saw the colour yellow she would say, 'that's Lello, like my trampoline'.

Every morning on the way to nursery school Holly would stand on the back seat of the car frowning strongly and holding onto the two front seats singing.

'If I had a donkey and he wouldn't go, think I'd beat him no, no, no. I'd put him in the barn with lots of corn, the sweetest little donkey that ever was born'.

Each morning on the road to school there was a man who used to shout obscenities.

'Ye in the County Council all piss in the one pot'.

As teenagers Poppy tended to mind and look after Holly.

'No Mummy, she is very careful. She won't get pregnant'.

I was afraid that when she stayed out late she would conceive Blue Hugh's baby.

Poppy and Holly's characters have continued to be very different and yet they love each other very much. They both understand each other. It's a pleasure to see them getting on well through life together.

Many's the boy would stand around Holly when school was over. Poppy fell for one boy, gentle Conor, and it remains so to this day. After many boyfriends, Holly fell in love with an Italian man, Luca, who is now her husband, a perceptive, jokey, attractive Tuscan builder.

I went up to Dublin for a mixed exhibition at the Bank of Ireland, full of chatting socialites, art lovers and artists. I had driven up through Listowel and dropped into the AIB for some money. The man next to me in the queue started to tell me how he was down in Kerry fishing. He went on, and on, and on, talking about his love of fishing. At the exhibition I joined Maria Simonds-Gooding. We walked around looking at the paintings. We almost tripped over a large man with dyed blonde spikey hair. He was lying flat on the floor. Around his neck he had a torch tied with a rope and a large wooden African spoon. He caught hold of my ankle and said.

'Hey, I want to talk to you. I want to tell you what is happening in your life'.

His name was Mick Mulcahy, a wild genius of an artist. I was afraid of him but Maria said.

'Sit down, Pauline. Don't be silly, let him tell you'.

The first thing he said was.

'You have just met a fisherman'.

Mick's eyebrows met in the middle. He was very intense, making one feel uncomfortable. We continued to go around the exhibition, I looked back and Mick Mulcahy was pursuing us.

'Hey, hey, can I join your group?' which now consisted of Brian Bourke, Camille Souter, Michael Farrell, Maria and me. I did not answer Mick's request, hoping he would lose us, but he pursued us out of the exhibition and down Baggot Street and across to the United Arts Club, taking from around his neck the African spoon.

'Have this, have this'.

'No, no, it's ok', I said.

'I will have it', Maria said, taking the spoon and putting it around her neck.

'He is beautiful, Pauline, he even looks like you', she said.

Finally Mick left us, and we heard the next day that he had been put in prison for lying in the middle of O'Connell Street with his torch switched on, to avoid getting run over.

The next day I was back in Killarney. Poppy and Holly were watching *Sesame Street* upstairs in the bedroom. I was downstairs in the front room and, to my surprise, a white Garda car pulled up at our gate and out of the car stepped Mick Mulcahy! This time he was wrapped in a large white sheet. Around his neck hung a pair of black boots, a Swiss pen knife, a fishing rod and a saucepan. He had travelled all the way to Kerry to find me. He walked slowly up the drive. I answered the door, my heart thumped.

'Hi Pauline. Can I come in?'

Before I could say anything he indicated to the guards to go. I was glad that Pat was soon to come home from work.

'I have come because I wanted to see you again and I also needed to talk to Pat, your husband, as I believe he is a psychiatrist'.

It transpired that he had gone first to St Finian's Hospital where Pat was working. Mick apparently stood in the hall of this enormous building and shouted.

'I am looking for Pauline Blewit. She is married to a fucking psychiatrist!'

It echoed all over the hospital.

At five-thirty Pat arrived from work. I ran to the door and whispered.

'You know that man I told you about. He is in the sitting room'.

'Oh, no!' Pat said.

'Mick, this is my husband, Pat'.

'Pat, this is Mick Mulcahy'.

Mick stood up to his full six foot height, the items round his neck clanking and clattering as he shook hands with Pat. The first thing he asked Pat was, could he stay the night.

'I am afraid not, I am packing for Dublin, Mick'.

I was alarmed when Pat said that, as Mick would now know that it would be just me and the children alone in the house.

It resulted in all four of us – Pat, myself and the children – leaving the house and heading for Dublin. I was too afraid to stay. Mick had clanked off to stay in the local youth hostel in Beaufort.

When we returned from Dublin we were told Mick had spent the day in front of our house, in the yoga posture beside a mound of mouldy old hospital boots he'd collected from the wood. Apparently he sat in the yoga position chanting *om, om, om* all day. There are many stories about Mick. I consider him one of Ireland's geniuses. I have known him for so long now, but still fear these periods of wildness that he gets.

Apparently, in Stephen's Green he waded through the lake to greet Mike Kane. He walked around and around the Rathgar church at Easter time carrying an enormous wooden cross on his back. He shouted into Davy Byrnes pub.

'We are going to have a general erection'.

He was the male version of Lady Gaga or Madonna or Salvador Dali. He sold one of his huge paintings for quite a price, the deal was done, he then proceeded to piss on the painting, shocking the collectors.

On one of these occasions Mick woke up the town of Cahersiveen as he strided naked through the streets, roaring and singing. A lot of women are attracted to his wildness. Lainey Keogh, the famous designer, voluptuous with her long wavy red hair, fell in love with Mick. What a couple they made, they inspired a big painting of mine, 'Two Muses by the Skelligs', now hanging in the permanent *Seven Ages Collection* in Waterford. I bought one of Mick's paintings having just sold one of mine. It was a predominantly navy blue and white work, depicting a shark just under the surface of the waves and above the shark a navy blue Skellig Island and on the same horizon a low moon.

Living in Killarney had a strange atmosphere. Lonely, I questioned what would I want to do and where would I like to be and could not answer anything. I suppose it was a kind of waiting game until we found a proper home for us all. Alone in this hospital house, looking out at the main road, cars whizzing and sometimes crashing on that corner, and on the other side of the road a thick woodland, a golf course that led down to the lake. I started to take flight in my mind and out came this story which I feel illustrates how I felt.

FLIGHT
In order to keep her stretched bedroom slippers on her heels she had to sway stiff-leggedly downstairs to make the breakfast for the family. Outside the large windows of their new house there was a land mist. Above the mist the bright sun had just risen over the McGillycuddy Reeks. The German factory had sounded its siren and the cars whizzed to work on the road at the

front of their house. Bobo the dog's tail wagged hitting the cupboard doors at her arrival. He knew it heralded food. His tin of Chappie was opened by She, Fin. In fact, Fin also thought it all came from her as did the breast milk when she fed the babies. Sean felt it was all from her too. Occasionally, he would get a little cross. Realising they were all dependent on him and his steady wage, but it was a lovely cosy life with Fin at the helm. As Kavanagh, the poet, once said, 'It's great to be fed, bedded and cleaned out'. The smell of toast and good coffee wafted upstairs to Sean's bed. It made him stretch with pleasure. The snap, crackle and pop bowls out for the children, Chappie in the dog dish.

'Breakfast is ready', Fin called. There wasn't a delay, all slip-slopped with their loose slippers to the table. Fin, being inclined to overweight, tried not to eat a third piece of toast, but enjoyed the first two so much, she indulged. The blackcurrant jam so lovely with the cafe au lait. The children finished first as always. Siobhan set about ironing her gymslip, then collected the violins for their music lesson. Jo-Jo brought in filthy runners and complained about them as he had sports today. Fin brushed off the dried mud. 'They will do'. Jo-Jo accepted this. Next, Fin made them all sandwiches. Sean was keen on boating, and often took a row out onto the lake at lunchtime to eat his lunch.

She felt a lonely pull when they had all left the table and the house. She immediately regretted the third slice of toast after all the joy of breakfast was finished. The children were now in the car. They were good children, well-loved and sensibly reared. Sean, all clean and looking outside-worldly, gave Fin a hug, smelling of aftershave and warmth. He had a great deal of love for her and she for him. Any differences they had never lasted, and this hug each morning thoroughly set them up for an angst-free day. The car now filled up with Siobhan, Jo-Joe and two neighbour children. The engine started and they were off for the day.

Silence. No cars now. All at work. The cuckoo and the birds 'tweet-tweet' from the woods behind the house could be heard quite clearly. Newborn lambs called, dogs barking in the distance, her peace totally uninterrupted. She had a mental list of her day's duties; fill the washing machine, no need to hoover today, bring in the turf, very little to do. She could shop when she collected the children after their late music lesson. A full day to do with what she liked, provided it was either in the house or within a five-mile radius. Just what she pleased. In the kitchen, when she had put away the last cup, she stepped out of her slippers, and wiggled apart her toes.

Outside the large windows, there was just the grass garden and across the road the woods. She shouldered off her dressing gown and her nightdress, and stood, with all her clothes about her feet, naked and warm, pressing her shoulder blades back together. She raised her chin to the ceiling, then out to either side she stretched her arms. They had a swift, strong determined feel about them. Slowly she turned her head to admire these strong arms to see that they had feathers growing all over them, big strong ones on the underneath, layered with finer, shorter feathers on top. They were an incredibly beautiful colour, pale shades of blue and yellow and white. The feeling of strength was enormous. Both arms were now large, strong wings, her body still a woman's, yet with a streamlined feel to it. She had, on other occasions, got this feeling during exercises or while swimming, but accepted it as a limited pleasure. Never did she think it would get to full fruition, this feeling to be to amazingly able …

In fact, she looked about her as she cautiously tiptoed to the back door, Bobo watched Fin's every move. Now her feet felt hard and thin. Opening the door a crack the spring air really made her feel like trying out her wings. The cuckoo cuckooed and she knew it meant, 'This is my place', and he was calling to another cuckoo,

'Come now, come now'. She also knew the other birds were saying the same thing in different accents. They were as happy as she. She looked left to the O'Connor's garden. It was empty. She looked down at her body, half woman, 'How crazy my bum would look to Mrs O'Connor if I flew off over those woods', she thought, 'Imagine what she would think'.

Fin retreated to the kitchen again, but didn't quite want to close out the thin spring air. She stretched again, backwards, arching the spine, raising her chin sky wise, her eyes closed. 'I'll go, I'll go', she said, 'just a little way and return in a while to write the shopping list'.

The back door clicked closed behind her, the key kept always under a flowerpot. She knew all was okay in the house. The cuckoo, the air, the lambs, the trees, the sky, the clouds, the arms into wings, the fields below, the houses from above, the air, the wings, the air, the stretch. She was flying and soaring as naturally as if she had always flown without clothes, shoes or her watch But she knew, she knew what time it was, She knew where to fly and then it would be time to return.

The McGillycuddy Reeks were to her left. She had flown along the route of the Laune River. Underneath the brown water she could see still fish, only their tails slowly moving to and fro, to and fro. She knew what they felt like. She knew how their gills opened and closed to let in the cool water. She knew the way to hide still under dark brown rocks, the belly touching sandy floors, the light waving in wiggly lines down through the brown water.

The air started to change to salt and sea. She was over Glenbeigh, the little village looking vulnerable to the open sky. She swooped out to sea between the Iveragh and Dingle Peninsulas, the breeze restricting her a little, pushing up against her chest. She saw a small island with black rocks, whitened in streaks by seagulls' droppings. In the centre was a patch of grass and sea pinks and wild bladder campion. They grew in clumps about the nooks and crannies. She couldn't see any sign of life for miles and miles except for four grey seals lying flat out on black slabs, sunbathing with their eyes closed, the black slabs sloping into the sea at the base of the island. She circled three times to make sure that landing was safe and wise. The hardness of her feet gripped the earth and the rough grass as she landed.

A rabbit leaped up into the air with shock and ran into one of the many holes. Fin stood and looked about her. She felt warm and tired. The earth smelled hot and dry. She found the dryness wonderful on her belly and on her chest. She nestled down, making a hollow in the dry, orangey-brown earth. All about her was the thin sea grass, and to her left and right she was protected by large cushions of sea pinks. She felt safe to fall asleep, no anxieties. The children were safe and attended to as was her husband. Her house was clean and after their violin lessons she would be there to collect the children.

Sleep was much the same as human sleep, but with air about her, air into feathers, air on cheeks, earth and warmth underneath, warm smells, sharp and thin air cutting its way into the lungs, making the rest more refreshing than a rest in the bedroom. Her head turned to her right wing, she entered her nose into the pale soft feathers to get into a full sleep.

Time passed. At the correct time, she rose instinctively. The sky had darkened with a passing shower. She was not late. The full moon looked untimely at this hour, shown up by the darkened sky. She landed softly on her doorstep. Inside, she dressed, putting on her vest, her panties with a pad, as her period had just started, and then into her jumpsuit, her runners and her cotton socks. She felt all healthy, cosy and warm. Her shopping basket and list in hand, she set off for town to collect Jo-Jo and Siobhan. When Sean arrived, they sat down to dinner. One white feather zig-zagged onto the floor and landed beside the dog's bowl.

All this time we were looking for a house or some land to build a house on. I tended to say 'yes' at every house we saw, but Pat was more cautious. We eventually found a beautiful spot in a valley near Glenbeigh, two acres, on a sheep-bitten field, this was to be our future home.

It was Maria Simonds-Gooding who said, 'let's try that road'. She was brought up in Dooks, Glenbeigh, but had never been up the Boherbue and down into this valley. We first asked about a piece of rocky mountain with furze bushes, but Pat O'Sullivan said, 'you'd be better off with this place'. That was it. We bought the two sheep-bitten acres, half-bogland. We got a local Glenbeigh builder, Paddy Brennan, to build our cottage.

One day on one of our visits from Killarney to see our new piece of land, we met on the road a farmer neighbour called John Shea. His large ears were flapping in the wind.

'Does it get windy here a lot?' I asked him.

'No, it is always grand like today', I then asked him.

'Is it all right to park our car here, on the grassy side of the road?'

'Sure, cars don't eat grass', he said.

In order to stay the weekends and be involved in the building of the house we bought a Barna hut. One Saturday night a raging storm flew down from the east from the McGillycuddy Reeks, shaking our Barna hut. We packed the few clothes that we had brought from Gortroe into our bags. The cat had disappeared, we gave up calling her and went home to escape the storm. The next day the hut was lying around the land in bits. A folder of my paintings was lying under a furze bush and our cat, Shelley, was still missing. I was so concerned and spent a couple of hours calling her, finally she meowed back at me. My folder saved, and the cat safe, we breathed a sigh of relief. The Barna hut people had not secured the lightweight wooden house to a base and so it was deemed in court that they were in the wrong. I was cross-examined in court by the lawyer for Barna huts in a harsh and severe manner. After we won the case, the Barna hut lawyer swept over to us and, to my surprise, he shook my hand with a big smile.

Paddy Brennan and his men placed block upon block until our house was suitable to move into. At first we camped on the cement floors on mattresses. In the village of Glenbeigh was the Towers Hotel, owned by Ernie Evans. Among his regular clients were famous stars, such as the actor, writer and folk singer Burl Ives. The receptionist was a blonde, vivacious girl called Anne Chute, She had a naughty wicked sense of humour.

'You must have nothing better to do than to come on time'.

One night she teased poor Major Simonds-Gooding, Maria's father, by tickling the palm of his hand with her index finger. He knew that it must have some meaning and couldn't wait to ask his Canadian friend, Duncan, what it meant. Duncan said, 'what? she did that!' She flirted outrageously, her blouse was always revealing, not that she had that much to reveal, but it all added up to an irresistibly attractive girl.

Major Simonds-Gooding brought up his family in India before he came to live in Dooks, Glenbeigh. He brought with him the skins of tigers covered in bullet holes for the living room floor. They later became moth eaten and hairless. He would throw many's the cocktail party to the high and mighty of the surrounding area, tripping over the tiger heads as he served the pink gins.

He also was a flirt and when he did his shopping he would lean very close to the shop assistant to read her name tag and say, in his very upper-class accent, staring straight into her eyes, with a suggestive smile.

'Thank you, Suzaannnnh'.

One day, his housekeeper announced proudly to him.

'I've tidied up the living room and I've cut off the dirty old heads and legs of those tigers'.

When Major Simonds-Gooding was dying, he was being cared for in the local old people's home in Glenbeigh. Maria wanted to be by his side, but got cold and very tired sitting beside her father, so she decided to creep off to look for a bed that she could lie on. She found one right next door to her father's room and fell into a deep sleep, only to be interrupted by the butcher, whose bed it was, as he climbed in beside her. It was the next day that her father died.

The Evans era ended tragically due to his wife's death, after which Ernie took off to Bray, near Dublin, to run a restaurant there. Shortly after the Towers Hotel was taken over by Brendan Sweeney, who successfully runs the hotel to this day.

In our mews house in Dublin whenever we needed a shelf, a nail or a curtain put up, we always got hold of George Pope, who lived in a fixed rent basement flat in a Georgian house in Baggot Street. He was good fun and a good carpenter. He had turned down a stage job for his whistling skills simply because he did not know how to write his own signature on the contract. So we had the pleasure of George's whistling as he put up the curtain rail or the shelf. We would hear the dulcet tones of 'Life in an English Garden', complete with blackbird songs and thrush trills. He always liked to joke and play and would ask:

'Is my next job to dig a hole in your garden for Pat, Pauline?'

So when we moved to Kerry we did not know anyone at the time who would do odd jobs in our new house.

'Let's ask George', I said.

George always asked me to read out the instructions on the paint tins, etc, pretending that he had forgotten his glasses.

'I'll come down to Kerry for a week. What is it you want me to do?'

'Oh, shelving, a hen perch, a bit of paint work, lots of things, George'.

I brought George on the train from Dublin, and as the train pulled into Kildare, George got nervous.

'I will get off here, Pauline and go back to Dublin'.

'George, you would be lost altogether if you got out here. Stay on the train with me, and I promise I will put you back on the first train to Dublin'.

Not only did George want to get off at Kildare but every other stop on the way to Kerry.

'Ah, Pauline, I will get off here!'

When we arrived and drove to our newly-built house in the valley of Treanmanagh, George eased up over tea of boiled eggs and toast. We did not have a bed for him, just a mattress on the floor, as we all just had mattresses on the floor at that stage. The next morning, his first job was the perch in our hen house. Elsie O'Sullivan came over. I brought her into the hen house to meet George. He took to her immediately. He had a speech defect, a sort of a 'Eccchh'. He called her 'Elchie instead of 'Elsie'.

'Elchie, hop up on the perch there; we will see does it work. Let's try it out before the hens'.

Elsie tucked her chin into her chest and coquettishly laughed at George's flirtations. That evening, George went to visit Elsie and Pat, her husband, at the farm. When he came back, he complained.

'Ah Elchie and Pat are lovely people, but would ya look at my swhade shoes, they are covered in cow shite'.

I loved the way he talked to 'Foxy' our dog.

'Where were ya?' he asked. 'The geese looked as if they were off to a match'.

He forgot his panic to go home to Dublin. He went to Mary Fox's pub, a mile away, down the Boherbue at the bottom of our mountain. This became a regular after his day's work. He sat on the same stool next to an old man from the Boherbue who spoke non-stop to George in a broad Kerry accent.

'I love that man, Pauline. I don't understand a word he is saying, and I tell him all about the banshee along the Grand Canal'.

Our other neighbours, the wonderful intelligent twins John and Pat Piggott would join George at the bar.

Mary Fox's was a solitary pub that had a row of old stools where a row of farmers would take their nightly pints. Mary Fox, slow moving and silent, would pull their pints and hand them up to the bar. A little dog sat at their feet.

'What breed is your dog?'

'Ah the mother wasn't fussy', answered Mary. Silence then.

'Tis good to be out of the cold. Sure heating is half of the feeding'.

'Yerra, I was at the doctor today with a sore throat. The doctor looked down my throat and said he could see nothing there. I told him you should. You should see two hay barns, a farm of land and a dozen cows. I drank them all'.

'I think', said George, 'I am going to ask Mary does she want me to give that pub a coat of paint because you can see conversation running all down the walls'.

George, showing off, said, 'I can drink twenty-five pints and it have no effeck'.

That was not quite true because we would hear him returning when the pub closed, coming down the Boherbue singing 'take these chains from my heart and shhett me free' at the top of his voice. We knew he was accompanied by Pat and John Piggott, but they remained silent. George would make his way by torch (we didn't have electricity yet) to the mattress on the floor and the next morning the mattress would be thoroughly drenched; presumably the twenty-five pints poured through his skin onto the mattress. He would set to work cheerful as ever, and sure enough the twenty-five pints had no effect on him.

He stayed with us for the week and then asked could he stay on another couple of weeks and work for his keep. We were delighted, and so was George. When dropping him back up to Dublin, he could not stop raving about the great time he had in Kerry.

Since the George Pope days, Treanmanagh has flourished. The garden now has a Tuscan chestnut tree, globe artichokes with their purple flowers, huge juicy Victoria plums, blueberries, rows of spuds, two pear trees, wild boletus fungi, and many apple trees that Betty makes apple crumble after apple crumble from.

Now Poppy and Holly were going to the local National School in Curraheen two miles down the Boherbue. One day they saw Paudie holding a newborn lamb by its back legs, to clear its breathing. He waved hello to them by swinging the lamb in the air over his head. Each day they joined the neighbouring children, Patrick, Eileen and Mary to walk the two miles to Curraheen.

'If you went up that cliff and fell off, you'd be glad you never went'.

On cold winter days the children would take a lift in Pat's car as he went to work.

The headmaster was a huge overpowering man who very often heated up a sally stick to whip the hands of any child who was naughty. It was a relief when he retired and Miss Roche took over as head mistress. She was stern, but not punishing.

'Miss Roche uses such long words you'd need a sledge hammer to break them up'.

A third teacher called Michael Morris was a breath of fresh air. He brought the children on tours around Kerry, believing that if they got to know their local county thoroughly they would get to know the wider world. They would camp by Killarney Lakes and cook in the open air. He taught them the penny whistle, how to dance and he gave céilis in the school.

Michael Morris asked me to direct the pantomime in the school, like the ones that he had seen the children do in our house. For instance, our old rust-red velvet curtains were hung up to divide the kitchen, the stage being the range and dresser end, the audience sitting at the open fire end. We had our rehearsals on Saturdays and Sundays. I wrote a condensed version of *Cinderella*.

Each rehearsal was a different and very funny version. The parents and neighbours were invited, forty in all, they sat on cushions, a bench in the fire alcove and on armchairs. As we had no electricity, the candles were blown out and large torches made good spotlights.

John O'Shea struck up on the accordion and the cast behind the torch-lit curtain sang:

'I love Cinderella, don't you love her too?'

'Yes, I do, I do, yes, I do, I do'.

'Would you like to see her in her wedding dress?'

'Yes, Yes, Yes, Yes, Yes, Yes, Yes'.

Eileen O'Connor and Helen O'Shea opened the curtain. The faces of the cast looked magic, spot-lit by the torches.

'Come hail, rain or snow, be *Jaesus*, I'm going to dance a set with the prince', Jer Connor ad-libbed.

'Tis fierce weather, I'm perished with de cold, you'd need to wear your woolly knickers, girl', shouted Patrick Moriarty, twelve years old in a wig, and a huge, pink boned corset, borrowed from Elsie.

Jer wore a flowery, frilly dress, a wig, big pink and white boots. The wooden trunk was always full of dressing-up clothes from swap sales. The ugly sisters exit into the pantry. Enter Cinders (Mary O'Shea) and Buttons (her sister Geraldine O'Shea).

'Oh, Buttons! How I wish I could go to the ball'.

All the torches went out, a sparkler was lit inside a big old butter churn that the Piggotts gave us and out springs the fairy god-mother.

'You *shall* go, my child'.

A toy mouse was to be the horse and a vegetable marrow the carriage. Again lights out and in rumbles a wheelbarrow draped in Christmas glitter. Portly Patrick was sitting in it, with tall, thin Jer pushing it. They tippled about and off to the ball.

Then Cinders appears, dressed in a turquoise evening dress and the barrow comes in to take her off to the ball. The curtains are closed, the tin whistles play with two accordions.

During all this, Pat Murphy ate a box of chocolates on the blue pew, his stubble chin turning circles with delight. The curtains open again to a rousing Kerry set dance, the ugly sisters, the prince, played by Johanna Naughton, Cinderella and all whirling around. Then the losing of the slipper, the prince trying it on to the huge feet of Patrick and Jer.

'Go on, go on, will ye. Push, have ye no strength, boy?'

'Maybe if you put both slippers on the one foot it would do'.

For the wedding, a real wedding-dress, Betty's, was used, then a procession at the end.

The evening was a success. The dressing-up box was closed again with all the junk, red lipstick etc until the next pantomime or the next whim of one of the children to dress up, just for fun.

Michael Morris's enthusiastic behaviour made Miss Roche cross ('Nellie Cockroach' as George Pope nicknamed her). She didn't like his popularity. She felt he was taking over from her and she was the headmistress. The school became blackened with their row. People took sides. He would call at our house and almost in tears would talk of the prohibitions. He soldiered on and included his pupils in all kinds of entertainments such as going to Tralee to listen to the Garda Band in Siamsa Tire. He fell in love with a tall confident girl and when they married he had the children all sing at the wedding held in the tiny Glencar church. He and his wife Catherine had six children, when a melanoma developed on his leg, penetrating his body, killing him within a matter of months. Catherine lived on bringing up the children and kept her spirits up as Michael would have liked.

Catherine's father, Gene, had many beehives across the lake. It was always something I wanted to do was have our own bees. In fact, the word 'Bewick' means 'bee keeper' as well as the Viking word 'beautiful harbour'.

'Of course I'll sell ye some bees'.

We didn't know when to expect him to arrive. Certainly we didn't expect him to arrive just as night was falling.

'I have a gang of Yanks in the car and a couple of boxes of bees in the boot'.

He swayed out of the driver's seat and opened the boot, where upon the bees swarmed all over the place.

'Oh Christ, they're stinging my arse. They'll settle, don't worry', he said.

We had bought two new hives for our bee friends and sure enough they did settle in a large clump on a furze bush.

'Have you got a white sheet', he asked.

I ran into the house for one and he spread it under the cluster of bees.

'You have to hit the branch with a sudden whip so that the whole lot will fall down on the sheet together', he said and again sure enough the whole lot fell and they all marched into the small hole of the bee hive.

The bees provided us for many years with the most delicious honey. Sometimes, depending on the pollen, the honey would be dark amber, other times it would be thinner and pale yellow. To eat the wax was just as delicious as the honey itself. We loved cutting the sections of honey and placing the clumps into large jars for the winter. Pat, like all men, loved all the bee gear and got a kick out of putting on the white spacesuit with a large white hat, hanging from it a green vale, on his feet he wore tight boots so that no bee could enter at any point. Quite often Pat would float silently in his white bee suit on his way to the bees, past my studio, looking neither left nor right while I would be in the middle of showing a work to a collector.

One evening Poppy and I were due to meet Pat in Killarney to go to a film.

'Oh no, the bees have swarmed'.

It was important to house the clump of bees as they might have chosen to nest in one of the O'Sullivan's garage cars. Again they had attached themselves to a rather thin branch of a furze bush. Poppy and I spread the white sheet and I, thinking I knew exactly how to deal with the situation, gave the branch a sharp clip. The branch, instead of yielding the bees with the shock, swung up and down, dislodging the whole lot, dispersing them all over the place.

They seemed to take a notion to follow Poppy and about a hundred of them or more landed in her long brown hair.

'Oh mummy, mummy, they are stinging me'.

I yelled back, 'bees can't sting when they swarm'.

'They are, they are, they are stinging me'.

I finally shook them from her hair and sure enough her head was covered in little black stings that had not penetrated, therefore their sting was mild and Poppy recovered quite quickly. We waited until they gathered again in their swarm and this time the whole process was a success and we drove to Killarney to go to the film.

Another day a bee managed to get through the green veil and sting Pat under his chin. His chin proceeded to get huge and finally swelled, covering his neck down to his chest. He realised to his horror that he was highly allergic to bee stings and that was the end of our bees.

We sold our bees to Mickey Junior and to this day they have survived the epidemic that attacked bees in Ireland and provide his family with their bounty.

17

ART STUDIO

LIMERICK
CITY GALLERY
OF ART.

BOOK 6

It was in our new house in Treanmanagh that I got my first real purpose-built studio. It was a bit of struggle to persuade Pat that I actually needed a special space to paint in.

'But you have always painted so well in bedrooms, living rooms and kitchens', Pat said.

'Maybe'.

However, I persisted, which got me a studio. In a funny kind of a way I felt I had lost my femininity, feeling I had become self-important, like a man; but Pat saw the moment it was built how necessary it was, and how right I was. The studio gave me an open powerful feeling, my own space dedicated purely to painting.

As soon as the studio was built I went straight into a commission from RTÉ Television of Louis Lentin's production of Eugene McCabe's *Cyril, the Squirrel*. It was in six parts, a story that he had written for his son to entertain him while he was in hospital. The story had double political meanings, which to this day I do not quite fully understand. I should keep away from things political as I have my own thinking about human beings and how they behave. I consider politics to be blind and on the surface; the grassroots being problems like dealing with over-population and the desire in us humans to kill each other. Politicians find another country's religion or skin colour a good excuse to pick a fight with them. They are blind to the real reasons of these problems.

This commission from RTÉ broke the ice for working in the new studio. After that job I went on to paint large works of the surrounding lakes and mountains, the moss and ferns, foxes and otters. We had landed in heaven.

There was no electricity in the valley that first year, which suited us fine. We would light up the oil lamps, put the turf in the solid fuel stove and we also used a little gas stove. I would cook the local fish, potatoes and cabbage, while Pat helped the two girls brilliantly with their homework. I was grateful to have dyslexia to get me out of that job.

We gave a dinner party one night, there were about 10 of us including the well-known founder of *Kerry's Eye* called Padraig Kennelly. After the desert, Padraig suddenly stood up at the end of the dinner table, taking one of the candles in his right hand and proceeded to tell us the story of Kerry before 'ural' electricity came. His story was about two brothers, one had a mouth crooked to the left and the other crooked to the right, neither of the brothers could blow the candle out and Padraig had us all in fits of laughter demonstrating with the candle from the table in his hand how difficult it would be to blow out a candle if your mouth veered left or right. The next day two of our guests, the Holdicots from across the lake, asked us, 'where did you hire that wonderful storyteller, Padraig Kennelly?'

The Kerryman had a notice in the planning section applying for planning permission for electricity to the valley of Treanmanagh.

'How awful', Pat and I thought. 'That will bring poles and wires'.

We had got completely used to life without electricity. Our milk was kept on the north side of the house in a dug-out and anything else was kept on a wire, safe on the north site. We loved our oil lamps even though the smoke blackened the ceiling.

We went to the Planning Authority to find out that, in fact, the planning permission was put in the name of Dr Patrick Melia by the County Council. We still do not know if they applied on our behalf or was it somebody else who applied for it using our name. We eventually accepted electricity into our lives, even though each pole that was erected was an eyesore until it became part of the landscape.

The phone rang, we were the first people in the valley to get a telephone due to Pat being a doctor. It was useful when the neighbours' cows came into heat. They would phone the inseminator to come. Hospital phone calls were made.

'Could you get me the eternity ward please'.

Electricity brought television into the valley, it released the children's tongues, they wouldn't gossip about the valley but they could gossip about *Dallas* and its goings-on.

I invited the artist and writer Bridget Marlene to come and paint with me, she stayed in the Clochán. She wore a large sun hat and brought many boxes of paints and canvas. She was inspired to paint the twins, John and Pat Piggott.

'Oh Pauline', she said. 'I have fallen madly in love with Pat Piggott'.

By the time she had finished their portraits, she said.

'Oh Pauline, I have now fallen for John'.

She had painted an exact image of them both sitting beside their open turf fire. Every Sunday she would attend Father Kelly's mass in Glenbeigh.

'Now lads, we're going to have a *shlow* mass with reverence'.

She told us many very funny stories. A man in America had fallen in love with one of her paintings of a beautiful young girl. He paid for Bridget's fare to come and visit him. When she arrived at the airport she noticed his face smiling in the crowd, but when he saw her, his mouth dropped. He expected her to look like the beautiful young girl in her painting and he more or less told her you can go now he was so disappointed.

I am proud to say that being an artist isn't a useless talent in our area. I was asked to paint the Virgin Mary which was placed on the island amongst the unconsecrated gravestones. Fr Crean gave a ceremony in his white habit, standing amongst the bluebells, blessing the beautiful lichen-coloured gravestones with holy water. When Pat and John Piggott's mother Nonie died, they asked would I make some wreaths for the occasion. I was so touched they asked me to do this as I was just a blow in.

The other time my painting was useful was when Poppy and I were driving into Killorglin on the narrow Caragh Lake road when we saw an old woman sitting in the grass.

'Mummy she can't get up'.

'Of course she can', I said, continuing to drive.

'No, no, go back'.

I was persuaded to reverse, Poppy was right.

'Thank you, thank you, I've been here a good while, my legs won't let me get up. Thank you, thank you', she said again as we heaved her to her feet. She then asked us in to her cottage for a cup of tea which we accepted.

'You see that clock up there, all the numbers have worn off it and it's hard for me to tell the time'.

I went to the car and got out my paints, took down the clock and painted each number from 1–12 and placed the clock back on the wall.

'Oh my God wait till my brother comes home from the bog and I'll say to him what time is it and he'll look up at that clock and I'll tell him it must have been the fairies that painted it'.

The phone rang. It was David Shaw-Smith, filmmaker of the RTÉ *Hands* series, enquiring if he could make an hour-long documentary on my work and life. As we had not yet bought various electrical equipment, I quickly hired a fridge for the food for David's visit.

On the eve of his coming, the cat had caught a wren. It was so beautiful I really wanted to make a painting of it, but there was no time, so I popped it on a plate and into the fridge, the only item within. The wren came in useful as at the end of the film David said, 'I want to film you painting something', so I placed the sweet, little speckled wren in the palm of my hand and proceeded to draw and then paint it, all the time being filmed by David. He had a subliminal way of working. Not for a moment did I feel self-conscious of the camera. Peter, his assistant, quietly would climb on top of the studio bench to shine a light where necessary. Everything was going well, until I made a large blob of dark, right in the centre of the picture, spoiling the whole atmosphere of it. I struggled on, and it only got worse.

'Sorry David, I will have to stop, it is all going wrong', whereupon David slapped his forehead.

'I've got to get out of here', he said.

He and his assistant Peter got into their van and drove off to Cahirciveen to visit Regine, leaving me weeping my heart out at the disastrous centre of my painting.

First the children came home from school and I wept to them both.

'I have spoilt the painting and David spent hours filming its progress'.

Later Pat came home.

'Oh, Pat, I feel awful, the painting is wrecked, it all went wrong in the middle. Poor David, he is gone off in an awful mood, a whole morning wasted, yards and yards of film taken'.

'Calm down', said Pat. 'We will have our dinner and then you can go back into the studio and work on it while we do the homework'.

It was hard to stop trying with the painting and crying, but I took Pat's advice and after dinner set afresh. It all came right, and with a great thrill I wrote a note to David and Peter, placing it on the door of the little round house that I had built for Harry, saying 'I have corrected the picture, it looks great'. He told me that he was so happy to get that note, and the next day we continued filming. 'A Woman and Wren' became the last visual in the documentary *A Painted Diary*. The editing was by Maurice Healy, music included Roger Doyle, Bessie Smith, Jelly Roll Morton, Brian Boydell and Luke Kelly singing 'Raglan Road'.

John Ranelagh of Channel Four was the first to buy this film, plus he became a collector. Subsequently, it was shown at several film festivals, many times on RTÉ and on Channel Four, as well as in the Pompidou Centre in Paris. David went on to make three more *Hands* films about artists. I suggested Barry and Philip Castle and Brian Bourke, and later David filmed Danny Osborne. His previous *Hands* films for RTÉ had been about crafts people, half an hour long. He is a filmmaker supreme.

My exhibitions in the 1980s became more and more successful. From being just comfortably well off with Pat's earnings, I found I could now start taking the family abroad, buying any piece of clothing I should want and any art materials I needed. I would spend till I ran out, then I earned more and then spent that. It was great fun.

I should tell you at this point how I gauged the prices for my paintings. One day back in 1957 Maura Laverty asked me how much for my drawing of her daughter, 'Barry at the Sewing Machine'. I suggested fifteen pounds, as I had my eye on a pair of boots. That was my first sale ever. The next sale I had was an exhibition in the Clog Gallery which provided me with a full cupboard of art materials. It's a good feeling to have a bundle of good paper, just one or two sheets can be inhibiting.

This method has lasted me throughout my career. I get the best handmade papers especially dyed, to tapestries woven in Aubusson by Bernard Battu, Aubusson being the *Tiffany* of tapestry making. After journeying to France Madeleine would speak to Battu in her perfect French about all the technical details. It was the dress designer and art collector Ib Jorgenson who advised 'you could get much more for your work'. I decided there and then to double my prices, and it worked. I raised the price from £400 to £800, the average size being 24" x 30", the paints being top quality, A-listed watercolours that do not fade. The paintings were selling well, right up to the recession, when the sales dwindled.

A flow goes on in my life that never has the effect of money worries. Something good always comes of what other people might call bad, like a recession. I found that within the flow of my life to share my talent for somebody else's talent was most fulfilling. It was not a question of sums and numbers. This exchange brings out in both parties, a feeling of fulfilment. So a recession brings about for me exchanges. I exchanged my work for building materials, years of organic top quality dog food, customised jewellery, beautiful handmade furniture and uniquely designed clothes.

Seamus Cashman ran a publishing house in Dublin called the Wolfhound Press, a friendly good-looking man with a grey beard and thick grey hair. Seamus suggested to Dr James White, the director of the National Gallery of Ireland, that he might write the story of my work and life, to which James, to my delight, agreed. Seamus asked me to provide photographs of all my childhood works and up to age of 50. I found a photographer, Danny Fernandez. He photographed each drawing and painting, which amounted to over 3000 works. I put all these photographs in perfect order, making it easy for James White to take one decade at a time, to study and write about.

At our first session, James and I sat for two or three hours at a shiny dining room table in their Victorian House in Herbert Park, while Aggie made our lunch,

James tapped away on his old-fashioned clickety-clack typewriter, looking over his glasses to question me and then tap away again without comment.

Our first lunch started with dark brown beef soup. They had not remembered that I was a vegetarian. I hoped that this would be the only misunderstanding! James never put on a smile if he did not want to. He frightened me a little. I battled through this fear, digging out the truth of my life. Perhaps in his opinion I was being outrageous. He and Aggie were very religious and, compared to Harry, they were very civilised. It was a contrast to sit in this dining room talking about my mother making love with a stranger on the kitchen floor or sleeping out on a corrugated tin platform by the stream.

After lunch we continued our work, his serious, straight mouth expression, his eyebrows raised seemed intimidating. He made no comment, he studied all the works. When I was twelve my feelings about the womanising headmaster, the famous film stars of the day, the big-breasted spotted monster women, the sailor and the two-faced Nicandra. James' lack of response made me fear I was being misunderstood.

Eventually, he broke his silence.

'You *must* have had influences from other artists'.

It felt like the time when Desmond MacNamara and his arty friends made me and Harry cry. It seemed that people found it hard to accept that one could paint without being influenced by other artists. I battled with that opinion and insisted that Harry had sheltered my childhood from all types of education, other than life around us, like the Carnegie Theatre productions and the cinema with its selection of films.

It was on the second visit to James White that he read aloud his first chapter. To my surprise tears rose to my eyes. He had understood everything. This work together continued for a year. I began to love all our lunch meetings and talking about their formal garden and the various interesting artists that he knew, such as Louis le Brocquy, Jack B. Yeats and Oskar Kokoschka. He told me about Kokoschka coming to the National Gallery in Dublin, and on seeing some paintings he asked:

When did I paint these?'

James had to explain that they were in fact by Yeats.

I asked James why he had red thread sown onto his jacket lapel. He explained that he had been given the Ordre national de la Légion d'honneur in France, consequently each of his jackets had a red thread sown onto the lapel. He told me that his father loved dogs, and how he hated them. The time he worked for Carroll Cigarettes and how at weekends he would fill his car with paintings by artists such as Norah McGuinness and Anne Yeats. He would take the paintings around Irish country towns giving lectures filled with his passion for art; a passion that had led him to become Director of the National Gallery of Ireland.

The book was titled *Pauline Bewick: Painting a Life* and was launched at the Guinness Hop Store in 1985, to coincide with my major retrospective exhibition of all these works from the age of two and a half to fifty. James White inscribed my copy of the book: 'Writing this biography was one of the most rewarding experiences of my life and has enlarged me'.

John and Pat Taylor curated this big exhibition that took up three floors of the huge Hop Store with 2500 works.

They said that they were worried that the amount of pieces I was showing could destroy the rarity of my work and that I was perhaps prolific to a fault. Despite that comment I could not be dishonest, I wanted to show how prolific I have been throughout life.

Luckily down in Kerry our neighbour Stam Mintz, married to the artist Raymond, was a trained librarian and highly qualified to help me sort these works before they were delivered to Dublin. She would say things like:

'Hey, do you really need this one, honey?'

So we ended up putting it into the reject pile that grew to 700 pieces.

On the opening night we arrived at the entrance of the Guinness Hop Store, people in evening wear were parking their cars and with a festive atmosphere they stepped into the Guinness Hop building. Margaret Heckler, the American Ambassador, Taoiseach Charlie Haughey and many dignitaries had accepted their invitations. Seamus Cashman sat at the entrance desk with copies of James' book, and a slim catalogue which described briefly the journey of the works.

We all climbed the stairs to the first floor. Guinness provided tray after tray of Black Velvet, a mixture of champagne and Guinness. The three floors were nicely packed with Dublin's beauties, the elite, the press, photographers, intellectuals and artists.

Our attention was drawn and James White launched the exhibition with a very serious face, lifting his right nostril as he gave emphasis to his description of 'how Pauline had developed'. He then spoke of Harry and her encouragement.

I remembered with a sadness Harry saying:

'To think all this publicity is because of me holding onto your pictures'.

Harry felt that I was prostituting myself by becoming well known and commented:

'You are sticking your neck out'.

She had become disturbed by many aspects of my way of life. She had made me feel sullied, she pointed out that art had no use to people. I found myself justifying the need to paint. It was fulfilling to see so many of the visitors standing before their appropriate subjects, such as pregnant women studying the works that I did when I was pregnant. I noticed little children talking to their parents about the pictures of their age.

'Look, look, Mummy, I can do a horse like that'.

It was gratifying to feel that buzz.

When the opening party was finished and everyone descended the stairs, we met outside the door five local teenage girls covered in make-up, chewing gum with their mouths open and a scornful look on their faces.

'Yez are all snobs'.

'You wouldn't let the likes of us in there'.

I put on an act of sarcasm and raising a hand in a foppish manner said:

'Oh yes, excuse me, I am going to my car'.

Then I turned back and said to them seriously:

'Will you all come back to the exhibition and I will give you a tour of the paintings'.

Sure enough one day they did come back, it was just as I had finished a long, exhausting tour, but I could not let these five girls down.

They had arrived where the contemporary work was hanging, the work I had done in my thirties and forties, one of which was a couple making love. The man had his pyjamas pulled down. I said:

'They were married so long he could not be bothered to pull them off fully', to which their cynical faces softened. It was fortunate that there were some raunchy sexy pictures in this part of the exhibition. That definitely broke the ice with the girls. There were many pictures also of animals, cats, chickens and foxes, which they enjoyed the stories about. At the end of the tour they had completely loosened their attitudes and we were all laughing our heads off.

About a week or so later, their Social Worker/Probation Officer came and said:

'You made a big impression on my girls. They used to tie cats up by their tails, twisting them onto the clothesline and they would stone them to death. Since your lecture they have stopped being cruel to animals'.

If only Harry could have witnessed that.

One day Pat Cahill, from the Frankfurt Avenue days, came to the exhibition and said:

'Harry's spirit came to me on the ouija board last night'.

I dismissed that immediately, having no real belief in such things, even though we had played around with it many times in Frankfurt Avenue, just for fun.

Pat Cahill subsequently came again.

'I wish you would let me tell you what Harry said'.

This time I allowed her and the words were few but gave me enormous comfort. They were:

'I now know what Pauline is doing'.

People from all walks of life queued up to see this exhibition. Each day before the doors were opened, queues had formed. Children and adults, rich and poor, came to see this exhibition.

One stormy afternoon the electricity in the Hop Store went off due to lightning. I noticed a huge muscular man in jeans and a black Guinness vest standing in front of the 'Gort Dromach Sneem' painting. He stood there for the full duration of the storm. When the lights came on he walked over and explained to me:

'I was there, I was in those mountains. Every time the lightening flashed, everything came alive. I have never enjoyed looking at a painting so much'.

He was one of the Guinness barrel rollers.

The exhibition was helped hugely by the public relations man, Frank Lewis of Killarney, who I had asked to assist me. He and Mary O'Shea organised many workshops and lectures. It was they that made the public aware of this exhibition. (Later I exhibited with Frank's gallery in Killarney; one of these was memorably opened by Páidí Ó Sé – 'these girls have balls').

Frank's programmes consisted of Ulick O'Connor telling the story of *Irish Tales and Sagas*, with my thirty-six illustrations taken from the book hanging behind him. Clare Boylan gave a lecture on the sensuality of the work, Patrick Murphy also gave a lecture. Tours were organised for each day. I took at least 30 to 50 people at one time on a tour throughout the whole exhibition. I knew I kept their interest and to my delight the children never flagged.

One day I noticed a cynical face standing at the back of the crowd during a tour. He followed us around. I guessed by his manner he was from the press. There was divided opinions about the work, and this man showed cynicism on his face. He was from *Circa* magazine.

Groups of old women sat on little camp chairs and cushions and copied the paintings with their watercolour sets. One day a young girl student came from the National College of Art. She said:

'I am here against my tutor's advice'.

He had told her not to go to the exhibition because 'Pauline Bewick is not a real artist'. She was obviously fearful of him finding out that she went against his advice.

One day when Pat came up from Kerry, I had just finished a tour. I met him at Heuston Station. The first thing I said was that my heart was doing strange things, banging against my chest.

'You have been working so hard. It is nothing to be worried about', he said and it never happened again.

The 2–50 exhibition was over. I had sold a number of works from the contemporary part of the show. I was tired, I wanted to go away, around the world. I choose the South Pacific. As far back as the conversations in the 1940s on our boat, Jaunty, I had the idea that the South Seas were an ideal society and I was so interested to find out for myself.

'Why don't you take a year's sabbatical, Pat, and we can travel, maybe to the South Seas and around the world'.

Pat did not take up the idea. I was noticing more and more that Pat did not take up any of my ideas. For instance, I said.

'Let's make a duck pond at the bottom of the garden'.

He said no.

'Shall we put in an Aga cooker?'

He said no.

It was not that I was asking him to pay for it. I was prepared to buy these things. It was that change did not appeal to Pat.

He did not exactly say a definite no to the sabbatical year. Meanwhile it was previously arranged, following the 2–50 exhibition, that I was to have a show of my most contemporary work in the Odette Gilbert Gallery on Cork Street in London [1987], so I travelled over for this exhibition and decided to buy a year's supply of handmade paper and top quality Winsor and Newton watercolours for the South Seas. Although in one way I did not think that I would paint as I was so tired, yet I bought these special materials anyway.

I had asked Professor Anthony Clare to open the Odette Gilbert exhibition. His speech started with:

> She is married to a psychiatrist and even worse she is married to the psychiatrist who is responsible for my early training. I should say that Pauline Bewick, as an artist, is an interesting psychiatric study because, and it is indeed a real problem for psychiatrists, she is unclassifiable … the energy, the extraordinary power of these paintings, the warmth indeed of her portrayal of women, the interesting ambiguity of her portrayal of men … This has in the end created an artist and an individual who is very difficult to classify.

Albert Roux of Le Gavroche restaurant gave a gift of party foods served by a team of young flirtatious waiters. Albert, along with his brother Michel and his son Michel Jr have collected over the years more work of mine than anyone else. Throughout, John Minihan was taking pictures for the *Evening Standard*.

Albert Ross
looks on
into the kitchen

Sara Jane
P.R.   Academic Gentleman

Paul

After the Odette Gilbert exhibition opening I gave a dinner party in the Chelsea Arts Club. I sat on Bob Geldof's left, on his right sat Odette Gilbert. He had come to my exhibition every day to look at one of the paintings, 'Tuscan Dream'. I later realised it was to look at the beautiful Odette, with her small breasts and big blue eyes. Throughout the party Bob had his right hand pressing and clasping Odette's thigh, while his left hand banged on the table as he shouted:

'I send loads of lorries with food and medicine across the deserts of Africa, so I should not feel guilty at spending money on a jacket that could keep an African person for a year. Our societies are so bloody different'.

All this time Odette's eyes were rising to the ceiling in ecstasy. I always enjoy the exhibition parties, this one consisted of a mixed London and Irish bunch.

The day after the party I felt in a buoyant mood, making my way to the exhibition in Cork Street. I dropped into a black shiny-painted shop with the letters FMR written in gold, the black-covered magazines, each numbered, each exciting. I choose the 1986 volume 20, it was to be £18 but the young glamorous girl said:

'You are the artist who is exhibiting in Cork Street right now? I love your work. Please take the magazine as a present'.

It had the full story in it of Kokoschka's love for Alma Mahler. Alma was the widow of Gustav, she also was a composer and a raving beauty. She was an intellectual who had the reputation of falling in love with men of genius. Kokoschka's large paintings and the painted swan-skinned fans expressed his passion for Alma. After a passage of time Alma rejected Oskar's love, so he went to a seamstress to make him a life-sized doll of Alma, instructing the seamstress:

'Use only the softest of silks for the inner thigh. I must never be aware of seams. I want to be able to dress the doll'.

When the doll was finally finished, Kokoschka would take it to the opera, to parties etc. Everyone in Vienna knew of Kokoschka's Alma doll.

When I read these amazing letters they inspired an idea for an opera. I not only wrote an opera synopsis, calling it 'Obsession', but also painted the set and costume ideas. These I took to Jeremy Isaacs and Anthony Russell Roberts of the Royal Opera House, London, whom I had an introduction to by one of my collectors, Sheila Kutner. They were excited by the ideas. I received a letter from Anthony Russell Roberts – 'it would be wonderful to work with you when you return from the South Seas'.

Royal Opera House
Covent Garden
London WC2E 9DD

26 April 1989

Dear Pauline

It was a very great pleasure to meet you and to talk about life, your painting and your specific proposal of your scenario (on K Love for Alma) entitled Obsession. As promised, I will talk to one or two of our choreographers to see if I can interest them in the idea. In any event I believe you were kind enough to say that I could hang on to the proposal as you have kept. Quite apart from your specific idea, I will do what I can to interest our stable choreographers in your work as it would be wonderful to have some designs by you here. I did manage to remember to video your programme, [*A Painted Diary*] which I have now watched with much enjoyment. If you find your South Sea Island, please let me know – but do not tell anybody else!

Yours sincerely
Anthony Russell Roberts
Administrative Director, The Royal Ballet.

In London I visited my actress friend Shelagh Fraser. I had known her ever since we collaborated on a cookery book that she had compiled for young people, *Clare Goes Cooking* (1962). She threw a party to celebrate my going to the South Pacific. Her elegant living room was filled with actresses and actors, Barbara Flynn, her husband Jeremy Taylor, Dame Eileen Atkins and film makers Derek Grainger and Kenneth Partridge all crowded around as I told them the stories of their lives through the psychological game. The singer Elizabeth Welsh said that her favourite animal was a large white dog and that she'd like to lie on it.

I always enjoyed Shelagh's stories. One day she gave a tea party for five or six of her famous actress friends. When one of them stretched her arms into the air, she closed her eyes and sighed.

'O how I would like to have one last fuck before I die'.

'Don't you think that's a bit much to say over tea?' said Shelagh.

When Shelagh's party was over I returned to the Chelsea Arts Club to find the photographer John Minihan, who had brought with him singer Van Morrison.

'What do you do?' I asked Van.

To which he turned to John and said, 'come on, let's go'.

He couldn't wait to leave the place. I sat and ate my dinner, witnessing a kafuffle going on in the dining room. A bath was overflowing above and was coming from the ceiling onto the dining table. Leso was seducing Dudley Winterbottom's wife. She tried to make Dudley jealous by kissing at the dining table.

John Minihan on another night brought John Calder, the first publisher of Samuel Beckett, to meet me. We hit it off and he invited me to Paris! In the billiard room and bar sat the writer Edna O'Brien and at the bar stood Henrietta Garnett. She asked me did her lipstick need repairing. It transpired that she had been photographed by Alan MacWeeney for his Bloomsbury set book.

'Oh do tell him I love him', she said.

Marianne Faithful was never to be seen either going in or out of her room which was next to my room. At night there always seemed to be a passionate argument. One was with the beautiful blonde, the 'club's bike' as she was nicknamed because everybody rode her. I opened my door a crack to see a fat drunken man crawling up the carpeted stairs trying to catch her. Next day at my exhibition I was greeted by the Queen's chef who enthusiastically raved about a collaboration we should do – his cooking for the Royal Yacht and my sensual paintings, but it all crashed down when somebody spilled this story to the newspapers and the headline was 'Irish Artist to illustrate the Queen's Cookbook'.

'I will subpoena you to court', said the man who had planned the cookbook.

Somebody must have overheard me in the club telling my news.

The next day Shelagh brought me to the theatre makeup shop. It had a glass counter with every colour you could think of in pots of makeup.

'Why on earth do you want just yellow', said the makeup artist.

By the time I had finished telling him the story of the Yellow Man, he proffered a full box of yellow powder which would have cost me £90.

'I enjoyed your story so much, this is a gift'.

I asked him did he know of anyone who makes prosthetics?

'I know Christopher Tucker', he said and he immediately contacted him and I was introduced over the phone. He did prosthetics for *The Elephant Man*, *The Company of Wolves* and *The Phantom of the Opera*, to name but a few.

'Where are you?' he asked.

'I'm staying at the Chelsea Arts Club'.

'Oh that crazy place', he answered. 'I'll be in London tomorrow'.

We met in the billiard room and bar. He had brought with him a very white-skinned woman who stayed very still and serious throughout the conversation that followed. I explained that I wanted to make a film about the Yellow Man and instead of using a cartoon I would prefer to use a human being.

'You're crazy'. He looked at his partner and asked, 'where did this crazy woman come from?'

After much laughter he invited Shelagh and I to his mansion to discuss the Yellow Man.

'I know that you would probably be very expensive', I said to Christopher. 'Would you consider exchanging work for work for the Yellow Man antennae prosthetic'.

Again he said, 'you're mad', and then said, 'I'd love you to come and see my ideas'.

Since Shelagh Frazer had been in one of his films, *Star Wars*, she was excited to come with me. We drove through the luscious rolling hills past large trees till we got to an impressive entrance gate which took us down a steep hill and facing us was what looked like an enormous cardboard stage set. It was the flat front of his grey mansion. Shelagh sat in the car while I banged the huge knocker. The door was opened by his white-faced friend. Behind her I could see wine-coloured, velvet-draped curtains and a wide staircase with a deep red carpet winding up what seemed like forever.

'Do come in'. I called Shelagh and we both entered.

Christopher Tucker welcomed us and brought us into a darkened room where he was watching the film, *The Company of Wolves*.

Halfway through this showing he said, 'come with me, Pauline, I'll show you some of the pieces I have made for this film'.

We climbed the red staircase and entered many rooms where he pressed buttons and switches which showed the skin on the wolf's face drawing back revealing his bloody jaws, the ears rolling backwards and the hair standing on end. In the next room we saw strange hands that moved and grew. I was beginning to really get spooked out.

It was in the last room way upstairs that he triumphantly showed me what he had made since we had met. It was a lifesize head with long antennae of the Yellow Man. It had the eerie quality of all the pieces that he had showed me in the other rooms. I couldn't express my feelings about his work other than to say how quick he was to make the Yellow Man as we joined Shelagh and his partner for tea.

When we left, driving up the steep avenue with the grey mansion behind us, we were both flabbergasted at the amazing place. A few weeks after I received a letter.

'Where are you? Is your crazy idea going to come to fruition?'

A telephone call came through to the Chelsea Arts Club from Pat.

'I am afraid I can't go abroad because the Southern Health Board won't allow it'.

The idea of putting off this trip made me cry. The very idea of staying at home, with no duck pond or Aga, and having the feeling that I had exhausted myself with the Guinness Hop Store experience filled me with a dull feeling. Yet, the very idea of travelling alone filled me with fear. I spent a gloomy evening in the Chelsea Arts Club with all the papers and paint from the shops waiting in my room for an adventure trip to the South Seas.

When I got back to Ireland, Pat and I had an argument.

'I knew one way or another you would make sure that you would not come travelling with me'.

'Don't be ridiculous, the Southern Health Board won't let me go'.

'You could somehow have got away, I know it'.

It was after this row that I made up my mind. I will break the second umbilical cord which I had formed with Pat. I bravely intended to travel alone.

Holly and Poppy heard that Pat was not going.

'Can we go with you, Mummy?'

And as I had earned quite a hefty sum of money from my exhibitions I said I would pay for the two girls to go.

There was great excitement from them.

'What shall I pack, Mummy? Do you think they will have sanitary towels in the South Pacific?'

'I have no idea. Pack what you think'.

The only advice I gave the girls was to bring art materials, as they had both become artists. Holly got a year off from the art school. The other thing that surprised me was that the two girls were going to leave their boyfriends behind in Ireland. Poppy was madly in love with Conor, the boy she went to school with, and Holly's boyfriend was a handsome young man called Paul who went to art school with her.

However I had still to fulfil a journey to Canada before we could leave for the South Seas. I had previously made an arrangement to go to McGill University in Montreal, Canada who had asked me to join a conference on Irish literature. They wanted an exhibition of my tapestries and etchings.

At Montreal Airport, eighteen-year-old Adrienne was waiting in her Mercedes, daughter of my hosts, Denise and Stephen. Her jeans were torn at the knees in contrast to the elegant interior of the car. Huge iced-over lake, cars on it, deep dark holes bored down in order to fish from. 'Ugly fish, too damned ugly to eat'. Hills with skiers, we whizzed along the snow and ice-lined road to their very beautiful large house.

Denise opened the door, her soft cheek to kiss, her thin eyebrows over lovely lidded eyes.

'We're having a party for you tonight', she told me.

In the top-of-the-house, my bedroom, I took off my heavy red coat and got a crack-click of shock from the huge brass bed, static, lots of it! Two hours' rest. The party had already started. Jennifer Johnston in shiny bronze, dark glasses, blonde, lined face and glamorous. On the table a huge vase of exotic flowers and around it rows of salmon, salad, cheese, fruit, a bounty from all over the world.

Next day Navadine called for me to help hang my etchings and tapestries. A beautiful negress, her black hair in teeny plaits mixed in with grey. Lots of Canadians go grey too young. Maybe it's the bitter cold that hits you in the shadow of the skyscraper's or at bus stops by lumps of ice.

The conference was fun, Paul Durcan had us rolling about with laughter with his poem about making love to a Russian girl in the top bunk of a train on his way to Moscow.

Down in the dungeons of McGill University I was shown ancient archives of Thomas Bewick. There was a will that had been changed, Jane had been scratched out in blue ink.

St Patrick's Ball, green bow ties, green cummerbunds, green dresses. Divorce causes old, bald men to be gaily dancing with their new young wives.

On our last day was a 'sugaring off' party held out in the country. In the distance we saw the Laurentian Mountains, the celebration held amongst the maple trees for us to see the draining of syrup into the little containers from pale barked trees.

Then back again to Kerry, with its dark blue mountains, its subtle colours, silver birch trees with purple tops, rusty orange dead bracken, black-green holly bushes. My memory of Canada – amazingly-hospitable people. Bright blue, white, red and black are its colours in my mind.

In spring the lambs were being born. On one of our walks in Lickeen we heard a baby lamb *baahing*, it took us a while to detect where from. There it was slipping slowly into the rushing stream, its bum in the water and its little black hooves trying to hang onto the bank. Pat lay on his stomach and pulled the lamb to safety where it joined its mother, shaking its wet tail. It was from then on that I sketched for the book, *Ireland: An Artist Year* (London, 1990) that I had been commissioned by

Methuen to do. I took off up the west coast, randomly stopping at places that appealed to me on sight. St Bridget's holy well, standing on stones that looked like telephone booths with statues of St Bridget within them and behind; the holy well covered in trinkets and wishes that had hung there for many years and dripped onto mossy stones. On past the Cliffs of Moher. I walked into a potter's studio; to her and my surprise a young woman was painting from one of my postcards, the painting of 'Yellow Iris and Blue Mountains'. She told me it was a commission from a man in Galway.

I stayed that night in the village of Roundstone where I got talking to the cleaner woman. She was English and had married a man who lived in a thatched cottage on the edge of the sea. He was incredibly romantic, until she realised, instead of her, the love of his life was going to the pub every night. Alcohol kept him away from her. However they had seven children so she had to make a living cleaning the hotel rooms.

Then I went on to Clifden where Michael Hartnett read his poetry from a low wooden stage, his face and hands covered in congealed blood patches. He had fallen off the Dublin train. When he had finished reading he said over the microphone, 'now can I have my cheque?' All went down in my sketchbook.

On the way back I went over to the Aran Islands where I hired a pony and trap to take me around the island. We clipped, clopped along the roads framed in stone walls, past the little white-painted cottages, stopping to talk to Gráinne who told me she loved Harry's *A Wild Taste* (Methuen had reprinted it recently).

10.8.88
Horse fair PICK

18

THE SOUTH SEAS

See fish chart for this painting

COCOnut CRISA

At last the time had come for our trip to the South Seas. Poppy and Holly's bags had been packed weeks ago. Pat was to come with us for two weeks, as part of his annual holiday. We arrived in Los Angeles for a one night stopover, marvelling at the hotel with the large red hibiscus flowers that circled the large swimming pool and the iridescent humming birds taking the nectar from those flowers with their long beaks.

After our huge Mexican breakfast of sweet waffles, we boarded the plane and took off for the island of Tahiti. On arrival at the airport the doors of the plane opened and we felt a blast of humid hot air. We went down the plane steps, caressed by this warm air and entered the terminal where a group of beautiful brown-skinned islanders played South Pacific music on ukuleles accompanied with their harmonised singing. One of the men, with a coloured cloth wrapped around his hips, handed us a tiara flower; the perfume was overpowering. Near the airport was our hotel, right on the edge of the sea, where we could hear the swoosh of waves beating on the reefs. I knew I had come to the right place. I was overwhelmed by the atmosphere, despite the fact that we were near the airport and in a hotel not far from a busy road.

Alan MacWeeney had been to the Cook Islands and he recommended that Aitutaki was where we should stay for our year in the Pacific. So the next day we boarded a small plane for Rarotonga, the capital of the Cook Islands. The Rarotonga people were rounded and smiley compared to the Tahitians. We were to stay in Rarotonga for two nights before going to one of the fourteen outer islands of the Cooks called Aitutaki.

'Let's go to Maurauki, it would be the most ideal island', I kept saying.

'But Mummy there is no such place', Poppy said.

We landed at this tiny airport, the terminal building was the size of a cowshed, thatched with coconut fronds. The runway was dusted in pale yellow coral and palm trees blew in the warm wind. The small airport bus trundled us along four miles into the tiny village of Arutanga.

We got off at the Rapae Hotel, a series of huts on wooden stilts, placed by the sea. To the left was the dining room, which consisted of poles holding up a roof of coconut fronds. It was not long before some local children came with curiosity to talk to us.

'What's your names?'

'Pat, Pauline, Poppy and Holly. And yours?'

'Training, Travel, Temata and Muia'.

Next day we hired a small catamaran sailing boat, driven by two youths, Peka and Utanga. The two of them were very lively and witty, very playful. They took us to the small motu where they prepared a picnic for us, cooking fish that they had just dived for. They climbed the coconut trees for sweet coconut water drinks. They were like two agile monkeys, legging it up the tall coconut trees kicking down coconuts.

After that Peka and Utanga would visit us each evening in our little wooden hut on stilts. They brought us small sweet local bananas and eggs. Then they invited us to eat with their people; where were looked at like museum pieces by the children, leaning on us and stroking our white arms as we ate.

It wasn't long before it was time for Pat to return to Ireland. I decided we would go back as far as Tahiti with him as my curiosity of that island had not been fulfilled. I also felt it hard to be left without Pat. I had a very sad wrenching feeling.

'How will I manage without him?'

And yet how dull it would be to go back to Ireland with him.

Holly was disappointed to leave Aitutaki, as she had fallen for Peka.

'Don't worry Holly, we'll return to Aitutaki for our year'.

So we said goodbye to Tamata, Tie and Retie and then to Peka and Utanga and promised faithfully we would be back.

Peka had written Holly a love letter that she read on the aeroplane.

'Will you marriage me?'

'Ah Mummy, isn't that a sweet letter!'

From then on, Holly could think of nothing else but Peka.

The sun came up, it was now Poppy, Holly and me. We booked ourselves on a ferry to the nearest island off Tahiti called Moorea. It was an early morning journey lasting two hours.

My plan was to stay for two weeks on a selection of Tahitian Islands, and on each island we would spend the first night in a hotel where we could clean up and then look for a cheaper abode. The two girls were having a sleep after our lunch in the luxurious quiet hotel. We had been served by waiters and waitresses with flowers adorning their heads and bodies. The garden around the hotel had volcanic stones, grass patches and rampant tropical flowers that grew for a great distance up alongside the beach.

While the girls were resting I walked along the dazzly white sandy beach, the turquoise water on my right, the reef with its white hissing waves only meters away. I came across a tiny sandy inlet and there set amongst hibiscus and coconut trees on a sandy grassy lawn were three wooden huts. I ventured to ask a large lady about the three huts. She was dressed in a blue pareu, her white hair drawn back in a bun. She sat under a huge hibiscus tree that dangled with shells, old CDs, beads and various artistic bobbles. She was an old Tahitian artist. Her husband was collecting breadfruit from the tree near their wooden house. He wore a crown of leaves to shade his face and a piece of old brown cloth tied around his hips, his bare feet moved like hands as he climbed down the tree.

'Aloha', they both said to me.

'I am looking for a place to rent for me and my two daughters'.

'We have one of these huts for rent'.

It was a reasonable price. I looked around the hut and choose my bed on the semi-open balcony. It had a yellow hibiscus flower cover. I placed the girls in a room with two beds that also had bright coloured hibiscus covers. Our kitchen had a cupboard made of wired windows to keep the flies away, a gas stove, a hammer to crack open coconuts and other practical utensils. I booked it immediately. I told Nannie and her husband Benjamin that we would be back soon.

When I got back to the hotel Poppy said.

'Mummy I have got a very bad earache'.

Poor Poppy was in tears.

'Poppy, Holly, I have got a beautiful place just along the beach'.

Poppy was still complaining of her ear as we settled into our new hut.

'What is wrong with your daughter?' Nannie asked.

'It's her ear'.

Nannie leant over Poppy and inspected her ear.

'I have a Maori medicine for this complaint'.

And for two days Nannie tended Poppy's ear, dropping oils from various plants until the ear got better. Benjamin showed us how to make breadfruit chips, we swam endlessly as yellow flowers dropped at four o'clock each day into the sea water from the large hibiscus tree. The flowers bobbed away with the current, slowly turning a deep orange as they went.

Each evening we could see a woman with a crown of coloured flowers, named Cecile. She would fish with a large white net that she threw into the lagoon like a lasso. She let it lie and then pulled it in, full of small white glistening fish. She had an outdoor fire lighting on the beach where she cooked these fish. We were invited to join her to eat this fish with our fingers dipping each piece in coconut cream, a large bowl of watercress went with it. Whenever she caught a larger fish she used a metal bottle top nailed to a stick to take the scales off the fish. It was here we started to paint.

At first I could not get the shape of the Tahitian head. It was like a tilted egg, our European heads are more like upright eggs. The wraparounds (pareus) I had painted on my figures were too bright, Poppy said, as I cried.

'Mummy you are trying too hard. Your colours are far too bright'.

Poppy's words relaxed me back into painting and out came large wonderful paintings from Holly, Poppy and me. We had well and truly begun our South Seas experience. I was pleased with my plan to settle for two weeks on these outer islands.

The two weeks went by and the following morning we set off for the next island of Huahine. It was pouring with tropical heavy rain, the raindrops seemed joined. Our luggage got drenched, this was an overnight ferry. We settled ourselves and luggage to lie in a dark part of the deck.

'Oh Mummy look'.

We saw it was the favourite spot for lots of brown shiny cockroaches, so we moved to some benches further along the deck. The wind got up and the sea got rough. Not only were we wet but we were now cold, but the fresh breeze stopped us from feeling too sea-sick. The sun was rising when we arrived and the warmth began to melt our uncomfortable bodies.

The quay front of Huahine looked promising for a guesthouse but they were all unavailable, so we went by bus to another 'luxurious' hotel. This island had an unfriendly atmosphere for us. The hotel staff seemed slow and unwilling to give us anything that differed from the menu. For instance I asked if I could have this dish without meat and the answers I got to all my queries, 'no!' Poppy and Holly kept joking about the name of the hotel 'Re La Mohana' and kept saying 'relax mohana'.

The beach had large plastic water toys, such gaudy orange paddle boats, blue dolphins and yellow dinosaurs. It took a while to find a cheaper place to settle for our two weeks. We stopped a young Chinese boy who circled around and around us on his bike with curiosity.

'Are there any guest houses around here?'

'I take you', he said, so he twirled and whirled on the road in front of us leading us to a pathway that led to Tina's guesthouse. It was again a wooden house with much the same type of kitchen we had at Nannie's. Over the beds hung old yellowed mosquito nets covered in holes.

'Oh! You are from Ireland, I love your Johnny Logan'.

She had fallen in love with Johnny who had won the Eurovision Song Contest that must have been beamed thousands of miles to this small island in Tahiti. She stroked Poppy's hair and said when she was young her hair was brown and dark like this.

'Oh your Johnny Logan would have loved me'.

At night Tina brought her ukulele and sang to us magical songs.

The Chinese boy came to hang around our hut every day of the two weeks. However he kindly helped us carry home our shopping and showed us the ancient fish traps. There were many ancient sites to be seen on these islands. The large fish traps were made of volcanic stones set in circles in the shallow waters. The fish were able to find their way into these pools but the stones were set down such that they could not get out. The islanders still use this ancient method to this day.

Holly found pieces of coral from the small inlets by the sea and with them she wrote out in large letters 'I Love Aitutaki' encircled by a big heart. We each painted good paintings on this island but our skin was covered in large uncomfortable mosquito bites, we had never been in such an infested spot. Mosquitos swarmed around our nets and every night they managed to get through the holes to feast on our blood. Holly joked that if she wanted to have bigger breasts all she would have to do is place her breasts beside the holes of the net and the mosquitos would do their job, enlarging them.

The one thing that we found hard was that the islanders did not want to commune with us. I stopped to admire a girl's carving of a fruit bowl but she would hardly look at me and there was no such thing as a smile. But I was determined to fulfil the plan to stay two weeks to try to really get to know each place.

The next adventure was the islands of Western Samoa. The plane arrived to humid breathtaking heat. We took a bus for Apia, passing fales with coconut roofs held up with a circle of poles. Each fale had a base of volcanic stones and underneath the flooring we could see little pigs rushing in and out. Never before had we seen so many churches, huge whitewashed buildings. God definitely had the best houses. Each window of the bus framed a painting; people working in the coconut groves, the breadfruit trees, and small outrigger boats bobbing on the water. Our hotel was the famous Aggie Grey's, in Apia, the capital of Samoa. The bus stopped outside and men in sarongs carried our luggage up the steps into this open hotel. The centre held a large swimming pool with a coconut tree on a little island in the centre of it.

The first person we met was a beautiful long legged girl named Cindy, who turned out to be a fa'afafine, a young man. We made a close friendship with him/her during our stay in Aggie Grey's. Each morning there was a typed-out sheet on our breakfast table beside the glistening pool which gave us world news. The Berlin wall had been knocked down, Europe this and Europe that. Thank goodness I was not there. An old Samoan

Chief asked could he join us at our dinner table. He pissed off Poppy as he smoothly flirted with me, offering to take us here and there on the island.

old 10,000 yr old came held in the pigs as in a pen —

Cindy spent a lot of time in Aggie Grey's hotel. She did not work there but she flirted outrageously with any of the sailors that happened to come in for a drink. She would lay her beautiful body stretching across three bar stools, swinging her legs and pointing at the ceiling. The sailors were intrigued, she was so luscious. Cindy often took us out at night. We went to a nightclub, music playing very loudly. The floor was empty, there seemed to be four or five people sitting in the darkness, Cindy, Poppy, Holly and I were the only ones that danced together on this circular floor. Walking home was quite scary on the empty Upolu streets. Dogs barked and it was a relief to get back into the well-lit Aggie Grey's hotel. I developed flu, so we had to stay on longer than planned. Cindy called for Holly and Poppy to go to the cinema. I lay sweating in bed when there was a knock on the door from one of the waiters who heard I had flu.

'Would you like a massage?'

I turned down this surprising offer.

When I got better we went to look for our usual cheaper abode and found an enclosed complex called Olivia's Casual Accommodation, and casual it was. The place was surrounded in wiring and large iron gates were locked each night. We chose a dirty turquoise wooden hut which had cockroaches in every crevice. At least six dogs lay on our veranda. A procession of little pink and black spotted pigs and piglets would rush through the coconut trees, the dogs would leap from their prone positions and chase them. I have never seen such bony dogs. Any time we left the barriered premises, little children would throw stones at our ankles. In the next hut to ours there was the most glamorous young German, she was travelling the world alone. When she went out at night, locking Olivia's gate behind her, she walked the dark road in revealing European-type clothes.

'I don't know how you dare go out at night', I said to her, she answered.

'I have a special way of walking with confidence. I am not afraid of being attacked, so therefore I never am'.

She wasn't the only female traveller we met. We met several who dared to travel these islands and the world on their own. We decided to take tours as it was a great way to see the island.

We were taken to the house of the writer Robert Louis Stephenson. It was strange to see a fireplace in his house in this hot humid country. Our tour bus took us high into the jungly mountains, the driver pointed out a blue wooden hut that was famous for marijuana sessions. We descended the jungly hills to have our prepared picnic on the beaches overlooking small tropical islands. Behind us a local man was killing a pig with the family casually sitting around the umu that the pig was to be cooked in. The umu ovens were used on all the Pacific Islands, consisting of a four foot deep hole that they dug into the ground and lined with black volcanic stones. A fire was lit to heat the stones, then the meat and the vegetables were wrapped in banana leaves (that do not burn), then placed into the hole and covered with earth to cook overnight.

They laughed at Poppy, Holly and I as we squeamishly *oohed* and *aaheed* as we watched the pig's belly being slit with the flies buzzing around our heads. Then along the black cindery road appeared a procession of local men, the old followed the young, each carrying fishing nets, rows of fish speared on sticks, heavy pigs, branches of green bananas, tarro and all kinds of foods. Our bus driver explained to us this was to be shared amongst the villagers.

The next morning we went to the big market in Apia. Women sat cross-legged on hand-woven mats, selling fruits and craft work, men sat around at low tables playing cards and drinking Kava. Obviously it was having its effect on them as they totally looked out of it and in a world of their own. This kava drink is made from the ginger tree roots. The South Sea islanders worship it, it has the effect of turning one numb from head to foot, transforming the men into Buddha-like figures, sitting still and content. When the missionaries came they banned kava, and lo and behold, our European drinks appeared on the market. It then transpired the South Sea Islanders do not have the enzymes in their DNA to cope with our type of alcohol. It can send them into murderous rages. They are far better off to stick to their own kava drink.

While we were choosing a watermelon Holly suddenly screeched.

'Wait for me', she was crying and shuddering.

'What is wrong with you, Holly?'

'A man pinched my bottom'.

'Don't be so ridiculous, Holly. He can't do much more harm in this place full of people'.

'I don't care!'

Walking ahead of us, she shivered with rage.

'I want to go!'

We filled our shopping bags with the food that we needed for our next trip which was to the island of Savai'i, a one hour boat trip away.

We were booked into the Safu Hotel, the owner was called Moelagi. She was a talking Chief. Her role was to give ideas and suggestions to the island people. The most important rank is that of a silent chief, who nods his or her head at the best suggestions. Moelagi was a good-looking, heavy, light brown woman with tattoos circling her smooth thighs. She was about 58. She said:

'They call them dancing tattoos, and very rarely does a woman let anyone see them'.

Holly, Poppy and I were privileged. Moelagi was an intelligent liberated woman, very in touch with the world. To my surprise she adored our Irish man, Conor Cruise O'Brien. One of her many interests was archaeology and she had also a great interest in the writings of the anthropologist Margaret Mead.

One of her guests was the anthropologist Derek Freeman who completely opposed anything that Margaret Mead had written. Moelagi was riveted to talk with Derek. He said Mead 'had lied through her teeth'. Moelagi talked to us a lot about her. Mead had taken up residence in Samoa in order to send back her written findings on Samoan youth to Professor Boas in America. He was convinced that Mead would find the Samoan people were without guilt or complex. Boas was delighted that her research matched his beliefs and the subsequent Mead books became world famous for influencing western society. The start of free love.

We were invited to spend Christmas in Moelagi's fale, it was next to her hotel. The Christmas dinner was laid out on oiled banana leaves placed on the floor, huge fish and pork was served from the earth oven. There were delicious rubbery banana pancakes, mangoes, papaya, coconut milk, all part of our tropical Christmas and there was one small Christmas pudding, sent to Moelagi from a friend in New Zealand.

Moelagi gave us bracelets and earrings made from coconut shells. She danced a seva for us, stepping sideways and swaying her large hips, her hands and fingers swaying in the air, her head jerking side to side in time with the seva music. Then Holly and Poppy showed everyone present what an Irish jig was like. When the party was over and the banana leaves chucked away we unrolled our sleeping mats to sleep on the floor of the fale, open to the night breezes of the South Pacific air.

After Christmas it was time to move on to a little yellow wooden house that we rented from a friend of Moelagi's called Dr Ceferalli. It was set in a large lawn with three huge breadfruit trees and behind this complex a whole jungle of coconut trees and various tropical plants. It was only 20 metres to the little sandy beach where we could swim each day. Holly, Poppy and I settled down in our hut making shelves for our clothes and paints from boxes found at the market.

We loved going to the market, our shopping would be wrapped in green leaves. Apparently American Samoa has been ruined by the introduction of plastic bags. People were used to throwing leaves onto the land and they would rot, but when they threw plastic bags away they remained and gathered all over the island.

One day we were sitting by the sea and heard a broad Cork accent behind us. He was a teacher in the local school, dressed in a long Samoan lava lava. He had been living in Savai'i for many years and didn't miss Cork at all.

Dr Ceferalli, the owner of our hut, was a very skinny, sun-shrivelled Italian medical doctor who over many's the evening philosophised to me in a very sad voice.

'I came here to Western Samoa to be as near as I can to nature. I married a local girl, falling first of all in love with her feet, broad toes, well set apart. When I took her home to Italy to meet my people the first thing she wanted was shoes. We tried every shoe shop in Rome including the men's department to find anything that would fit the broadness of her feet. She ended up crying with a feeling of dreadful inferiority. Now all through our marriage she seeks the things that I was running away from, cars, fridges, television. She saw me as a provider of these things. As a doctor my philosophy is the survival of the fittest and yet I had to give caesarean sections to some of the weakest women, thereby perpetuating that weak strain in the female. When I first came here all the village people would gather round to watch a woman giving birth, they would sing to her, oil her head and soothe her. Now they are not so open. Since I have been living here things have changed', as he stared into the distant sunset over the reef.

There was a New Year's celebration going on about twenty coconut trees away from our hut, it was New Year's Eve. Holly, Poppy and I crept over in the moonlight. Two of the larger fales were lit up, each filled with dancers, female only in one and male only in the other. As we kept ourselves hidden in the shadows, the thump, thump, thump of the feet of eight lads had a very deep frightening drum about them. Their skin had been oiled so that they could not be caught, they raced by with the intention of raping some unsuspecting girl, said a woman in a hush hush voice.

In Samoa the elders always placed the young girls in the centre of the fale for safety at night, but the cunning boys proffered what they called a 'love stick' into the centre for the young girl to feel the little carving that was attached to the end of the stick. Recognising it as her boyfriend's carving, she tiptoed over the elders, only to find a young rapist who had cunningly copied the love stick carving.

Throughout the weeks that we lived in Savai'i we were often taken out by Moelagi's friend, a sensitive Englishman who owned a coffee plantation on the island. He took us on long drives into the deepest wilds of the island where we might swim in dark pools under strong tall waterfalls directly flowing over the black volcanic cliffs. He was an intellectual who would tell us all about the island, like the huge fox bats that hung upside down by their feet from the elephant trees. We would stop off to buy green cooking bananas from a remote jungle fale. We would be taken to the lava fields where we excitedly collected the green crystal oliveens that the volcano had created in the depth of its baking furnace. We were shown a church that sat in a little green oasis where the black lava had completely surrounded it, leaving it untouched. Of course the local people called it a miracle. Each village that we would drive through, crowds of adults and children would beckon us to join them.

It is such a good idea for women to travel together. People wanted to take us under their wing, show us things and look after us. We would not have experienced so much if we had a man with us. We felt so at home with Moelagi and Dr Ceferalli it was very hard to fulfil our plan to go back to the Cook Islands, but that we did. Packing our bags and saying goodbye was a very tearful moment.

On the ferry back to Upolu I noticed a fly hovering above Holly, Poppy and me. It hovered over the white-skin, black-suited Jehovah Witness, over the mother with her little child who started to vomit with the sway of the sea. That fly stayed in the air all the way from Savai'i to Upolu without landing. To this day I can't work out whether it flew that distance, or because it was under an awning, the measure of its flight being considerably less.

I have many tales of my South Seas years, told in a thick manuscript which sits in a drawer. Part of it was edited and published by Art Books International as *The South Seas and a Box of Paints*. One day I would like to put together a full book to detail all the extraordinary experiences amongst these amazing islands.

We returned to the Cook Island of Rarotonga, re-uniting with our little girlfriend Mee. On the first night of our week there she took us to her sister's engagement party on the beach. The dancing and the music in front of that South Pacific sunset was beyond description. The next day our little friend, her brothers and sisters, took us up the mountain and banged red flowers on our hair which oozed jelly-like juice. They called it their conditioner. They pulled green and yellow passion fruits from a tangle of leaves and gouged out the yellow seeds for us to suck from the centre. They showed us their horse that stood on a rock by a waterfall. Their mother adopted young prisoners.

'I look after them, Mama. Nobody loves them. I love them, they are good boys really. I make them into good boys with my love'.

We met a huge striking man called Kauraka. He had an enormous brown body. You could see if he was slimmer he would be incredibly handsome. His long hair hung like a waterfall down his back. He had written many's the slim volume of poetry about Cook Island legends and his deeply romantic feeling about women. Tucked into his pareu he carried a small wooden flute which he played through his nose. He lectured in literature in the University of Rarotonga. He gave me a Maori name, Te-Pua-Renga-a-Tepaeru. Kauraka's friends talked of some of the negative influences that white people had on the islands. A colleague of Kauraka, who also taught in the university, made me feel 'very white', but when he saw my art work he told me I was different. He asked me to lecture in the university about my work which I later did.

Arriving back to the tiny island with its necklace of motus, Peka and Utanga had found us a ramshackle green wood house to live in. It had a large lawn which the South Sea islanders have around each of their tin or wooden houses.

Once again Peka and Utanga came to take us to football matches, to their parents' houses and to the Motu islands. Gradually Poppy and Utanga became smitten with each other. They would take off around the island together on Utanga's scooter, Peka and Holly likewise. I would paint, tucked in under some exotic tree, wallowing in being warm, alone and peaceful. I did not miss Pat and I did not miss Ireland. There was a wonderful feeling of aloneness. The girls were happy and time stretched out before us.

The evenings were spent playing games on the lawn, screeching, running and yelling. I became a teenager again. We had a visitor one night, a skinny bony old man. He walked into the hut and announced:

'I want to fuck the mama'.

Poppy kindly squished between the old man and me to protect me. The boys laughed till they cried. It became a household joke. We eventually got rid of that old man and he did not call again, thank goodness.

Poppy and Utanga would tell me of how they went deep diving for clams. Poppy became an expert at getting her body to the bottom of the sea. We would cook up their catch, listen to the ukulele and Utanga's singing until it was time for me to get into my bed and the boys go home.

On another occasion we had a second intruder.

'I think the two boys should stay in your house, Mama, because that intruder could be dangerous', said Peka's mother.

We had been stalked by a stranger. I was in my bed when I heard the click, click on my slatted window. I froze and did not dare turn to see what was happening behind me.

'Click, click, click, click'.

I picked up my pillow and turned around and in the deepest guttural voice threw the pillow at the window and yelled 'go away!' and saw a dark figure in the moonlight, running away between the coconut trees. So yes we were glad to accept that the boys should live in and protect us.

The young man later stopped me in the village and said.

'I am sorry I thought yez was your daughter', as if that made it any better.

Holly and Poppy had been taught by the islanders how to do the hula. They were able to dance beautifully, swaying their hips and twisting their hands in the air. On Saturday evening the local women made Poppy, Holly and me crowns of flowers. We were to go to the Rapae Hotel for Island Night. It was organised that Holly and Poppy would dance for the tourists.

'Ladies and gentlemen we now have the beautiful Poppy and the fabulous Holly to dance for you. They have been living on the island for eight years. Both married an islander and have eight children each'.

The drums were banged and swaying from the dark outside came Holly and Poppy.

Underneath the coconut roof of the Rapae Hotel the audience sat at their tables having eaten a traditional Maori feast and they whooped and hollered with enjoyment at the dance. Next Utanga and Peka scissored their legs, flashing their white teeth, shuddering the leaves that were around their ankles, hips and head. I had rarely seen such magnificent energetic dancers, especially Utanga. Towards the end of the entertainment, all the dancers male and female, spread out amongst the tables choosing a tourist to come and hula on the floor with them. The white people (Papa-a) looked stiff and awkward in comparison to the fluidity of the Maori dancers.

On one of these Saturday nights Peka fell off his scooter bike on the turn before the Rapae, his two front teeth were knocked out and he believed it was the spirit from the leper colony that used to be there that pushed him off. There was a streak of strong superstition in the Maori people.

'See that coconut tree, the nuts are empty. That is because it is a haunted tree'.

There was also a strong belief that dreams were in fact true. They believed that if you had your period you must not walk past the garden tomatoes and plants because they would die.

Utanga would joke and say.

'I like the girls, but I really like the Mama'.

And he would bend to take off my flip-flops in a joking manner. He seemed to be preparing himself for Poppy's departure, which was eminent.

The sad day came when Poppy had to leave, the date had been pre-arranged for her to rejoin her studies. She went back and reunited with Conor, leaving Utanga heartbroken. Holly and Peka were still laughing and playing in their fun relationship.

Before Poppy left, Utanga had started to pay a lot of attention to me and my paintings. He subsequently told me that he had fallen in love with my wrist, the way it moved when I painted. He would sit so close beside me like a child watching my every move. It transpired that he was a brilliant artist. I gave him some of my materials and I knew that if he should have an exhibition in Europe it would be a success, but he was a young island man with no such ambitions.

'I know where you would like to paint, Mama'.

They all called me Mama.

'I know, Mama, where you would like to paint – the old bakery'.

Utanga would bring me on his rattley scooter bike that was made up of bits of pram and wire from the island dump. We would sit for hours silently concentrating on our paintings. At first he talked of

Poppy and how he looked up at the aeroplanes in the sky and thought of her being taken from him in one of those planes. Poppy sent a box to all our islander friends, including football boots, trinkets and necklaces. Utanga was so delighted with these boots that he wore them despite the fact they pinched and squeezed his very broad feet. The trinkets that he hung around his neck were soon ripped by a branch as he collected fruits from the top of the trees. The studs of the boots fell off and the sides burst. Life on these islands was rough, possessions did not last long.

When Peka's birthday came around, Pauline, his mother, laid a banquet for his party. The priest gave a sermon saying:

'Every boat needs an outrigger in another colour', referring to Holly. They all knew what he meant as they would like to see Holly and Peka marrying.

My feelings for Utanga puzzled me. There was this beautiful, and at times extremely ugly, young man, yet he had a certain caring way about him, an understanding of the way I would paint.

'I know how your mind works. You become that tree and you become that animal. It all comes down your wrist from your brain'.

Holly, Peka, Utanga and I would roam around the island visiting the black aunty or the leader of the dance. I had rarely felt so free or laughed so much, everything seemed funny, almost everything seemed in the wonderful 'now'. I was happy that all was well with my family and myself, and the company of Utanga was refreshing and new and mind-boggling. Sitting behind him on the bike along the hot dusty red roads, I could smell the warm skin of his back. I wanted so much to touch him, but would not dream of it.

On most days Utanga would read to me. I would lie my head on the crock of his arm with my eyes closed, listening to his soft voice. He was replacing Pat in a funny kind of way. We decided one night to sleep on the veranda, his body close to mine, which somehow seemed quite natural. The Maori people are very close and touchy. In the middle of the night he pulled his arm from under my body and I put my hand on the skin of his arm, which felt as smooth as the bark on a birch tree.

'What are we doing?' I said, as Utanga leant over to kiss me.

'Going to have a fuck I hope'.

I found that an irresistibly funny reply and we made love.

The next morning we had tea as usual in the kitchen, both of us obviously shy and speechless at what had happened. Utanga went to his home to tend his tarro patch. I took off and hid myself way along the beach. I felt incredibly embarrassed and puzzled and did not want to see Utanga with this awful feeling that had overcome me. As I sat in my hidden spot drawing, I recognised the *put, put, put* of his scooter. He had followed my footprints and had the Maori instinctive hunting talent of finding wild animals, fish and me.

He sat beside me giggling like a silly boy and started to tell me about the girls he previously had. In no way did I feel attracted to him until that evening when his humour got to me again. On a walk he started joking about how he had to pay me for a haircut I had given him the other day and that payment was love making, and yes neither of us resisted each other, so laughter once again relaxed us both into a deeper relationship.

Holly was totally accepting of this turn of events. Nothing seemed to surprise Peka or her, indeed the whole village had got used to seeing Utanga and me together. There seemed to be a complete acceptance of this extraordinary difference in age. I later read that in ancient times young Maori men would take an older woman as their lover before they married and settled down. Perhaps this was an old gene surfacing in Utanga?

The shopkeepers used to say:

'Get your son to carry that, Mama'.

There are no such words as mother and father in the Maori language, just the word relation which can refer to mother, father, aunt, son, daughter, grandmother.

Holly and I had to go back to Ireland, as Holly was returning to art school and my book *Ireland: An Artist's Year* (Methuen), was being launched in Bewley's, along with an exhibition of my South Seas paintings in the Taylor Galleries. The book got good reviews in the press and the exhibition sold well. At that launch the publishers admired my South Sea paintings and commissioned me to return to the South Seas and just write:

'We have enough paintings already here for a book'.

This idea I gladly took up. Subsequently Art Books International published the book, *The South Seas and a Box of Paints*, thanks to the suggestion of my friend John Krupnick.

My life in Ireland went back to the way it was before I went to the South Seas. Pat continued to read aloud to me in his comforting voice. I was selling my work and meeting my friends, but on the many walks that I took on the Kerry mountains, my tears mixed with the rain and wind as I thought of the South Seas.

One year later. I handed my ticket for Tahiti and the Cook Islands to a jolly Los Angeles airport official:

'Lucky you, wish I was going to the Cook Islands'.

It was as if my whole mind and body was in the shape of a question mark, there was so many mixed feelings going on in me. I arrived in Tahiti at night, the porter in the hotel was called Adolphe Gauguin. It transpired that he was the great grandson of Paul Gauguin, the artist, and his father was the first Tahitian son of Paul Gauguin called Emile. My book *The South Seas and a Box of Paints* had begun.

I invited Adolphe to my little coconut house, set in the hotel tropical garden. He came the next day, walked over the little wooden bridge where huge eels swam in the brown water and sat in my little balcony. I made him coffee and had bought him some banana cake.

'My father, Emile, used to sell fish traps on the steps of the market. One day in 1963 a woman came from Chicago. Her name was Marjorie Kovler and she say to my father, "are you related to the great painter Paul Gauguin". My father say "yes". She then ask him would he paint for her if she bought him some paint, canvasses and brushes. "I will try it", my father said. So she brought him many paints and he try and try but he could not do it. So he take the paint and brushes to his friend, a China man and the China man paint many pictures for him and my father sign them, Emile Gauguin. Oh Kovler was so so pleased. She took all these paintings and my father on the plane to Chicago and she have a big exhibition of the China Man paintings. Many many people come and many many pictures are sold until they are all gone, then Kovler say to my father, "you must please do more". She go to get more brushes and paint but my father stop her and he say "we go back to Tahiti to my friend, the China Man and he will do more paintings for you and I will sign them Emile Gauguin, ok". Kovler was so surprised that my father did not paint them himself. She say we must tell everyone the truth about this. The museum kept one of the China Man's paintings, which my father sign Emile Gauguin, as a record of this event'.

Then for me, in my sketchbook, Adolphe drew the way his father Emile tried to draw a person. 'He do a round for his head and two sticks for arms and two sticks for legs. He do two dots for eyes, one dot for the nose and one dot for the mouth, that's all my father could do'.

So I am the proud owner of an Adolphe Gauguin in my sketchbook.

I boarded the plane for Aitutaki, nobody knew that I was coming back. The same tiny turquoise airport hut stood on the yellow coral of the island. The airport bus trundled us passengers, first stopping at the familiar Rapae Hotel and next I asked the bus to stop at a youth hostel that I had discovered previously.

I was given a small bright room and we all shared the cooking facilities in the kitchen. I decided to hire a scooter bike and took off for Peka's home. His family were excited and happy to see me again. Peka wasn't at home but he came to visit me in the youth hostel. He had told Utanga I was back. Peka was intrigued as to what Holly was up to back in Ireland. He missed her terribly, I could tell.

It wasn't long after Peka went home that Utanga came, carrying a large cooked orange-coloured crayfish as a gift for me. While eating the crayfish on the front lawn we once again bonded with laughter. One of the villagers shouted over the hibiscus hedge, 'ah ha, Utanga stills loves the Mama'.

It was an emotional return to our love-making. We moved into a long wooden house belonging to Utanga's friend. Many islanders came and played cards, fell asleep on the floor, drank their bush beer, sang, cooked and even fought in this house where Utanga and I lived. I placed a tiny padlock on to a dark cupboard where within I hid my return ticket, a little money and my clothes. Apparently if anyone broke that padlock they could go to prison in Rarotonga for breaking and entering. However anyone could take the clothes off the line or shoes off the doorstep, it was a case of what's yours is mine.

As well as Utanga there were other natural artists who used to come along and we would all paint together. I eventually decided that we had enough work for an Aitutaki exhibition. The Village Bakery allowed us to use their veranda where we pinned up all our works. The hurricane was threatening and the wind had started to arrive on the island of Aitutaki. Each of the paintings flapped and tore from their drawing pins and Sellotape. At last we secured them and waited for passersby to visit our exhibition. Our only visitors were those that had done the paintings. Utanga climbed the wooden steps of the veranda, bent double, using a stick. He was pretending to be a very old millionaire. He shakily lifted the stick into the air, going around the veranda saying:

'I'll buy this one, that one, that one, that one, that one and that one and now I'm going to talk on the Coconut Wireless about this exhibition'.

We got such a laugh, but had to take down all the works as the hurricane was arriving in earnest.

The radio hissed and crackled with news of the hurricane. It was travelling strongly towards us. We made sure we had torches. I missed my hurricane lamp which had been stolen and taken up to Nannie's tarot hut. We also had to have ready our sheets to sleep in should we have to climb to the highest point of the island if the waters reached our house. The sea turned a threatening yellow colour and heaved its way up the beach, bringing with it yellow lumps of coral. The coconut trees bent and waved:

'You better watch those trees, sometimes the heads blow off'.

Everybody seemed to get excited rather than frightened of this hurricane. They leapt and jumped into the yellow waves screeching, 'hee haww, hee haww'.

'Come on Mama', stupidly I entered the angry sea, where upon I was knocked over and was rolled and sucked along with heavy lumps of coral. I thought I would never get my head above water. All night the wind raged and sang its threatening song. The next morning things were calmer but the island looked like the morning after a drunken party, debris on tin roofs, fallen trees and flattened taro stalks wherever you looked and a dead hurricane bird lay dead on the lawn. The storm moved on to the next island.

A letter arrived at the post office from an American couple called John and Elaine Krupnick.

'We have followed your artwork around Ireland and our mutual friends, Hilary and Gerry Collins, told us you were on the island of Aitutaki in the South Seas. We are coming to look you up'.

The day came and Utanga and I spent the whole time asking couples.

'Are you the Krupnicks?'

In the evening we went to each dining table with the same question. It became quite a joke. The next day the Krupnicks turned up at the funny long house that we were living in, immediately joining in the fun we were all having.

The publishers had asked me to retrace my steps in order for the stories to match the paintings and sketches I had done. I asked Tangata Haurua, a young very beautiful girl to type for me. Not only her, but Joe Campbell, the Maori schoolteacher, Utanga and anyone that dropped by were well able to write out my dictations.

I first went back to Western Samoa on my own, to Savai'i. Moelagi welcomed me and told me more about Margaret Mead and also the words of Freeman. I asked her many questions, including how do people make love in their open fales. She said we either are very quiet or we go into the jungle, not like white tourists. The noise they make shocks everybody here when they make love. The girl that I painted called Sarafi could hardly make eye contact with me as she still felt her status was of a lesser person.

'Why paint her, she is only a waitress?'

Road workers from Australia sat on the bar stools and crudely quipped at me, had I burnt my bra yet. Moelagi brought me through the ceremonies that Poppy, Holly and I had witnessed with the kava making, the weddings, the funerals. We would take walks in the evening together, passing local women all naked but for a small cloth around their loins, washing themselves for their evening meal. The men would be vigorously shouting and playing cricket.

I returned from Samoa to everyone's and Utanga's welcome. It was now time for me to write about the outer islands of the Cooks. As Utanga was quite knowledgeable about the islands he wanted to come with me and he arranged for us to stay with different relations on each island.

The first island that we flew to was Atue, where we stayed with one of Utanga's uncles. Holly, Poppy and I had been on this island before and we met Kauhe. Kauhe had asked me would either Poppy or Holly marry him.

'Which one do you want most', I asked him.

'Either would do', he said.

He took us to the caves where Maori legends abound. We drank from the deep clear pools within the caves.

'When you drink that water you drink Atue'.

Bats were flitting in and out in the fading light.

The next island, Mauke, was like a tiny flat pancake set in the Pacific Ocean. The airport was a mere shack, our little white plane trundled to its landing. We passengers were taken in the back of a lorry, one of two trucks on the island, into the village. I overheard a young girl say.

'What does that woman want with that young fool?'

I was flattered that she did not say:

'What does that young man want with that old fool?'

We stayed again with another relation of Utanga's who told us that the airport truck nearly went down into the ocean when they downloaded it off a ship onto a raft outside the reef.

Each delivery from the big ship would be placed on this raft. They would wait for a wave that would take them over the coral reef. Many's the goat, motorbike or wheelbarrow lying at the bottom of the sea.

The second truck belonged to the Chief on the island and he allowed a whole group of us to visit the small beach where there was a legend of a man called Pi.

'Pi left his sweetheart, until she died of heartache wailing at the top of the cliff. Her bones remain there to this day. Pi travelled in his outrigger, first to Rarotonga and then to New Zealand, never returning'.

What remained was the profile of his handsome face cut by nature into the cliffside. Strangely enough the old and the young who had come to this little beach had not ever actually seen this profile, it was me who pointed it out.

'Look that's his nose, his chin, his neck', the old grandfather made a guttural sound with surprise and scuttled back to the truck with fear. I began to feel like a witch for having pointed this profile out and a truckload of scared islanders returned to the village. I made sure that the Chief, who owned the truck, explained to them all that the profile of Pi has always been there so that the islanders didn't think it was just me that pointed it out.

Utanga's uncle who we stayed with had the usual rusted wreck of a motorbike. He was forever tinkering with it as they all do. In his toolbox, amongst all the rusty cogs, nuts and bits of pipe, lay an ancient stone age tool that he had found at the top of the island where the mahogany trees grow. They used to carve outrigger boats with these tools.

I tried to refuse to take such a precious gift when I was offered it. Utanga whispered:

'He will be very insulted if you don't take it'.

So I took it with the resolution that Poppy and Holly would take it back to the Rarotonga museum one day.

It seemed totally acceptable wherever we went that Utanga and I should be put in the same space together.

We went to see the divided church. It came about as the two villages could not agree on who should do the carving and painting within it. They solved the problem by using a carpenter and a painter out of each of the villages. The altar was placed so that the priest could have one foot in one village and his other foot in the other village. It really was divided in design, one side vied with the other in the brightest of colours and the ornatest of carvings.

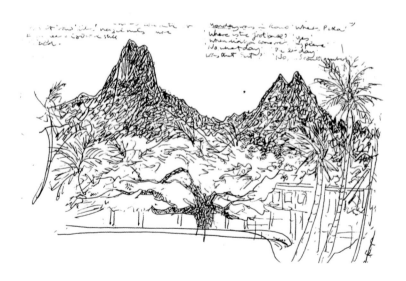

The next island was Mitiaro, where a Japanese archaeologist spent much of his time researching its underground passages. These passages were made by nature but the islanders now use them as eel traps.

Utanga sat amongst the fishermen as if he was part of their everyday life, chopping heads off the eels and flinging them into buckets. I busied myself jumping from lava stone to lava stone as the sea swirled around and a little brown and white dog jumped with me.

When we arrived back in Rarotonga we stayed with the George's, both artists. They gave us their tiny beach hut. Both Utanga and I knew that I should be boarding a plane from this airport soon to finally leave the South Pacific. By chance there was a party been given by his relatives, so we were invited. It was there that I felt most upset as Utanga was obviously attracted to a lovely girl called Anna and gave her the largest stalagmite that he brought back from the caves of Atu. Doing the same funny bow that he did when he took off my flipflops ages ago, 'this', he said, 'is for you', bowing low and holding his offering on both hands.

As the party proceeded Utanga did something he promised me he would never do while I was around. He drank bush beer mixed with European beer with abandonment. It was as if he was trying to annoy me on purpose. Maybe it was because I was soon to leave. I decided to sneak back to the George's as I was not only upset about Anna but also feared Utanga's aggression after drinking bush beer. He caught up with me on the moonlit beach and aggressively flung me to the ground.

'Utanga, please, I am too old for this, just let me go back to my friends to sleep'.

I attempted to get up and was pushed rudely back where he started to rant and rave about how I must have been unfaithful to him when I went on my own in Western Samoa. He was obviously in a turmoil between me, Anna and the beer. The mixture of beers I found out was the reason why nearly all the little fragile huts that they lived in had holes punched in the walls.

We made it along the beach together and slept in a small seaside shelter. I so wanted to crack him over the head with anger and finish everything with him. I was awake before him and walked up the lawn of my artist friends' house and told them how frightened I was of Utanga. They knew him and they also knew the temper that mixed beer brings about. My friends insisted that I report it to the Rarotonga police. When I did they recommended I go back to Aitutaki without him.

Just as I was about to leave for Aitutaki, to my surprise the police fetched Utanga and brought him to my friends' house. He was still inebriated and kept shouting at the top of his voice, 'I love Pauline'.

'Come, get on the back of my motorbike. I will take you to the airport', said my artist friend's husband.

It wasn't long before I heard Utanga's loud voice echoing over the airport.

'Pauline! Pauline!'

I got through the turnstyle without him seeing me and sat into the aeroplane with one empty seat beside me.

When I got back to Aitutaki, the New Zealand Maori schoolteacher, Joe, offered to put me up in his house.

'As long as they don't all think there is something going on between us', he said.

I had hoped upon hope that Utanga would stay in Rarotonga with Anna. I remembered the things I had loved him for saying so much such as 'an octopus brain is good enough for an octopus' and the wonderful drawing he did of me in the shape of a tree with golden apples and he was the roots. The next day there he was sitting under the large banyan tree on the back of his 'Kelly' bike. It would have been stupid not to say hello to him. By now he had quietened down and was apologetic and it wasn't long before the two of us were together again. My desires overcame my wisdom.

Time went by with us fishing, lamping crayfish. Groups of us camping on the beaches, Mo telling me about her time in Rarotonga prison where she shared a cell with another woman; one of the porters 'asked us to put our bums against the bars so he could do us'. It was a beautiful life studded with strange and difficult moments and soon it was time that I had to use my return ticket back to Ireland.

I went up the narrow steps into the small plane sitting on the weedy tarmac in Aitutaki. I felt the heat on my back, as did those who were seeing me off, standing under the shade of a coconut shelter. Little babies were being held up and made wave to me. Utanga had moved off to a clump of coconut trees, kicking stones and sand with his head down. I could not read his attitude. On the journey to the airport he seemed sulky and to dislike me. I knew I did not want to stay and I knew I did not want to go.

I could see the small cluster of my Aitutaki friends from the window of the plane. Even though I knew I wouldn't or couldn't stay. I sat back into my seat. I could smell the perfume from the many eyes of the cool Aitutaki flowers that were placed around my neck. The wind from the propellers pushed dust towards the group and we were off into the sky.

A terrible tight feeling from my chest up to my neck, an awful grey scene loomed up of Europe; leaving behind this sun, wind, sea, mosquitoes, dirt, singing, laughter, love, hate, perplexity, and going back to Pat. Pat, who had said 'no' to a sabbatical year. I remained stubbornly convinced that he could have got away, the word 'no' echoed in my head. Somehow the future seemed to hold the noise of the solid fuel cooker being riddled and rattled by Pat. Everything at a regular time, lunch, dinner etc.

What was I leaving? A half-man, half-boy, so many laughs, so physical, so sexy. Was Utanga and island life to be my real life? Yet I found the people at times to be sulky, lazy, ugly, unintelligent and violent. I was flying between these two aspects of my life.

The arrival in London was as I predicted; veiled in cold and greyness. There in the Chelsea streets was the old tramp wheeling his supermarket trolley piled high with the plastic bags of all his possessions. I stepped into the Chelsea Arts Club where Pat and I were to meet. There he was at the bar, the garden outside the window dripped with rain. I sat at an angle to Pat at a window table, it was like sitting beside the father that I never had. The usual faces were around the bar and billiard table.

Pat and my relationship had always been totally honest. It was now facing him that I told of Utanga. This news was met with extreme calmness from Pat. Then he said:

'Well, I have had an affair too, but nothing quite so exotic as yours I am sure'.

It was a relief.

I knew it would have been with Gale, as he had said in one of his letters that he had met up with her again. Gale was one of his girlfriends from his Trinity days. She was a small, blonde girl interested in the same men as I. She had an affair with Luke Kelly, in fact many's the man fancied Gale. I impulsively said to Pat:

'I would like to ring Gale now to tell her that it is perfectly alright for you and she to continue with each other'.

In fact I found it a relief that Pat had been unfaithful.

'That would be very nice of you', Pat said.

We went into the small yellow phone booth in the club. Her voice came over the phone, light and posh.

'Oh, Pauline, you are sweet! I do love him so'.

Pat and I left the phone box, having settled with Gale that my return was not to break up their relationship nor our plan for Pat and I to go to Paris before returning to Kerry. Pat had booked our flight and we sat next to each other, with both a small distance and a large distance between us. He had booked us into a small hotel in St Germain des Prés, an enormous double bed. Pat's habit of siesta had not changed. We lay a distance apart in this big bed, and talked with friendship and sadness. We ate dinner that night and talked of things that we always had in common; the flight of the Brent geese at home in Kerry, how the river Lickeen had overflowed its banks, the plays and films that Pat had seen, the fruits and plants that I had left behind in the South Seas.

We slept with that distance and awareness. I awoke to the navy blue light of Paris and cried. We went for breakfast at the Les Deux Magots again where we used to go when we were students. We visited the Musée d'Orsay, and at the Monet there was a large canvas of water lilies filling the room. I said to Pat:

'I will just go and stand on my own on the balcony for a while'.

And so our Paris weekend came to an end and we arrived back in Kerry to low grey sky.

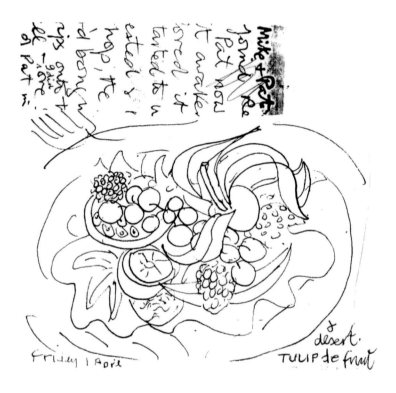

Friday 1 April

desert.
TULIP de fruit

Betty had cooked us dinner. I did not keep up any pretence with her or anyone. It would not have worked with me. In a funny kind of a way there was an acceptance from Betty and people. Goodness knows what fun and gossip people had about our lifestyle.

Pat was travelling to London and Monaghan to visit Gale. He would get Betty to iron his shirts. I felt sad and jealous to hear Pat on the phone booking tickets for himself and Gale for a play or a concert. Off he would go. I would be alone to walk the mountains, my tears and the rain rolling down my face. Pat was so good at finding a play or a concert, and the things that I liked about Pat, like reading books aloud, going to the theatre etc, and here was I without that pleasure and without the South Seas. I said it to him when he got back:

'We are both sharing the same house, so why can't we both share a film or the theatre together'.

Poor Pat was now torn between Gale and me. He could not attend plays and films with us both.

It was Christmas Eve. We were all in the kitchen, Poppy, Holly, Pat and I, having just had dinner. I was lying on the couch, and I said:

'It is great that you will let me get an Aga. When shall we put it in?'

'O Pauline, don't spoil Christmas talking about the Aga', said Pat, whereupon I exploded with temper.

'What, spoil Christmas? I feel so happy about getting an Aga and you say, spoil'.

Poor Poppy and Holly witnessed everything.

'She is like the banana republic', he said over the phone to Gale.

On one of these phone calls I asked could I speak to Gale to suggest that he go and live with her.

'O Pauline, I do love him so, and you are so sweet. The one thing I don't want to do is break up a marriage'.

'Gale, I would find it a relief to be alone. He is sick with a prostrate problem and I will have to look after him with all this resentment'.

'But Pauline, I can't take that on. I just can't'.

Poor Pat was tossed between us both. Pat quickly forgets arguments. He asked Betty the next day to iron his white shirt as he was going to Leitrim for the weekend with Gale. Betty duly ironed his shirt and once more I was struck with a strong feeling of loneliness that I had never felt in my whole life. Again I knew they were going to the theatre.

It was on New Year's Eve that Poppy and Holly sat with us and asked Pat to choose between Gale and me.

'I suppose it would have to be Pauline', he said. 'There is such a bound history to us all'.

To which I burst out again, disgusted with the word 'suppose'.

'I think you should leave this house', I shouted.

'Why me?' Pat asked. 'Why should I leave?'

'Because this is not your workplace and it is my workplace and I would have to set up a studio and you have your workplace in the hospital'.

As the argument went on, I impulsively suggested.

'Perhaps it would be a good idea if Gale came down to live with you in the garden house'.

'Well, if that is all right by you, it is a good idea', Pat blandly said.

It was hard to take Pat's quick recovery from each of our arguments. He didn't see it in any way difficult for me to accept all his 'no's' to the studio, the Aga, the duck pool and the sabbatical. Basically he hated the idea of any change. He would miss filling the solid fuel cooker and riddling and rattling it until it came to its feeble flame. Everything to him was just the way he liked. It appealed to him to have Gale come and live in the garden house because he would have everything around him: Poppy, Holly and me as well as Gale. To Pat that was an ideal solution and perhaps it was. Even though I had suggested it I got furious at his quick acceptance.

Once when Pat went to Leitrim to see Gale I had a visit from Caroline, a friend from Dublin and the South Seas. She brought a bottle of gin, we gossiped and drank till the early hours. Gin was never one of my drinks. When Carol left the next day an almighty wave of depression, sadness and extreme loneliness came over me. I was slim and fit and would walk long distances every day, twice a day. The rain came sideways from the west hitting my face. I did not know what I wanted. I did not want to go back to the South Pacific and I did not want to be here in Ireland. No place came to mind to give me a happy feeling. It certainly would not have been Pat, and I was not content with my suggestion that Gale should come and live with us in the garden house. So when Pat returned I once more said he should leave the house and go about renting somewhere to live.

In amongst all this was arranged a trip to London for the launch of the book *The South Seas and a Box of Paints*. The launch was being held in the Catto Gallery, London, along with an exhibition of my South Sea paintings. We asked a voluptuous Samoan girl who brought along a team of drummers to dance for us in the middle of the launch. John Krupnick had bought a lava lava especially for the occasion and a necklace of South Sea shells. He danced with abandon and pulled the publisher into the circle, in his English socks, to join in the fun. We afterwards celebrated the evening with a dinner in the Chelsea Arts Club where John and Elaine were told not to take photographs.

When I returned from the launch Pat told me there was a cottage available on the other side of the lake, which to my relief he took. When he left I got a sense of freedom and started to paint. This brought with it happiness, yet not complete. Friends visited me. Too many. I discovered that living alone renders one vulnerable to unannounced casual visits. Having a man prohibits people from just crashing into daily lives.

The yellow topaz engagement ring had snapped in the middle. I put this ring into my jewellery box and commissioned a new engagement ring and wedding band made by the jewellery designer Sean Osborne. I am always giving myself things, to show how much I love myself, such as clothes, jewellery, shoes etc. Maybe with these new rings I was marrying myself. The broken engagement ring spoke to me of wear and tear.

I began to feel a little invaded and possessed by some of my friends. They came into my studio uninvited. One day a friend called throwing her two hands in the air.

'O, I thought that was somebody in my space'.

It was a cut-out of the Yellow Man. I really loved that friend, but she had become possessive.

Pat was still in his rented cottage across the lake. He persuaded me to go to a marriage therapist with him. There was something repugnant about this idea. All they want to do is to put you together again. The trip on the train to Dublin for our first appointment was embarrassing. The appointment with the therapist was strange; sitting outside his door, waiting for our turn, hearing emotional muffled voices from his room. He was a middle-aged man wearing tweeds, smoking a pipe. He indicated for us to sit on two leather chairs opposite him. He then leant back, slowly puffed at his pipe, and asked us.

'Who wants to start?'

Pat was always intimidated by authority figures and seemed very shy and reluctant to start, so I poured out all the grievances about not going on the sabbatical year, that he did not try hard enough, the Aga cooker, the duck pool, etc, which made Mr Shanahan smile around his pipe. It was then Pat's turn.

'Well, the Southern Health Board did not want me to take leave … and an Aga is so expensive, and our solid fuel stove is perfectly all right … and why have a duck pool when the garden was beautiful as it is …'

Mr Shanahan nodded throughout.

Our first session being over we left to spend our evening together at the cinema. The next day we had time before our appointment for a coffee upstairs in the atrium of Bewley's. I was beginning to feel more at ease with Pat. We then caught a taxi to St Patrick's. On the journey I asked Pat.

'Have you seen or heard from Gale recently?'

'Well actually I saw her just now, from Bewley's window'.

'What! And you never told me! If I had seen Utanga I would have blurted out. "Look, there is Utanga". How could you have kept it in?'

I was amazed at his secrecy. Here he is trying to win me back, yet behaving in a sneaky undercover way.

This was the first thing I told the marriage consultant when we sat down, whereupon he flung his head back roaring with laughter, looked at me and said:

'But he told you in the taxi, didn't he? You have to understand that people time things differently. Pat and you are so different'.

'Yes, we are. When I am hungry, I eat, and I ask Pat "are you hungry?" and he looks at his watch'.

Again, Mr Shanahan puffed his pipe and laughed.

'You speak out without pre-meditation, Pat thinks first. Pat, I want you to take off your watch and live without looking at it for a week. You are a little too guided by time and routine. Pauline, I want you to count to ten before you criticize, before you make a judgement'.

We left his practice laughing; willy nilly we were patching things up together.

However once again we saw Gale. This time she was going into a telephone booth in Baggot Street.

'Get off the bus, Pat, and go to her'.

It was perverse of me; perhaps I was testing him. He went to get off the bus, then relaxed back again into his seat.

'No, no, she would have left the telephone booth by now'.

As we walked up Heytesbury Lane, I continued to pester Pat to go back to Baggot Street and talk to Gale. He continued to oscillate between that idea and staying with me, until finally he said.

'No, Pauline, I don't want to. It is you I want to get together with'.

In Kerry, Pat often organised lunch in his rented cottage for Poppy and me. I was put in the best chair, facing the view. The conversation was a little awkward, all about nature, birds and flowers. Poppy seemed happy to see us together. Our lives were getting back together again.

19

TUSCANY AND THE YELLOW MAN

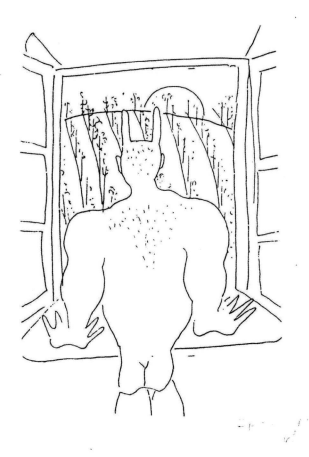

naïve Vile
teeth
Post, pastels

SAT.

Alone as all went to Siena — 9 painted
Thunder coming sky — Dinner at Rach
+ Pino's wonderfull creative house full of toys +
all of found furniture painted to look like works of ai
lino teeses + is intelegent, though city said he also
'acist'. — The Thunder + down pour nearly stoped "
 my — Sunday swim is colder
+ i.e. we go to the church in
evristio for the cristing of
Siucia to the footballer, + his
emtfull wife related to Lucia he turns
ik — balcony, tables laid
close — Ganille so beautifull, Then thunder + rai
sheets of water de hid in food the inside
full of folk — bent on serving all bea
into trays of foods + idk suits, brou
smart + ganzo — ugly man playi
sweet to the childe evisitbe
hander creed Lucia wo is sweet

The ora of milk
on baby mothers
its gets when
the baby is fish
+ the odor of sea
returns.

284

I had gone to the South Seas expecting to find the perfect society. After returning to Ireland I focused on creating the ideal being, which I called The Yellow Man. Looking through my sketchbooks I see that I first conceived of him in 1979 when the family had returned again to Tuscany. I was sitting under our grapevine when I doodled in my handmade sketchbook a small Yellow Man with antennae walking over the Tuscan hills. Two little boys from next door, Stephano and Roberto, saw the Yellow Man and asked me to draw more. 'Omno Jallow'.

Later I realised the little Yellow Man was our neighbour Gino the farmer. Gino who inspired it is small, balding, burnt dark by the sun, hunched and strong. He has little brown eyes that dart from one of us to the other. He giggles, yet seems to accept the inevitability of life in a silent unconscious way, making Gino a magical man.

He would climb the mulberry trees outside Briccano, muttering Italian words that I didn't understand, as he collected baskets of mulberrys. He fooled on with Holly and Poppy, turning them upside down and stuffing hay inside their t-shirts. He could be seen each day alone, opening up the centre of his many olive trees to let the sun in. Gino tended the grapevines, clipping the trendles. Over dinner when the television was on, he would cut the bread towards his chest. His brother Pierro was serious and didn't laugh, his sister-in-law, Bruna, always shook her head at Gino's joking.

'It is Gino that is the vagabond', she would say as they ate the cheese from their knives. I knew that Gino, Pierro and Bruna would not understand what I was saying in the book I started to write, *The Yellow Man*, but there it is, the inspiration for him was born here.

It was as if the Yellow Man had jumped into my head and had to express himself. Without being intellectual about it, I realised that his philosophical way of life was of course my philosophy. The side of me that was mindful of nature, un-cynical – basically wishfully thinking that all human beings could be like the Yellow Man. Not only did I write a book on the Yellow Man, I painted extensively, making Yellow Man tapestries, ceramics at the Rampini Studios, a doll, stained glass, a carpet. I used every medium to show the joy I felt about the Yellow Man.

Back in Kerry I was at one of Regine's parties in 1993 and met a gestalt psychotherapist called Helga. She said she had a tearoom in an old farmhouse in Ballinskelligs. One week later, I decided I would go and have a cup of tea and meet her again as I liked her. A weather-beaten grey farmhouse with cement steps rising out of a sheep-bitten field led to her front door.

'Oh! Come in', she welcomed me with open arms, one holding the door open, the other, the door frame; and there she stood, a handsome German woman with brown wavy hair and glasses, a big lipstick smile. The waves were bashing against the black rocks of Ballinskelligs beach behind me.

'We will have tea later, first come into my workshop'.

It surprised me to be told.

'Sit there, close your eyes and tell me about your parents', as she lit a stick of incense. The familiar smell of hippies filled the room. She put a stethoscope into her ears and dangling from the end was a metre long tube, which she placed on my stomach. This was to listen for gurgles to hear if I was relaxing. I closed my eyes thinking:

This crazy hippy ... but I suppose she won't kill me. I'll go along with her questions.

So I searched myself inwardly for my family.

'Well, my mother meant a huge amount to me, but not having a father around I thought nothing of fathers. No, nothing, and he might not have been my father anyway'.

'Nothing at all?' Helga asked.

'No, nothing'.

'So you have no memories at all of your father? I want you to relax and search within your body to find him'.

I willingly searched intensively, and much to my surprise I found down the right hand side of my body a grey stone-like male body, well established, cold, grey and dead. I felt that he had been there for all of my life. His head came up my neck and misted away, his arm went down my right arm and misted away, his legs went down my right leg and misted away, the centre part of his body, his head and torso were beautifully formed, a handsome grey man.

'Is he alive?'

'No, he is stone dead'.

'Now tell me, what is on the left hand side of your body?' and again I searched inwardly and found bright sunshine; a happy yellow aura filled my left side, reminding me of the Yellow Man that I had painted in Italy.

'I am going to ask you to draw out what you have found in your right hand side'.

She handed me a box of crayons and a pad to sketch out what I had found. When I had finished, she held the drawing up for me to see it from a distance, asking me.

'Has he got any life?'

'No, he is dead'.

'Ok, I will put this picture on its side. Has he got life now?'

Now it appeared like a grey ugly blubbery living manatee with its head lifted up my right arm, there was an eye, in its heavy face, lifting up to sniff the air.

'Keep that image alive, get into your car and go home. I want you to draw or paint as many pictures of this grey man, and if you feel like it, draw out the Yellow side as well', she said.

I knew the yellow side was my Yellow Man that I had doodled many pictures of that time in Tuscany. The Yellow Man, my ideal being, that for some reason I loved so much.

'Come back to me in a week's time'.

I had been surprised not to get my cup of tea and not to get to know Helga herself.

A 10 x 8 sketchbook was what I used to draw out eight grey men. Each one came out with a feeling of truth. I knew I hated one big aspect of men, and that was war. My Grey Man had an army of men shooting, killing and bombing; in other words I blamed the most severe bad things of the world on this Grey Man and men in general. You could imagine how I felt when

Helga explained to me that throughout life I had harboured a deep resentment of my father for having abandoned me.

'You know, Pauline, even at the age of two, you would have realised, in some away, that you had been abandoned by him, lost to alcohol'.

Pat, being a psychiatrist, was most impressed by the difference Helga had made to my judgmental side. I had softened towards Pat as a result of recognising this Grey Man. So within me were two men, the grey and the yellow, the blame and the acceptance.

On my fifth journey to Helga I was expecting this to be my last visit as I felt there was nothing more for her to point out. When the car shuddered to a halt outside Cahirciveen, near a guesthouse that was named 'The Last Furlong', I walked down the manicured path to the front door and asked if I could use their telephone to tell Helga that my car had broken down. Helga's response was:

'You are a very clever woman, you made the car break down, you did not want to come'.

'That is it', I thought, I had never heard so much nonsense. When a mechanic fixed the car, it was too late to go to Helga's, so I went home. I did meet her again, and threw politeness aside, saying:

'That was nonsense about the car breaking down!'

She explained it this way:

'If you were driving to pick up a Lotto win, you would have made it for sure. You would have got a taxi and would have done anything to pick up the lottery win, but psychologically you used the car as an excuse not to come for further analysis'.

Somehow I knew that she had hit a very real thing within me and I actually did not want to sully the water with further analysis about other things/problems in my personality.She had revealed something to me that was incredibly important.

Seamus Cashman of Wolfhound Press fell in love with the Yellow Man story and he decided to publish the book, even though bookshops said they had no shelf to put it on, as it was neither for adults nor for children, but he felt there was something about the philosophy that was unique. It appealed to him so he went with it.

The Yellow Man was published in January 1996 and launched along with a huge Yellow Man exhibition held at the Royal Hibernian Academy, Dublin. After Tony Clare's opening speech, the Café Orchestra played the Yellow Man tango with two dancers swirling around the floor. I had commissioned the Café Orchestra, after Poppy had heard them busking in Grafton Street, to compose this piece.

Theatre director Mike Scott put on in the RHA basement a stage performance adapted from the book. I gave Yellow Man art sessions for children that filled the basement. The sales were amazing. I sold 95 pieces and still had a further 90 works left. Crowds visited the exhibition, despite the cold wet January weather. I felt, having discovered him and brought him into existence, I could die happily fulfilled.

20

MARRIAGE AND GRANDCHILDREN

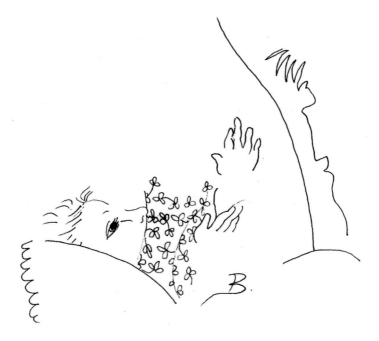

Hollys wedding

A pool of sun shone down on Caragh Lake. It was Poppy and Conor's wedding (1995). Dan O'Connor was rowing the bride and groom from Caragh Lodge, where we had our wedding lunch, over to our side of the lake for the wedding party in our house. Michael Morris and his children had another little rowboat. The children played the accordion, a violin and penny whistle as we bobbed over the lake. All the other guests came in boats, there were 13 boats in all. Unbeknown to us, Dan dragged a line hoping to catch a salmon, and just before arriving he shook the line and brought up a huge glistening silver salmon as a wedding gift. We were amazed and delighted with this catch. He later confessed he had pulled this fresh salmon all the way through the water.

To our surprise, on the edge of the lake stood a beautiful horse and trap. It was Pat Surely Griffin. He had heard about the wedding and wanted to give a surprise and bring the bride and groom the quarter mile up the hill to our house. The party got going instantly. All the neighbours brought musical instruments, many's the set was danced outside. As night fell we moved indoors, the hooley continued. Dan's wife, Mary asked Pat up to dance, her strong arms lifted Pat off the floor and his feet hit our dresser as she whirled him around to a Kerry set.

Poppy and Conor had decided to take their honeymoon in Nepal and visit, at the same time, her college friend Sophie Shaw-Smith and her husband, the Nepalese artist, Romio Shrestha. Their honeymoon coincided with a booking that Pat and I had made to meet John and Elaine Krupnick, also in Nepal. So it ended up with Pat and I going with Poppy and Conor on their honeymoon!

When we arrived at Kathmandu airport the sun was setting behind the vivid Nepalese mountains. The streets were crowded with brightly dressed people, amongst them rambled white sacred cows, one or two of them limping or deformed as they had been hit by the randomly driven cars. We stayed in the beautiful old-fashioned Varjra hotel. Romio and Sophie joined us for breakfast with their little girl, Amber, a tiny little brown-eyed baby. We ate breakfast outside in the garden. I felt rather sick having just taken malaria tablets. It soon passed and we were on our way down the hill towards the Bisnumati River that had dried up and all you could see in the riverbed were enormous pigs rooting in mounds and mounds of rubbish.

Over the bridge and into the city. We had arrived at the Dasain festival where it is believed that blood must be given to the cars that now line the streets, the reason being when the first car arrived in Nepal it killed somebody, therefore everyone believed that cars needed blood. The way they got over that was to kill animals. A poor goat would be stabbed and it was made to circle the cars. With every heartbeat a squirt of the goat's blood covered the cars. It was so upsetting to see these animals weakening as the blood poured out of their bodies, the streets were running with blood.

There had also been a strike resulting in none of the rubbish being taken off the streets. It had such an effect on us that we wanted to get on a plane and rush home. However time passed and this vivid city began to find its way into our hearts.

Romio's people sat us on their high-rise balcony and gave us a Nepalese dinner of dahl bat. Sophie was honour bound to serve us and then sit on the floor with the family. She was not expected to join us for dinner. Being married to Romio she had to behave in the manner of a Nepalese woman. After dinner Romio showed us the precious garments and wall hangings that were handed down from his Royal relatives. He had been brought up in a Catholic school and a Hindu school so he was torn between the two worlds.

Romio and Sophie travelled around with us to the outer Chitwan Jungle, onto a small plane to Pokhara where we all stayed, including the Krupnicks. Across a lake, in a hotel, the staff slept on the kitchen floor and cooked for us in the morning.

John and Elaine Krupnick have been friends of ours since meeting them on Aitutaki, both of them intelligent humorous travelling companions. John could not stop laughing at a notice in the town of Pokhara that read 'energy for sale'. Whatever it was, it was happening behind a very wobbly curtain. We looked at charmed snakes undulating out of baskets, we bought beautiful semi-precious stones from Tibetan women who roamed the streets. The climbs we did around Pokhara took us up steps upon steps, passing tiny villages and hearing many different forms of language, passing mules carrying heavy loads and little babies tucked up in baskets that hung from wooden roof rafters.

We visited the Chitwan jungle, riding elephants, hearing tigers, watching crocodiles dip under the water, and Pat sitting on the back of an elephant being showered from the elephant's trunk. The last adventure we had in Nepal was to climb the Langtang trek and valley. We stayed overnight in the village at the bottom of the mountain, the walls behind each room were separated by cardboard and newspaper. Our journey up the Langtang taxed us to the full, we had to cross rope bridges looking down on rushing rivers in deep gullies beneath us.

A farmer's filthy hands peeled a potato for me, scratching off the peel and kindly handing it to me to eat, because I had given him a piece of Elastoplast for a cut on his foot. We overnighted in teahouses on the way up the mountain. In one Conor, who is incredibly clean and fastidious, had to put up with his chips being cooked over a fire on the floor, the chef turning them with one hand; in the other he held his child with snot dribbling off the baby.

Upwards we went, the air getting thinner and thinner, passing mandala stones and people who lived in this incredible environment. In our last teahouse before the top, during the night I could hear Conor and Poppy endlessly making love. I thought it was a bit much even though they were on their honeymoon. I discovered later, when I descended down the rickety ladder to the loo, that it was a piece of plastic pinned to the window that rattled with the wind.

At the top of the mountain came a claustrophobic feeling that one could not get proper air into one's lungs. It was better not to panic. We settled in the big teahouse to eat and the panic of breathing subsided. The next morning Pat and I called into a tiny white stupa and met two shaven-headed monks, a man and a woman. They laughed a lot and welcomed us to come in, stroking and patting their little snub-nosed curly-tailed Nepalese dog.

Before we descended I bought a bedcover that was hanging on a line for sale by a man who had climbed over the mountainous border of Tibet to sell his wears. The journey down was a relief. The drive home was tense because the roads were in such bad condition. Parts of the road had fallen down into the valley below, leaving a very narrow bit of road for our truck to negotiate. We saw that one of the trucks had in fact tumbled miles down into the valley.

We stopped for lunch, the dishes were being hosed and laid out on the lavatory floor. As we were eating our dhal bat, a brightly-painted bus stopped, so full of people they were hanging out the windows and leaning from the rooftop. Surprisingly a man jumped from the roof and said 'hello Dr Melia'. He was a junior doctor from the Killarney hospital where Pat worked. On the last day we visited Bhaktapur. John, Elaine, Poppy, Conor, Romio, Sophie, Pat and I played with children, John joined in card games with the local men and Elaine played the mouth-organ with a circle of monks. We laughed our way around the streets and finally felt sorry to leave this raw, bright, vital city, monkeys jumping from wall to wall and flags flying from great rounded stupors with eyes painted on each. That was an amazing trip!

It was the middle of the night. Conor ran down from the garden house.

'The labour pains have started'.

Poppy's case was packed for this event. The four parents and Conor stood in the hospital corridor. Poppy was taken into the labour ward. It seemed an eternity before the swing doors opened and out she was wheeled with a little baby lying in her arms, naked, with a little willy – a surprise, none of us knew beforehand. I had no experience of boy babies. I looked into Poppy's relaxed, exhausted face and said:

'You've made a boy'.

You could tell that Conor's cup was flowing over with love for Poppy and his new baby. Conor does not jump and yell about things in life, one has to turn to him to see what is going on. He was incredibly happy. Little did I know that I would soon have a painting mate. When Aran was two he would sit naked at the end of my art table enthusiastically painting away with me.

In 1998 we travelled to Tuscany for Holly's wedding. The Tuscan weather was perfect. I decided to make our car look beautiful and hosed it down for the occasion. Holly was up in my studio putting on her wedding dress. We had chosen it in Brown Thomas on a visit to Cork. Holly was quite fat with pregnancy and each dress that she tried on didn't disguise her baby bump. An audience had developed in the Brown Thomas café. They would yahoo and clap at each dress that Holly came out in. Finally the winner dress that got the loudest clap was arty-looking, almost transparent and white. On her wedding day Holly looked gorgeous in her 'Ghost' wedding dress coming down the rustic steps of Briccano.

Just before we took off Luca came rushing from the village with Holly's bouquet of huge yellow sunflowers. When she took the sunflowers, a large praying mantis jumped onto her bump, the colours were so good. Our good Canadian friends, Ed and Nuala Cowan, as well as young Helena O'Connor, our neighbour from Treanmanagh, came over for the wedding. The wedding was in the hill-village of Radda where Luca was born. Great arches looked out into the village square where people stood on the cobbled stones and sat on the sun-warmed marble seats around the altar. The ceremony was short and jolly, the priest ended by announcing that a cypress tree would be planted in the village in memory of this wedding. Then we all went to a workman's café for the wedding lunch.

I sat beside Marchello, who mixed the oil into the salad in such a way that I copy him to this day. He spent ages lifting the lettuce leaves up and twisting them in the air and circling the leaves round and round, and yes, it tasted delicious. We had the usual course after course, finishing with black coffee and Sambuca.

After this huge lunch we went home for a rest. The evening meal was in a vineyard, tables were set out of doors with lanterns hanging from olive trees and an enormous television set placed outside for those who wanted to watch the football match. Helena sat amongst the yelping men watching the match. Children ran about having a wonderful time; there is no need in Italy to correct children because they are always allowed to be at these functions in the company of adults. A sexy little woman in a black leather mini-skirt belted out Italian love songs to dance to. The band tried their best to play an Irish jig for Helena to perform the brush dance. Everybody yelped with joy and clapped to the Irish rhythm. It seems that wherever the Irish go people love their abandoned way of enjoying themselves. We got home in the early hours of the morning and went to bed to the sound of nightingales singing in the Briccano trees.

Our family stayed on until Holly's baby, Chiara, was born. Again, Luca was running up the hospital stairs, two steps at a time, totally involved in the whole business of a new baby on the way. It was such a sweet relief to see the dark skin, dark-haired Italian-looking baby girl, and Holly lovingly looking down at the baby lying on her breasts.

Not far from where Holly was married she had an exhibition of fifteen paintings, one of which was bought by the business philosopher Charles Handy and his wife the photographer Elizabeth. It transpired that they had also bought one of my paintings from the Odette Gilbert exhibition in London. They had a villa where we were invited to lunch. During a conversation Charles quoted Heraclitus.

'No man ever steps in the same river twice, for it's not the same river and he's not the same man'.

It was this quote that inspired a painting which I later translated into a three-metre high tapestry.

Charles loved to cook and our lunch was a sophisticated treat which was discussed in detail. Holly's painting of 'Tuscan Fruits and Vegetables' seemed to glow down from their wall.

Shortly after our lunch with the Handys, Nerida (a pal I'd met in the South Seas) came to visit us in Tuscany. We were to paint together. We first chose to paint the tiny graveyard in Barbistio. As we sat painting amongst the graves and plastic flowers, in through the small iron gates walked a bent old woman dressed in black. She was dabbing her eyes with a handkerchief. Nerida and I looked at each other, feeling guilty that we might be sitting on her loved one's grave. It turned out that she was crying for her husband who died 15 years earlier. Nerida and I got the giggles, we could hardly contain ourselves, it seemed a long time to cry.

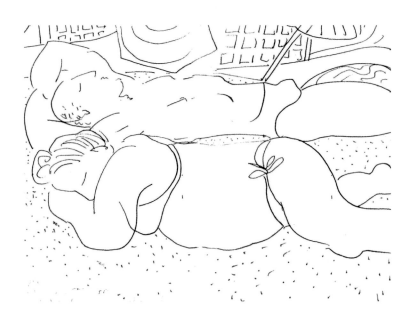

21

Here and There

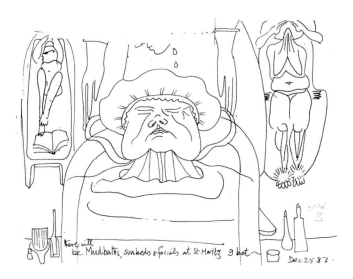

here will be Mudbaths, sunbeds & facials at St Moritz 9 hot

Dec 25·83·

BOOK II

(When ?,
the ...
in PB ...)

Pat suggested that I accompany him to a psychiatric symposium in Munich, it was something I was very interested in.

One of the tours we were taken on was to a historic museum, the Deutsches Medizinhistorisches Museum Ingolstadt. The psychiatrist gave us a lecture on the strange pieces we were looking at, a rough canvas and leather, strapped straightjacket, black handcuffs made of heavy iron and a helmet to protect the patient's head from self-damage. One form of treatment was a revolving bed which could be set in motion and would gather enormous speed which was to calm schizophrenia, the patient was of course strapped to the bed. Such treatments were used until Philippe Pinel said, 'let them free'. He is said today to be the 'father of modern psychiatry' and moral therapy. We were then taken out into a kitchen garden with geometrically shaped areas of therapeutic herbs, each labelled with their name and cure.

Instead of attending all of the lectures with Pat, I took off on my own to the Städtische Galerie and saw art such as Münter's painting of Paul Klee, Franz Marc's 'Blue Horse', Marianne Von Werefkin's school children and Kandinsky's train. These works gave me huge enthusiasm. I wanted to get out my paints there and then. After climbing up to the modern section, my mood changed. The first work of art had a grey curtain with a drawstring, revealing a grey featureless sky. My heart dropped. I took a piece of paper from my Filofax and wrote:

'This is such a depressing work with no meaning'.

I left it tucked behind the curtain. I had to relook at the train by Kandinsky, puffing through the German countryside, to cheer me up again before I left.

On leaving the museum it was the first time I ever saw street artists, painted in gold, standing as still as statues; to my surprise they would jerk into action. I passed the beer houses with glasses of beer the size of small buckets, to meet Pat on the steps of the Bundestag, where Hitler gave many war speeches, for a reception given by the psychiatric symposium. It seems that buildings soak up the history of what happened in them; on entering one picked up a very strong war-like atmosphere, despite the cocktails and chat.

'Wish *I* was going to Honolulu', the airline official said.

At last we landed smoothly at Honolulu on the Hawaiian island of Oahu. There were my two friends, Bob and Gery, who I had met in the Cook Islands, looking as healthy and fit as they did years ago. They go to Oahu each year to write their books. They placed a lei around my neck, frangipani, green twisted banana leaf, divinely perfumed.

I had a wish to get to know the Hawaiian Maori settlers. Of course, I knew that America had taken it over but I was still curious. Bob and Gery's apartment was on the top of a 34 storey skyscraper. When I stood on their small balcony, it gave one a tingle of fear looking down at the big drop.

They had made my bed in the corner of the kitchen.

'I am due for our hula class. Are you ok to join me?' said Gery.

We walked to a shopping centre where a banyan tree grew and dominated the centre space. The hula lesson had started. The average age of the dancers was 60, smiling, brightly dressed, retired American men and women. Gery looked stunningly beautiful in this setting and was able to sway her hips in the Maori way, better than any of them.

The class over and after all the friendly goodbyes, we went on to the Waikiki beach, passing a tramp in the shadow of a palm tree, an ideal place to be a tramp. We look at the statue of Duke, who brought surfing to the world.

My friend Easkey Britton comes here for surf competitions. Apparently there is no wave higher than on the north end of the island. The sea was clear, fresh and moving. I have never experienced such clean air, despite the fact that there was traffic everywhere.

Bob and Gery took me to all their usual haunts, where we heard the song 'Pearly Shells', 'I love you more than all the little pearly shells'. Their hip hop venues were teaming with full-skirted whirling dancers in their flat black and white shoes.

During my stay as we visited the whole island we encountered only a sprinkling of native Hawaiians, mostly selling goods in the market. We flew to another island, Molaki, where there was a leper colony situated at the bottom of a very high cliff. This cliff separated the lepers from the general public. We were taken on mule back down the zig-zag cliff, swaying on the mule's back from left to right, and on each corner their hooves slipped and slithered. It was a terrifying, vertical journey!

'Lepers get very sexy', our guide said. 'There's a woman there in that house that can't get enough. See that man, he is a pack rat. His wife moved out as their house got too full of rubbish'.

To fulfil my ambition to get to know the Hawaiian islands I booked a very expensive ticket on the 'SS Independence' cruise ship. I climbed the gangway. A tall Irish steward asked me:

'What type of people do you want to sit beside at dinner for the week-long tour?'

I specified local or arty people.

'I'll do my best, mam'.

The sun set quickly. *Waoooooo*, the ship's horn blew and we moved away. Slowly we left Waikiki lights in a cluster behind us, onwards over the dark sea.

I went down to the dining deck.

'You're at table number four with the ship's doctor and his wife. You'll love them. They've cycled all over Ireland, been to Alaska and Egypt'.

The steward was right. I liked Walt and Isobel immediately. Over dinner they told me about their trip around Ireland and drew a perfect map remembering every town and village. After dinner the band leader announced:

'We'd like to sing an old Hawaiian love song to all who are celebrating anniversaries or their honeymoon'.

The floor filled with very old, fat limping couples. One fell over.

Past enormous displays of tropical flowers, I went to my posh cabin. There was an orchid and a chocolate on my pillow. Lamps were fixed to the surfaces so there was no flat surface to work on in my little sketchbook. I went up on deck to smell the night air.

In the morning we were in Kauai Harbour and travelled by bus to the Weiema Canyon and Fern Grotto. We were told that film stars have their runaway houses deep in these mountains, such as John Wayne and Sylvester Stallone.

'The animals we have are wild boar and black-tailed deer', said our guide.

The canyon, all brown, deep furrows, high-ridged mountains, is another world. Scratched into the earth were these words:

'Listen to your navel, it knows things'.

'Let's heal mother earth'.

'I fucked DL'.

'Dimples was here'.

Maui was the next island. I chose a tour into a jungle. Our hippy guide gave us tabi shoes. You put your big toe into a glove-like shoe, 'best for slippery, muddy stones and root walks', he said.

We started the steep trail up through the Hana rainforest. Johnny, our guide, picked us samples of fruit and nuts growing along the way. We swam beneath a 30-foot waterfall.

'There are many micro-climates here'.

Maui is considered to be the greatest place in the world for humpback whales.

The next island was Hawaii, we had a frightening yet exciting helicopter tour which involved going high over the live volcano. They gave me the front seat which had a glass floor, as they saw that I was an artist. I sketched the deep red boiling holes of lava. When the lava hit the sea it sent billowing steam clouds into the sky, all of this I sketched into my book. It was so interesting that my fear left me as we swirled in the helicopter, veering on its side as it got nearer to this hell-hole.

Out of all the islands that the cruise ship visited, I chose Maui to be the island I would return to and get to know better. I had asked the guide who had taken us on a jungle tour if there were any artists living on the island that would rent me a room for two weeks. He enthusiastically said:

'Yes. Susan'.

Susan lived right in the middle of the island in a pineapple plantation, not far from a small cowboy village, with tie posts for their horses.

I was introduced to singer and actor Kris Kristofferson on this island by Susan, she was a friend. She told him I was an artist, sketching the islands.

'Why don't you take Pauline to my yurt in the jungle', he said. 'I won't be there but here's the code to get through the gate'.

You could see that his life was written in lines all over his face, and his voice was deep, romantic and gravelly.

It was at the weekend we took off for his yurt, driving through hot volcanic streams, through banyan forests, stopping to visit other friends of Susan who lived in a banyan tree. They had built a platform and on this platform they had a pipe supplying water to a sink, a cooker and all the necessary kitchen equipment. The bath was nearly swallowed up by a branch of the banyan tree. It had twirled around the taps, down the side of the bath under and up again. It would be quite a business to get into that bath.

We could see in the garden down below a beautiful girl, blonde and slim, planting salad. After a cup of fig tea we said goodbye and passed the girl. Up close we could see her skin had been baked into rivulets by the constant sun.

Kris Kristofferson's yurt was in the centre of a circle of smaller yurts. It had a pleasant creamy light within. There were shelves of coffee-table books, his record player and good expensive equipment. The other yurts were presumably for his visiting friends. There were futon couches everywhere, presumably to chill out on. He had built a small generator on the rocks below, and below that again we could see the swirling green sea.

On our way back Susan stopped the truck as she wanted me to meet a cowboy who was the subject of her latest portrait. He was a work-worn, weather-beaten, strong cowboy who was feeding his horse under a lean-to hut. Later in my stay we delivered that picture with others for an exhibition Susan was having.

The next evening she took me to an art session. We walked through clouds of tiny black fruit flies on our way to a large white colonial mansion. In the centre of the large room there were bejewelled long-haired women and tattooed bearded men standing at easels, confidently putting colour and charcoal on their large canvasses. They were painting an old Hawaiian woman sitting on a tapa-covered couch.

On other days we would go to the horse whisperer. I rode a heavy white horse down a steep hill. The two weeks went by quickly and Susan and I have corresponded ever since.

Then back to Waikiki for my last few days with Bob and Gery. We watched the surfers, looked at the pink flamingos in the zoo, ate spring rolls and visited the university where Bob and Gery used to teach.

When I got back home to Kerry I was determined to collaborate with Eddie Tadier, the Glenbeigh ceramic artist. He made me several biscuitwear urns, platters and wall plaques which I decorated with white glaze. Eddie fired them for me. It was as exciting as working with the Rampini Ceramic Studio in Italy, even though white was the only colour I had to work with.

One day I was on the bus in Dublin when I got talking to a young man, Rafal Slowinski. He was reading a catalogue on gardens and plants. He told me that he was looking for a job.

'I have a back field that needs cleaning up but it's down in Kerry', I said.

'I will come', he answered and sure enough it wasn't long before we had Rafal digging and sweating on our back field removing the dense tussocks and flattening the area into a field where we could grow apple trees.

A young, dark-haired Irish woman called Geraldine in a white blouse and blue jeans said she had always wanted to have a piece of my work hanging in her house in Auckland. Her enthusiasm that I would love New Zealand became a reality. The whole family packed their bags and off we went and landed in Auckland, with that feeling we were walking around in the middle of the night, yet it was broad daylight.

The first thing we did when we arrived was to hire a great big black eight-seater car. Pat not only had to deal with the new gadgets in this car but also the speed of the traffic. We found our friend Geraldine's suburban house and were given a huge breakfast. She wrote out for us how to get to Rod and Susan's place in the Coromandel where we were to rent two wooden houses on the edge of the sea. Huge avocado trees groaning with fruit, rampant herbs, lettuce, anything you desired grew in the garden around our little houses. We would do our shopping in Whitianga, taking our car over the inlet on a ferry. We all got to love a little restaurant that served sushi and after our lunch back on the ferry with the shopping.

We took a trip to Rotorua; the wide road was dotted with squashed possums. They are considered a pest in New Zealand and are a protected species in Australia. One night we heard loud noises in our hut. I switched on the light and there looking down from the ceiling were two huge eyes.

'You were lucky it didn't jump on you. They are quite dangerous. They always jump onto the highest thing in the room; it could have been you. Their claws are very sharp. I'm going to kill that possum', said Rod.

The smell of sulphur met us steaming out of grids in the streets. We visited the geysers; all bubbling, hot and steaming; champagne pools of yellow sulphur where DNA begin; pathways through coloured crystals. The tourists did not take away from the magic, it was like touching the world's beginning. Sue and Rod caught a fish for our return. We had brought a kauri tree sapling and planted it on their land, leaving our mark.

I always felt that New Zealand was a level-headed country politically. There were lots of things over the years that appealed to me about New Zealand, for instance, their involvement with Greenpeace and the Rainbow Warrior boat trying to stop nuclear testing in Tahiti. I admired the way they had a transvestite in a high-up position in government, and each New Zealander I met, while living in the South Seas, seemed to have a relaxed, common-sense attitude. They somehow knew how to live. I loved the film *The Piano* written and directed by Jane Campion. She also directed *Angel at My Table* written by Janet Frame. If I had my life to live again I would go and live in New Zealand. It has that cut-off feeling from the rest of the world and I would like that.

After swimming between the ocean-sculpted chalk rocks, and the volcanic peaks that jutted out of the sea and ancient trees that we had never seen before, we left the Coromandel for Auckland to visit Geraldine again.

Pat landed in heaven when Geraldine arranged with her friend that we go out on the Prada racing yacht. He took the wheel and we sailed out of Auckland Harbour and back again. If a human could purr we would have heard Pat purring all the journey. He had become a captain of one of the most beautiful yachts you could imagine, thanks to Geraldine.

On our journey back to Europe we took a detour to visit our friends in the Cook Islands. Peka was now married with several children, Holly and he seemed so happy to meet again. Utanga was by now married in Boston. We were welcomed by all the dancers in the Rapae Hotel and Pauline, Peka's mother, gave a banquet of a dinner for us where they danced and played the ukulele way into the night. It was sad to say yet another goodbye to them.

'Ye'll find Mauritius great altogether, 'tis all waterfalls and rainforests', said the man in the airport queue. It seems even the most broad-tongued mountainy men and women of Kerry travel far and wide these days.

'Yerra, she's off in India for herself', is quite an ordinary phrase to hear. We arrived to stifling hot humidity; *I'm Dreaming of a White Christmas* blaring in the arrivals hall.

The taxi man at the airport was called Noorani, a small, smiling man eager to please us; coloured medallions and ribbons dangled from his front mirror. We asked did he know of a suitable apartment and he recommended one across the island on the sheltered side called Clios. As we travelled we saw exotic palms, coffee-brown earth, air smells of growth, cement-box houses set among tropical blossoms with the craggy volcanic mountains, a banyan tree on the roundabout, designer shops and temples.

Noorani told us:

'We have many religions on this island. We do not fight, we never war, we have respect. If we had only two religions maybe we'd fight. Life is a bit difficult, we have to earn a living. Me? I'm a taxi man. I must work with many people. I am Muslim and I am very good with my neighbour'.

'Do you mix in school?' I asked.

'Oh yes. All religions go to school together and we all practice our different religions together. My mate is Hindu and my other friends at school were Catholic and Muslim'.

We saw wood and corrugated-iron houses blown down in the cyclone, hundreds of incomplete cement block houses, sweet green bananas and pineapples for sale. Plenty of bright red flame trees.

We settled on the apartment in Clios, it was inexpensive and beautiful. At the back of the apartment I saw many birds' nests on the ground, looking up I saw many more hanging from the branches. I learnt that it was a weaver bird nest. Male and female both make the nest by twisting round and round. A local man told us the female weaver bird starts the nest and the male finishes it. It is considered one of the most beautiful nests in the world.

We take off for a walk on the long white sanded beach in front of the apartment, paddling in the fresh turquoise sea. Two horses were being trained, all brown and muscular, heads thrown up, thick-necked with straight noses. They rolled in the sand and when they got up white sand had stuck to their sweaty brown bodies. Further along the beach a bony little man approached us:

'My name is Dr Beach. You wanna massage? I've been watching you, you need to kill stress. Dr Beach can de-stress you. I'm off now, but I'll be back. I'm not going to let the devil get me because I'm tired. The devil takes people when they're tired'.

He laughed and off he went, old and healthy.

The Mauritian people love being in the water, the babies and the grannies. They stand for hours in the water, talking and laughing.

The next morning we were delivered bread, fresh from the oven. The days went by so pleasantly while Pat read aloud Richard Dawkin in the shade. In all the hot tropical countries that I have visited, there is a very melancholy feel in the afternoons and this was no exception.

To our surprise every night the apartments were patrolled by a man with a dog and a gun. We wondered why the apartments were fenced in so thoroughly. We also observed that all the posh hotels had guards at the gate.

Noorani took us to the village market to fill our basket with fresh salad and fruits. I also wanted to find a Hindu shop.

'Miss Pauline she walk fast', Noorani said to Pat.

In the Hindu shop I selected about twelve colourful reproductions. I had an idea for a painting. This painting now hangs in the *Seven Ages Collection* in Killorglin.

Noorani treated us to coconut water on the street. As we were nearing home he waved at a young girl who shyly hid behind a lemon tree.

'That is my girlfriend'.

There seemed to be a game of hide and seek between men and women in this country. Another mysterious thing I noticed about Noorani was his dark beady brown eyes which seemed to give me messages. I wasn't sure what this was about. Was it flirting I wondered? Could it be a language of eyes, something to do with the wearing of a yashmak?

On one of our tours we were told how the dodo had become extinct. It was because they tasted 'delicious'. Typical of human beings, having eaten all the dodos to extinction in the past now they paint pretty little pictures of them to sell to the tourists. Noorani drove us into the centre of the island with its deep valleys and high white rushing waterfalls, the tree branches full of grey brown frolicking monkeys and out into a park where there was a religious ceremony going on around brightly painted icons.

On our last night the owners of our apartment gave a seva party and barbecue for us tourists in a large back shed where we sat on benches at long wooden tables. The 'de da da da da' of the drums beat into one's body. All the cultures mixed and ate the good seafood, smoky from the grill. *Da da da dum dum dum da da dum*, it's a party. A young girl appeared dancing the seva, her hips circled wiggling her feet which did not leave the ground, a tradition stemming from the days of the slaves, a way of dancing on sand.

We had our last swim saying goodbye to the sea, ate jam and bread, and packed. As the 747 took off, we looked down on the towering peak of Mount Pieter. Leaving Mauritius covered in bundles of white clouds, we were now over the deep blue sea, then miles and miles of Saharan desert to cross, before Paris, Dublin and Kerry.

I often treat the whole family to a holiday when I sell a bundle of paintings. This time we were off to Tahiti. On arrival we took the ferry boat to Moorea where we stayed once more in the little coconut houses on the beach that belonged to Nannie and Benjamin. Both looked older in the intervening years, their daughter had taken over the business to a great degree. The shape of the beach had been slightly altered by the building of a hotel. All the children spent practically every hour of the holiday in the turquoise water with the yellow and orange wild hibiscus bobbing around them while they dived and swam, occasionally getting a nip from a naughty little fish that did not seem to like any of us passing its path. We used the outrigger to go and look down into the depths of the lagoon wondering if we would see sharks again.

Luca took great pleasure in hiring a speedboat that created enormous back waves as he rushed across the bay. At night we often went to the glamorous new hotel for the after-dinner floorshow. The Tahitians dancers have quicker movements than the Cook Islanders. Their bodies also are trimmer, the men tattooed and superbly handsome. Each night as we left the hotel to walk home along the beach the dancers would throw their dancing wreaths of flowers around our necks. We would kick the seawater to look at the little sparkles of phosphorescence under the upside-down moon and the Southern Cross.

Holly's neighbours in Tuscany, Dolly and Brett, run a business taking twelve or so people on an old beautiful yacht around the Turkish islands. After a wonderful year of paintings in Treanmanagh, we decided to book one of Dolly and Brett's tours in Turkey. It was quite expensive but it was an experience that pleased each one of us. The crew consisted of three that managed the sails, the engine, anchor etc, the Chef, Dolly and Brett.

On the boat with us were Elaine and John Krupnick and four New Zealanders, friends of Dolly. I can't say it in Turkish but the crack was mighty. Brett took us into the remote hills where he arranged with a farming couple a lunch out under their fruit trees. He took us to graves that were carved into the mountainside, over hills littered with ceramic shards left there from the days when they cooked their food in an open fire and had to break the pottery vessel to open it. The captain took us to a nightclub. We all got addicted to a song that was popular at the time, *We No Speak Americano*. We smoked Turkish bubble pipes and I bought a dressing gown that was made of old antique Turkish material. We would go to bed at night listening to the chanting of the prayers from the nearest mosque. Another time we went with Brett to Greece, travelling around the islands in a similar old yacht where Brett took us to untypical tourist places, which he has a special gift for.

Back at home, Ann Kerins posted me a copy of *The Cleaner*, a brilliant film her brother Noel had made. I was so impressed I wanted to back his next film. It was a totally different subject to *The Cleaner*, he called the film *The Enchanted Island* and it took place in Bantry. It was about a mermaid and a gardener that fell in love. Each night the gardener would stay back on the island and wait for his mermaid to come to him. This film got an award at the Monte Carlo film festival.

'Who do you want to bring?' Noel asked me.

'Ann, your sister'.

We arrived at the Monte Carlo hotel, wheeling our luggage between the rows of Lamborghini sport cars, our rooms looking down on a myriad of huge expensive yachts. The film was shown and Noel and I were asked to give a speech. Every nationality seemed to attend, all swearing they would go to Ireland having seen Noel's film with the beautiful scenery of Bantry. At all of these parties a tall glamorous blonde attended bringing her giant white poodle on a lead, the dog's collar was studded in rhinestones and its large toenails were painted red.

'It's Donovan and Linda', I said to Ann, whereupon they turned around to the sound of their names.

They joined us to eat quales' eggs, sitting beside statues carved in ice. The music started, Linda asked me up to dance. She wore a long blue diaphanous dress, her long brown hair hung down her back, a very beautiful woman.

'That visit to your house with Romio, Pauline, was a life-changing experience'

And she went on to tell me all about the time she knew the Rolling Stones and what a wonderful composer Brian Jones was.

'Brian did not get enough praise for his compositions', she went on to tell me as the moonlight twinkled on the Mediterranean Sea beneath the balcony.

Our kitchen has a long French oak table. Around it are the six Chieftain chairs Edward Fitzgerald left me in his will, almost fifty years ago. The conversations around that table are so vital we almost levitate with interest.

Helena always comes up with interesting questions.

'Does the way we think change our genetics?'

'Why are fingerprints unique? We did not get them from our mothers or fathers!'

I might say, for example, isn't Mary dreadful, not tidying up her possessions, to which Helena would answer:

'That's not about Mary, Pauline, that's about you'.

Helena trips us up many times with those three words, 'That's About You'.

Intelligent, cool-headed Nina Finn-Kelcey would often quietly collect her camera, without us knowing, taking original shots of us, the house, the animals and the surrounding scenery.

When Poppy hooks in on religion, she is like a dog with a bone. She can't understand how people can be so blind as to think there is a God controlling everything. For instance Betty might ask for sunshine and Pat Piggott might ask for rain. Who does God answer?

Martin Bell, a Jehovoh Witness, shakes with energy around these ideas of God. He and all around the table have flourishing discussions.

Like Pat and I, all the bachelors along Callinska were getting old. Betty and Johanna arranged for Con Riordan to have an emergency button which they placed around his neck.

'Now Con, you press that button if you fall or think you are getting an attack'.

'I will, I will'.

It wasn't long when Con's emergency button rang out to Betty and Johanna. They raced to his house to help.

'What is it? What is it?'

'I have run out of spuds', he said.

One day I got a phone call from an uncle I had never met. He had read James White's book on my life and objected to my saying that Corbett Bewick may not have been my father. He knew that story and shouted down the phone:

'That mother of yours ran away like a gypsy. Massey Taylor was not your father. He fancied the dress your mother wore, not her', implying he was gay. 'You are a Bewick alright'.

It was Cork city's year of culture in 2005. A search of Cork led to an exhibition held on Lavitt Quay in the premises of Owen O'Callaghan. Pat Keegan from Solo Arte did the research for me. One of my collectors, Dermot Desmond, a Cork man, flew on his private plane to Cork Airport to open this exhibition. He gave a deep informed speech, I was so proud of him. Not only did he buy 'Cork Woman' to go with a work that he had already purchased, he bought a tapestry woven by Regine Bartsch called 'Woman and Swans'. He said when I was next in Dublin, I was welcome to visit his house in Merrion Square and his butler would show me around to see his collection. When I did visit, the butler handed me white cotton gloves to look through one of his many limited edition books. His garden was lush with flowers and shrubs, birds shaking out their feathers in a fountain. He had the only real garden, all the others had been turned into cement spaces for cars.

22

SEVEN AGES

all the five women of Welland
visited in
Vain for
us
your
Seed
till
be
long
long
& living
into
age

My life's work, from the little pencil drawings done aged two and a half, up to seventy amounted to 900 plus works including tapestries, paintings and sculptures. I needed to clear the past, but wanted to keep the collections together, which gave me the idea to offer them to the Irish State. I was delighted with the choice of venues in Waterford and Kerry (thanks to the amazing work of Pat Keegan, Madeleine Crowley, Peig and Gary Ledwith). The pieces were divided equally into three permanent collections, with great help from Kate Landers. The Kerry Collection hangs in Library Place, Killorglin and the Waterford Collection is at Waterford Institute of Technology. The third collection, entitled the Travelling Collection, I gifted to the family, and this is available to travel the world.

The announcement of the donation was made by Minister of Arts John O'Donoghue at the Abbey Theatre during the launch of the *Seven Ages* 70th birthday book in October 2005. *The Late Late Show* did a special piece, hanging the tapestries and bringing several of the works into the studio to show on camera.

The celebrations that followed in November 2006 included red carpets rolled up steps to the offices of Professor Kieran Byrne, head of Waterford Institute of Technology. A black shiny car arrived and out she stepped, the articulate, intelligent President Mary McAleese. After introduction and canapes, wine and water, we continued on yards of red carpet to the Walton Building where the 300 pieces had been hung by Martin Bell. When I showed her the Yellow Man section I explained that he was my ideal being and that I was looking for the perfect society when I visited the South Seas.

'And did you find it?'

'No!'

We continued laughing our way around.

After the tour, she sat amongst a row of dignitaries wearing cloaks and mortarboards. Dr Abdul Bulbulia introduced President Mary McAleese who said:

'This collection is one of the loveliest acts of generosity ever given to our nation'.

She showed her deep comprehension of the collection in her speech. The audience sat riveted as she explained what these works were about. When the ceremony was over Mary McAleese and her aide-de-com walked ahead to their car. Holly's husband Luca rushed up behind me.

'Paula, Paula. *Una photographie con la Presidente!*'

'What does he want?' the President asked her aide-de-com.

'It's all right', I said.

'He wants a photograph', said the aide-de-com.

'Sure, come here', she embraced the whole of our family for this photograph. Not only did Luca get what he wanted, so did the many photographers of the press. It transpired that Luca won a bet to get five free dinners from his friends back in Tuscany. Those friends did not believe that he was going to meet the President of

Ireland so he needed to bring back proof in order to get his five dinners.

Every time I visit the Institute there are clusters of students studying and looking at the collection, which is gratifying indeed. As well as Cathal Ó Searcaigh's introduction to the *Seven Ages* catalogue, I had asked Seamus Heaney to write a small piece as I knew he liked my work. I got one of the nicest refusals one could ever get: 'I often say yes, in my upstairs study, to that lily-looped Bewick-girl reading her Heaney pillow-poems with your dedication from 1982. It silkens the whole mood of the place ...' Clare Boylan once asked Seamus to write a small piece for *Image* magazine as she was then the editor. His answer was 'no, no, no, no, no, no, no'.

'Why so many no's?' she asked him.

'I hate to say no, so I must practice', he answered.

Library Place, Killorglin was shimmering with heat the day the Kerry Collection was launched in May 2007. The square in front of the building was filled with people, the hot sun shining on everyone's back as John O'Donoghue, Minister of Arts, gave his speech followed by other dignitaries. After the speeches classical music was played, people viewed the show as they ate and drank. To my surprise out of the crowd came the uncle that I had never met. I was told by one of my friends that he was going about proposing to several women. His daughter excused his enthusiastic behaviour.

The limestone statue of Niamh kneels under the tree in front of Library Place. During Puck Fair one year some young lads splodged her with white paint.

'I gave her a rub and now she is totally in her birthday suit again', the street cleaner told me.

The next excitement was when Pat Keegan told me that Kieran Byrne was enthusiastic that I should do a visual translation of Brian Merriman's baudy Gaelic poem, *The Midnight Court*. I fulfilled this commission with a huge burst of enthusiasm. I found Merriman's poem very vivid. What a good idea it was of Kieran Byrne. I ordered 40 x 80 heavy Saunders paper from Kennedy's art shop. Before I really started Pat and I went to research the area in which the poem was set, the village of Feakle, County Clare where Merriman lived for many years. We first found where Merriman had been buried. A group of four or five people stood around the grave and we became involved in a lively talk about Merriman. They told me that the village of Feakle was divided in opinion about Merriman and his bawdy poem.

The man in the post office directed me down to the exact place where the poem starts on the edge of Lough Graney and there it was, exactly like the poem, swans floating just as he had described and across the lake a forest where the fox and deer run.

My sketchbook was filled with very useful sketches that I took home to Kerry. I used sepia-coloured inks, drawing out first the lake, then the hag that ran towards him as he lay sleeping under an oak tree, then to the courtroom where the Queen was conducting a court case against the men of Ireland. I painted next the wailing girl whom no one would marry or impregnate, next the illegitimate boy. Back to the courtroom for the trial of the men of Ireland for not marrying and procreating with the women of Ireland, and the last picture was the moment Merriman woke up from his dream, running naked away from the women of Ireland who were just about to flog him.

When the paintings were finished and were set up in the glasshouse, I invited Professor Byrne, Pat Keegan and Claire Keegan of Solo Arte to view them. Kieran was ecstatic.

'They are better than I had ever dreamt'.

But when they got home I got a phone call from Kieran Byrne requesting that I do one more painting and that was of men and women frolicking on the bog. I really let loose with that one. They were framed in heavy oak with gold Gaelic quotes carved around them.

We had many celebrations for these paintings from Feakle village to the Shelbourne Hotel and to Paris where Pat, Poppy and I booked into a typical tatty Paris hotel. Alan Hayes came too and stayed nearby. We met up and went to the Center Culturel Irlandes in the Latin Quarter where the exhibition was hanging. I worried I could not do my speech in French but I was told that the sophisticated audience understood English. After the event, the Irish Ambassador to France, Anne Anderson, entertained us to a wonderful dinner in the Book Restaurant.

The next night we were free to go to the Moulin Rouge, suggested by Alan. What a laugh! We sat right at the edge of the stage and could see backstage as the dancing girls rushed by. Each table had a bottle of champagne on it. Several times feathers from the half-naked dancing girls swished across our faces, nearly sweeping the bottle of champagne off the table. Alan, Poppy and I sat gobsmacked at the whole show. Pat had decided to go to bed early in our funny little hotel. We ended the evening eating French fries in a Persian street café.

Since 1950 Barry Laverty had been one of my best friends. When we were young she and I shared our feelings about crushes etc. However there was one area that Barry kept to herself and didn't talk about, and that was her mother. The emotions between Barry and her mother, Maura Laverty, had strong undercurrents. Maura being so famous was constantly in the limelight and Barry's sister Maeve got a lot of attention because of her extreme beauty. It didn't help Barry to overhear comments like 'Maeve is the pretty one', the implication being 'Barry has brains' and in those days brains in women were not admired. Her brother, the youngest of the three, was muddled by his upbringing because the father was always talked about in a detrimental manner in front of him. As for religion they all pretended that they went to mass. There never seemed to be clarity or security in Jimmy's life. I once asked him:

'Why are you looking out of the window like that, Jimmy, for so long?'

To which he answered: 'I am waiting for a tree to fall'.

Barry kept her thinking to herself about the whole mother situation. It prevented her from painting and completely becoming herself. However after Maura died [1966], Barry burst into painting works of sheer genius and technical perfection. She also burst into writing and illustrating the wittiest of books, one being *Cooking for Cats* [Methuen, 1985]. In Barry's life she had to cope with the drug-related death of her brother Jimmy and the suicide of Maeve due to depression and the alcoholism of her mother who was found dead in her bed days after her death. It was a lot to bury in her mind. A lot not to talk about.

Barry tended to protect and pamper men. Philip often sulked like a child if the cake she had made for him was not big or creamy enough. I told her off one day when she pampered a yacht's man by carrying his two heavy buckets along the quayside.

'Maybe you are taking away his masculinity!' I said.

Pat always enjoyed Philip's mind.

'I am going to live forever'.

He was constantly inventing ways to be eternally frozen or putting his body into a space machine and coming back when they had invented a way for us humans to live forever. He seemed happiest when painting and called his painting style 'Sophisticated Primitive' – a good title for his little matchstick people walking through well-researched Florentine public buildings.

Philip died before Barry and she went into hiding. None of us knew what country she was in. She had properties in Villefranche, London and Dublin and no amount of phone calls got her.

The house in Dublin that she had converted for wheelchair access for Philip was a superb streamline small house just off Stephen's Green. One day a brain tumour was found in Barry (2006). She was diagnosed but chose to not really take her sickness on board. It was interesting to see how she gobbled chocolate and still painted in a very wobbly manner. She had picked up Philip's philosophy to not face death. It just was not going to happen to her. I got a phone call in Kerry in 2006 from her cousin, Conor Kavanagh, who advised I come immediately as she was dying. I literally heard her last breath as I bent over to whisper hello. Conor and his wife Eileen cared for Barry so well to the end. They held a celebration of her life in her house on Prouds' Lane. I had flu so couldn't travel, but Pat and Alan attended and said it was a great tribute to her.

Clare Boylan was commissioned to write an article on me for *Cosmopolitan* magazine in 1979. Clare knew the Irish editor Deirdre McSharry (an old friend from the Pike Theatre days). We met in a small restaurant and from then on restaurants featured in our friendship a lot, as one of her jobs was food critic. 'My companion had cheese soufflé'. We hit it off instantly and talked about anything and everything other than the interview she was commissioned for. Our long lunch over, we walked along South Anne Street in the pouring rain, the roof of her umbrella hitting the top of my head as we went along. She was so short and didn't realise. I had to keep reminding Clare to keep her umbrella higher. All the way to her bank we stopped to look at clothes. She had a habit of trying on clothes that were three or four sizes bigger than her, she seemed to have no concept of size. We finally parted, making a future date to meet after the photographer, Colm Henry, took his photographs at the Dawson Gallery.

Clare and I met up many times which included meeting her friends June Levine, Mary Kenny, Margaret Drabble, Michael Holroyd, Maeve Binchy, Gordon Snell, Fay Weldon, Ivor Browne, Molly Keane, Polly Devlin, Eavan Boland, Julia O'Faolain and many more.

One day I met Molly Keane on the train. Having already met her through Clare Boylan we felt comfortable sitting next to each other. The one thing I can remember about that train trip was her pointy nose and pleasantly wrinkled face looking intently into mine, saying:

'My dear, I went into the nursery and there I saw Nanny locked in the arms of another Nanny'.

Philippa Puller, Clare and I visited Margaret Drabble and Michael Holroyd in London. Margaret gave us a vegetarian dinner in her Hampstead house where there was an atmosphere of indoor plants and healthy garlic-impregnated food. We didn't go into Michael's house but it was right next door. Margaret and Michael were in love but were of an age where living together did not suit either. I have witnessed this in people a lot. It's a partnership that should be recognised where people don't have to live together. We would go on hikes over the Sussex Downs with Michael leading the way like a shepherd as we trudged after him. Clare and he talked together like the hammers of hell.

Maeve Binchy sat on a high stool in her tiny living room in Dalkey. She was giving a party for all her creative female friends. She emanated a feeling of warmth for us all.

'Go and see your drawing. Pauline. It's in the loo'.

I had illustrated one of her short stories and given her the original drawing. The party was influenced by Maeve's generous attitude.

Fay Weldon stood on the marble floor of the National Gallery talking at the top of her deep voice about her haircut. You could see at a glance that she would be a good writer. It was good to meet her as I had illustrated one of her stories called 'Out of the Light'.

Clare took me to one of the most interesting parties ever. It was given by June Levine and Ivor Browne. Though I had met them before this party revealed their characters. The guests were writers and artists. We had been asked to contribute to a fund that was being raised for a poor colleague. June had cooked a large curry-based buffet and Ivor played jazz on his guitar and Irish jigs on the penny whistle with his son. Paul Durcan stood up and read one of his poems and Clare read an excerpt from one of her books and so it went around the room with Ireland's literati reading their works. June was well suited as a researcher for Gay Byrne's *Late Late Show* and you could see during this party how well she organised everybody.

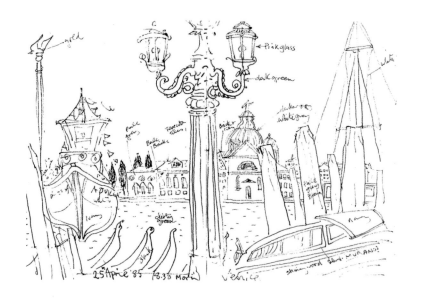

Clare and I took off for Venice in 1985. She had an ambition to include Venice in one of her books. She and I laughed our way around the streets, me looking at shoe shops, Clare looking at menus. We went to the theatre together for Handel's Orlando Opera sung by Marilyn Horne and we drank Bellinis. All this research was being jotted down in her little handmade notebook.

We were sharing a turquoise room in the old Seguso Hotel. I painted Clare sitting beneath a Venetian glass chandelier writing in her notebook. She wrote an article on this trip, full of wit and life of our adventure together and she wrote this poem in my sketchbook.

> My friend Pauline paints private parts
> To stimulate the visual arts;
> Hens and Cocks and bare vaginas
> (RTÉ said they are not suited to minors)
> But Majors love 'em, and sultans and (Boomtown Rats) –
> And she also paints fairly respectable cats!
> *To Pauline with Love – From Clare 1987*

Clare Boylan died of cancer on 27 May 2006. On one of my visits to her in the hospice I opened the door of her room to see her sitting at the windowsill, defiantly smoking a cigarette.

'They don't want me to smoke but why the hell not since I am dying'.

In my hands I held two gifts. One was a packet of Garibaldi biscuits and the other, two t-shirts that I had dyed a dark pink, her request I had fulfilled. It took me ages to achieve the exact colour of raspberries and cream and to find the Garibaldi biscuits. I wondered why Clare had set me these tasks. This was explained to me by Mary Clancy-Hatch – it was because Clare knew there was nothing I could do about her dying, but I could do that.

23

THE INTERNATIONAL WOMEN'S FORUM

Gemma Hussey, Minister of Education, invited me to be a member of the IWF. We met in Jury's Hotel for the first meeting where I mingled nervously with a dauntingly-intelligent group of high-powered women. But far from these women being daunting, they have a basic grassroots intelligence, whether they are the head of a bank, a hospital or a theatre. Whatever their profession each had this understanding quality that I hadn't experience en-mass before. The IWF introduced me to Karen Irwin, a strong clear-minded woman.

The Christmas dinners were always special. This particular one was held in the Unicorn Restaurant. There were about thirty of us sitting at round tables. I was next to Maureen Gaffney:

'Wouldn't it be interesting', I said to her, 'if we all put, anonymously, on a piece of paper how we got to where we are in our professions?'

Maureen immediately took up the idea and said:

'Yes, we'll call it Pauline's hat'.

So into this hat we all dropped our unsigned stories. Mine mentioned the encouragement of Harry. The CEO of a large bank told me what she had written on her piece of paper. She said she felt very inhibited for years in the bank, she had automatically felt the men folk must be far better than her at everything. Then one day she suddenly discovered that she was able to solve difficult issues much quicker and clearer than the men around her. She dared to speak out and it wasn't long before she became the Chief Executive Officer of that bank.

The desire to go to China was almost as strong as it was to go to the South Seas. The opportunity came when the IWF sent out a circular of their many world tours, the subject being a conference on 'World Without Borders'. I asked Poppy to be my guest, I knew she would love it and would be good at researching the tours and lectures etc. Taoism, Chinese art, prawns and bamboo all made me want to go to China. The title 'World Without Borders' has huge appeal to me as I believe the world will benefit from being without borders.

Hong Kong airport was full of masked people frightened of swine flu. At midnight in the Marriott Hotel Poppy announced she felt sick. We both imagined that we would create havoc as the hotel might think she had swine flu and would have to be quarantined. We finally decided to ring the receptionist and they sent up the hotel doctor, Dr Kung. Dr Kung laughed at our worries:

'You have got acute gastro-enteritis', he told us. His herbal treatment worked instantly.

The following morning we went on a pre-conference tour with six IWF members to see Guilin and the countryside of China. It seemed Guilin town was built of hardboard and cardboard, the only solid building was our hotel with a bejewelled lift. Rain had swelled the Lee River onto the street. Men in coolie hats with plastic bags over their shoulders were sweeping the pools of water towards the swollen river with hand-made brooms.

In the morning the tour bus took us six miles through rice fields, coming to the tallest conical-shaped mountains pointing like fingers into the sky, mist swirling through the large bamboo trees growing to the top. A boat was waiting for us, there were two decks. We took our table in the centre of the deck. A long glass display of traditional Chinese foods, steaming rice, sweet osmanthus and snake wine in a large glass bottle, with a curled up yellow snake immersed in it. I sketched as we went along the swollen river; one page after another was filled with wet indigo watercolour. I frequently changed my dirty paint water, chucking it over into the Lee River. On one of these occasions I threw it onto a young Chinese boy who had come up on a raft beside our boat to sell us jade pieces. He laughed forgivingly at my surprise.

Mighty bamboo trees bent their heads like swans; waterfalls gushed creamy white froth, the occasional round coloured temple set amongst the bamboo and the wet jungle. There were fishermen on large flat rafts, each had their own cormorants with a thin rope tied around their necks. The cormorants would dive into the Lee River catching fish, the rope around their neck was tight enough to stop the cormorant gulping down their catch. The fish were taken from the bird and dropped into a bamboo basket. Apparently at the end of the day the cormorant wins a feast of fish for its work.

We passed a mountain with horses carved by nature onto its cliff face. The boat stopped for us to inspect a row of stalls selling dried black ants.

'It is good for dying your hair'.

Scorched whole chickens, bone hair-combs and, to my delight, a stall of artist brushes made of mouse hair, wolf, mink and goat. This stall captivated me to the extent of annoying everyone on the tour.

'Pauline, come on we are leaving'.

I was indecisive as to what brushes I should buy, how many etc, so eventually I had to leave without buying any of them and run to the ferry. I would have loved to have had a collection of these brushes.

On our return the mist thickened to a dense grey-white fog before we got back to our hotel. That night Poppy and I went to a Chinese opera; between each of the front seats were little tables for people to eat their dinner during the opera.

The story of the opera was that of a beautiful woman who lived among the Guilin conical mountains. The stage became so believable, as an acrobatic young woman flew across it, hanging from ropes, singing her high-pitched Chinese opera as she went. In the interval acrobats tumbled like Nijinsky around the stage, a man hung two buckets full of water from his eyelids.

The next day we visited the Reed Flute Caves lit up with gaudy-coloured lights shining on limestone stalagmites and stalactites that form shapes of forests, castles and Buddhas. Then we climbed to Long Sheng; rain and mist hiding the rice-paddy mountains. Our legs ached as we went up and up the steps, eventually stopping to have lunch beneath hanging red lanterns, looking out to the pagoda-like tall houses.

On a balcony a young woman bent over to comb her long black straight shiny hair.

'We are only allowed cut our hair two times in our life'.

She then twisted it and coiled it around her head, securing it with a bone comb. Each house held a very beautiful Chinese scene, women sewing, minding their babies and hanging kimonos out under the verandas. The lunch was in one of these traditional houses. We ate rice grown on their terraces that every now and again we could see when the mist rose.

The next day it was time to leave Guilin. The bus splashed through deep muddy water to the airport, stopping off at the pearl shop where we were given a tour of different coloured and priced pearl earrings, necklaces, bracelets and pendants.

'Look I bought myself some "fuck you" pearls'.

She held high a long necklace of iridescent grey-toned pearls.

'I don't give a damn spending his money. I am doing what my friend did when she separated from her husband, she bought "a fuck-you jag"'.

At the airport Danni showed us fake designer bags.

'You get the best imitation in China'.

She purchased six of these bags and one enormous one to put them all into for the plane journey back to Hong Kong. Looking down from our Hong Kong hotel, soundproofed, scented and soft, we could see layer upon layer of spaghetti-viaduct roads. We went down to the conference area where breakfast was laid out with fruits, croissants and coffee which some of us carried into the larger conference room.

'We're entering into a new era of globality where borders are blurred and the very idea of foreignness is foreign'.

The screen on the stage showed a woman beamed from Pakistan saying:

'Business without borders competing with everyone from everywhere for everything'.

The sophisticated IWF women took notes, held their pens high to get a word in, the energy that emanated in the room was palpable.

Poppy and I took a tram to look down on the city and waters of Hong Kong. The tram seemed to take us vertically into the sky. In the evening we were separated into small groups, Poppy's group dined in a sky restaurant and my group were invited by Janet de Silva to the famous China Club. The walls were covered with 1930s paintings and photographs and Janet de Silva entertained us to dinner in a book-filled private library. When I got back to Ireland the China Club inspired a large painting of that name.

The last meeting was one of the best, a laugh. We nearly didn't attend as the subject was ageism.

'Remembering a name nowadays is as good as an orgasm', said Dr Kanwaljit Soin, the first speaker.

The whole room was abuzz with laughter and comments.

'As you age, you rage'.

Up leapt Lucy, a glamorous woman of 92:

'I think I am an illustration of what you're talking about. I haven't retired – I have re-tyred, like a car. At the moment I am making a film about artists who are still working over the age of 80'.

'Hey! Let's go up to Karen Irwin's room to the Irish contingent's party' said the deep-voiced Canadian journalist Ann Medina.

Once more we all had our temperatures taken at Beijing Airport to see if any of us had swine flu.

'What if I'm having a hot flush?' said one of our group.

Beijing was like landing in a shiny kitchen. People were cleaning between railings and on top of ledges. The flat-paved Tiananmen Square was our first tour; Mao, looking down on us, his portrait backed in red. Straight-backed soldiers stood in rows, a frightening atmosphere filled the square. It felt very different when we walked through the gates of the Forbidden City, surrounded by tiled buildings glazed in turquoise, blues and browns; large bronze stork and turtle sculptures, terracotta tiles and knarled trees that looked like bonsai, their roots growing over weather-beaten rocks, ponds of waterlilies and wooden bridges, brightly painted corridors leading to lake boats. We were shown the concubines' enclosed quarters and the back door where the dead could be discreetly removed. Bunches of tourists walked in groups as if they were all joined together.

'Um-Qoy', explained our friendly waiter is an expression of gratefulness and reverence. This used to be expressed silently by the Emperor's minions. They would bend their forefingers when the Emperor would leave to explore the outer world as a full bow would blow his disguise.

We visited the abandoned Olympic city, our IWF minds full of ideas of what could be done with these huge modern buildings from the 2008 Olympic games.

Such interesting women. I fell for Barbara, in particular, we had the same philosophies in life. Hillary Clinton and Barbara are best buddies. If that's the case, Hillary Clinton must be as wonderful as I thought she was.

At the silk factory the worms were busy weaving.

'Do you think this would suit me?'

Each IWF woman consulted Poppy and I about the Chinese silks as we were the only artists in the group. Poppy bought two duvets filled with silk for Aran and Adam. We were measured for outfits to be tailored overnight. At six the next morning two young tailors knocked on the door and we tried on our outfits. By evening the boxes were waiting at the reception desk.

Reaching for miles and miles into the blue mountains was the historic Great Wall of China. Past conflict and architecture leaves its mark everywhere. Young vendors climbed the tall walls without permission from the authorities, their boxes of goods strapped to their backs to sell small carvings, hats and jade.

'China surprised me; my mind-set has been changed by this trip', said Barbara.

We were looking at the park full of children, old people, parents and young people – laughing, singing and playing extraordinary-looking instruments. It seemed a huge amount of people were happy. Perhaps the torturous events in history are slowly being forgotten and a new, relaxed China is emerging. Poppy and I flew back to Ireland with silk and bits of bamboo in our cases.

I still cannot get China out of my mind. The Nan Lian Gardens inspired a painting of huge goldfish swimming beside a sleeping woman with her fingers in the water. Guilin inspired many paintings incorporating those conical-shaped mountains; the strange legendary atmosphere that wafted through them haunting me to this day.

There were three of us, Poppy, Helena and myself. We had booked with the IWF for a trip to New York. It was my second New York experience. New York, like China, also has left a vivid print in my mind. We stayed in the Gramercy Arts Club, it was Christmas time. The wide carpeted stairs were hedged with huge red poinsettias going to the first landing, a Christmas tree in the bar glittered in the soft light, it was a very abundant looking Christmas theme. We met our Irish and New York friends at the club. We wined and dined under the Tiffany glass ceiling. Frannie said:

'No wine for me. I gave it up when I got into bed with the wrong twin'.

The dining room had to be reorganised for a lecture I was to give. The room filled with strong, witty confident women. Generous in their appreciation of listening to us, new visitors to their city, I have rarely spoken to such an appreciative audience.

On Sunday, we were all taken to mass at Harlem, the street was full of luscious fruity black people. The women dressed in designer clothes, the men mostly seemed to be in black with white shirts contrasting with their faces. The Abyssinian Baptist Church in Harlem rose to the sky. We entered and climbed the steps to our tier within the church. Onto the podium stepped a priestess, her hair styled immaculately, her dark robe covering designer clothes and on her feet shiny 8" heels.

Her voice started low:

'Gooood welcomes you. Halleluiah'.

Everybody replied, 'halleluiah'.

'We are all here in the presence of our beloved God'.

'Halleluiah', everyone shouted.

'We must be good in this world, help each other like God helps us. We must not be greedy'.

Poppy, Helena and I genuflected, knelt and stood copying the congregation's movements. Suddenly she shouted at the top of her voice.

'And you know, my dear friends, the Devil wears Prada'.

Helena and I looked at each other. We both had black Prada bags with Prada written all over the straps on our shoulders, and indeed I bet your bottom dollar we were not the only ones in the congregation wearing designer and Prada clothes. But guilt made us feel we should at least take them off our shoulders. The hysteria was expressed louder and louder to orgasmic heights. We were all risen out of our earthly state to the heavens above the church until the moment when we descended and exited onto the New York streets. Lunch was served in a barn in the country with wooden-built mansions and well-dressed villagers going in and out of Ralph Lauren's shop.

We have a lecture from Edie Weiner, a fresh looking young woman.

'Always employ happy people. We started as hunter gathers, then we farmed and now we use transportation. The rate of change is getting faster, faster and faster. Knowledge is all on the web, a nine-year-old can access it all. What we need is people with intelligence, inner wisdom. You women in the IWF are the brightest in the world. Society changes. World health depends on the marriage of mind and body'.

Looking down on Ground Zero our faces pressed against the thick glass, viewing way beneath us the flatness left by the tragedy.

He was a Russian taxi driver:

'I drop off a customer to the Twin Towers five minutes before the first plane crash into it. I turn around and was heading uptown when a man jump in and he say "drive me back, I want to take photographs of the accident". Then along comes the second plane. We think it was some guy trying to make history by flying between the two towers. We then think they make a film. Look they are throwing dolls down to pretend they are people. Then we realise it must be terrorists. The man he run out of film. I drive him to a store. I see those photographs in *Time* magazine. I nearly run over a woman who jumps in front of the car with her two-year-old baby. "Lady I nearly kill you", I say. "Take me out of here, anywhere", she cry and she cry. "My baby, my baby, I want my baby to be all right". It was like white hard rain pouring down on the taxi. I feel a bit of it and it's aluminium between my fingers. Then another man he open my car door, he is shaking, no jacket. "Take me away", he say. "Anywhere", he say. So I make for the Brooklyn Bridge. The woman and her baby are in the front seat. Then I see she is all blood and a big bump on the back of her head. "I must phone my husband. He work in the twin towers", she say. "My mobile won't work". She uses the man's mobile. "He is alive". She cry and she hug me. We drop off the sick man to a hospital, he is all sweating, he needs his medicine. He have no jacket, no money. We just make Brooklyn Bridge before all the bridges to Manhattan close. "Take me to Long Island to my mother-in-law", the lady say, "But I need your address to pay you, I have no money". I say "I don't need money" and I drop her to Long Island. Many weeks later the lady with the baby sent me $300 and she say in a letter you deserve more'.

24

THE PAINTING LIFE AND STUDIO VISITORS

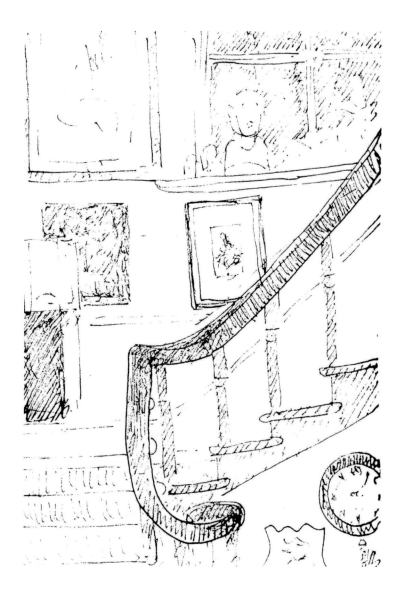

Saffron yellow, gold and amber, a cowboy walk. It was Romio Shrestha leading his visitors up the drive. Linda, with long brown hair and Donovan carrying his green guitar. Later came Bruce Lee's beautiful wife. It wasn't long before Donovan was singing *they call me mellow yellow* amongst the flowers.

On another occasion he arrived with Dr Horst Rechelbacher and his wife, founder of Aveda and Intelligent Nutrients. Antoinette O'Shea had just made a Thai curry for us which they shared. I think I embarrassed him by showing him a bunch of herbs from the garden. I suppose he was used to Himalayan and jungle herbs as he didn't know anything about my mint, thyme, lovage and parsley.

'May I see your paintings?'

I happened to have 'Reading and Thinking' in my studio. He immediately bought it, enthusiastically advising me to go bigger. Horst gave me the 'golden seed'. I did go bigger, with huge canvasses three metres high, and tapestries which I had woven at Aubusson, France.

The painting he bought was of a woman waiting for her lover, her eyebrows were her legs spread eagle wide apart to welcome him. One does not notice this at first. Charlo Quain of the Cork Art Society said:

'I looked all over the city and never saw anyone with such interesting eyebrows'.

One day a nun in plainclothes came and bought a copy of this print. However that night she phoned:

'I have just noticed the eyebrows. May I change it for a different print?'

A week went by and she rang again:

'I don't care. I want "Reading and Thinking" back again'.

Romio brought another visitor, Sinead O'Connor. Sinead said a few friendly words to Dan O'Connor as he was stacking logs into a wheelbarrow. She entered the kitchen and was heavily pregnant.

'I'm fucked', were her first words.

Then she stretched herself out on the settee by the fire. Romio massaged her head, neck and shoulders.

'The spaghetti is ready'.

We all sat around the table. Sinead, with great effort, dragged herself to the table and sat down. There was a bowl of Moo mints on the dresser behind her. She proceeded to eat them, one after another, pressing the sweet papers with her index finger into the centre of her uneaten spaghetti.

They say things come in threes; all in the one week came three psychiatrists. Firstly two beautiful blonde women. They had been camping on the west coast and wanted to do an interview for their psychiatric magazine called *Inside Out*.cThe next was a Professor from Oxford University. He bought a present for his wife's birthday, he stood tall in his brown leather belt and talked about his work in Oxford. I was baffled at his long words.

The phone rang:

'My name is Phil Moran and I would like to arrange a trip of over thirty Americans to see your work and studio'.

She explained that they were all old and incredibly rich millionaires.

It was early summer, the shiny white bus arrived at our gate with the visitors. The arrangement for this visit had been made the year before. I had got my friends to give me a hand with the paintings that I took out of storage, couriered from Macroom for the occasion.

The bus door opened. Each person took a very long time to descend the two steps of the bus, then the challenge to turn around in the direction of our house. Phil Moran stood on the wall gesticulating directions. In a clear voice she said:

'After our lunch we will go to the glass studio where Pauline will be giving a talk on her life and work'.

It seemed that nobody was listening to her. The Park Hotel Kenmare did the catering. John Brennan had made a beautiful job with the long table in the office. He covered it in a white tablecloth, laid out gourmet food on silver platters and bottles of glistening wines in silver wine buckets:

'Oh! I am so tired I can't follow a thing being said to us. I just want to sit down'.

Two of the men were still at the gate, they could not even make it to the house, they were propped against one of O'Sullivan's wrecked cars. The reason they were so tired, apart from being very old, was that morning they had been taken on a treasure hunt over the Dingle Hills, then Dunquin and then came in the bus to me.

I overheard one woman saying:

'I gave all my 13 grandchildren 13 million each, isn't that neat?'

The only time they seemed to perk up was when they were sitting comfortably on the golden chairs provided by the Park Hotel listening to the lecture. However one man must have been so comfortable he gave out loud snorting snores. By the time the day was over one book had been sold. However, nothing like that really disappoints me, but I did expect a complete clear out of all my paintings. When it was time for them to leave for Kenmare, getting them onto the bus again was even slower. I am sure they all had an early night.

John Ryan, one of the liveliest and tallest of them, asked could he come back next year with his extended family. They came with the grandchildren, the parents and the grandparents. We had such a good time painting together, laughing while the mothers and fathers bought a great number of my works and etchings. From that day on John Ryan sent me one of his painted photographs every Christmas. He had a very original talent but this Christmas no photograph came.

I washed each Staffordshire dog and antique plate in a bowl of sudsy water knowing that Carleton Varney was a collector. He had seen my paintings of 'Irish Animals' on the walls of Ashford Castle when he was doing their interior design and requested that I send him the limited edition version.

George and Michelina Stacpoole from Adare brought Carleton for a visit, the sun was shining when they arrived. Out of the car stepped a big, incredibly flamboyant man with pure white hair, a wide silk tie that fluttered in the wind, a yellow kerchief, white trousers, red socks and red leather shoes.

'My goodness you look healthy and wealthy', I said.

'Let's walk around the garden, it's so rare to get sun in Ireland', he said.

There was no shortage of laughter and chat. Lizzy had prepared one of her gourmet lunches, starting with delicious salmon and salsa. After lunch we took our coffee in my studio. I thought Carleton had a glass of wine too much as he was slowly falling sideways towards me. Finally he righted himself and held up the leg of the chair which had fallen off. Carleton noticed every little thing:

'I like the way you stack your toilet tissue'.

'Are we going to see your work?'

I had taken from storage my large tapestries, one of which Carlelton said:

'Hey, that looks like Obama and Michelle', taking a photograph which he said, 'I'll show them this'.

He is one of America's best known interior designers and has decorated the White House as well as castles and mansions in Ireland. What a colourful visit that was.

I was painting a large work I called 'Horse Eating Thorns' when Emer arrived to cut my hair.

'That's a fabulous horse'.

'It doesn't really look like one', I said.

I felt embarrassed that I had painted such large exaggerated teeth.

'Sure can't they go out into the field to look at a real horse', Emer said.

That painting was bought by a very interesting man. It is rare that someone calls without an appointment. He had a haversack on his back and wore mountaineering boots.

'I've never bought a painting before but I would like to buy one now. I don't want to spend too much', he said.

I showed him line drawings, etchings and small watercolours.

'I am going to go for a coffee in the Glenbeigh Hotel to make up my mind which one I'll take'.

On his way out of my studio he spotted 'Horse Eating Thorns' on my easel.

'My God, I like that one'.

'That is a brand new painting and would cost you a fortune', I joked.

Off he went for his coffee. Shortly after the phone rang:

'I have decided which one I will take. I want the "Horse Eating Thorns"'.

He came back to write the cheque and as he was doing so Ben, our dog, had found a pair of black knickers of mine which he proffered to this man, wagging his tail enthusiastically:

'That's a dog after my own heart', he said.

I enjoyed the impulsive way this man bought his first painting.

'Is there anywhere we can land our helicopter?'

It was Bill Cullen, Jackie Lavin and Norma Smurfit, a shy wise person. I took Adam with me down to Dooks Golf Course, I knew he would like to see a helicopter up close. After showing him the inside of the helicopter, its steering wheel etc, we jumped into the car, Bill sitting next to Adam.

` 'So what are you going to do when you grow up?' he asked him.

'I am going to put my seed into a woman and have a baby'.

'I don't think I'm going to ask you any more questions', said Bill.

It is always a pleasure to show my work to them.

I have enjoyed so many dinners and parties given by Bill and Jackie. At one such lunch, to my delight, they sat me next to Joanna Lumley. We talked of how upsetting it is to see lorries of live cows trundling along the road destined for their end. We both had animal welfare in common.

For many years in springtime I would go to give a weekend art session in the Burren College of Art in Clare. There amongst the Burren's flat stones and rampant wild flowers we would sit together painting and painting. Two of the many students who attended my art classes were NC Britton and her daughter, Easkey, age twelve. Now at the age of 27 she has become one of my lifelong friends. We paint together around Christmas time. One of my favourite Easkey paintings is of a grey monkey sitting on a rock. She would take a break from painting to play her silver flute and to contemplate on the swing in the glasshouse, a very easy-going guest. She also happens to be a famous surfer, travelling the world winning events and attending conferences as a marine environmentalist.

If I don't get down the idea of a painting, Now, another Now takes over. Don't think about it, do it. I almost called this book *Now*.

As a child with a piece of charcoal, chalk or pencil in hand, drawings would come out on a surface without any awareness that I was becoming an 'artist'. Just as a child would pick up a stick and bang, enjoying the rhythm that he created without the title 'drummer' or 'musician'.

A President of the Royal Hibernian Academy said:

'When I first saw your work, Pauline, my member kept moving'.

There is a perception that I am a free, 'sexually liberated' person. One doesn't necessarily paint what one is – it could be what one would like to be. A painting of a sleeping relaxed naked woman lying on moss with a frog and spawn about her isn't me. Perhaps it's a wish that it could be me in total abandonment to nature with no fear of man nor beast. To paint out the desire to be a dancer or a bird fulfils a desire to be those things. Artists like Cezanne or Pissarro approached painting differently to me. They are looking outside themselves. I work from inside out, more like Chagal, Rousseau or Picasso. Picasso once said that he painted with his penis. The canvas offers therapy to express horror, violence and beauty.

Fear of change never entered me, in fact it's exciting:

'You should have stuck to your line drawing'.

Or:

'You should just paint Ireland, that is your *métier*, not anywhere else'.

Those restrictive comments hurt, but the drive to keep moving is compelling.

Drawing and painting is a way of unconsciously sorting out what puzzles about love, beauty, hate and things that upset and disturb. It is a tool to suss out unclear feelings. Viewing and being influenced by other artists is rare. If there is an influence, it springs from life.

Going through the menopause brought about a painting I called 'African Woman's First Period', simply because each month I wondered would this be my last. It was a painting of a young black woman on her honkers with blood dripping onto her hand from her vagina, a look of bewilderment on her face; behind her the jungle, a flowing waterfall, a giraffe.

A couple flew into Farranfore Airport in Kerry in their private plane with the intention of buying a painting. As they were looking through my folder, to my embarrassment they came across this very personal painting, 'African Woman's First Period'.

'You don't want to see that', I said, attempting to remove it from the folder.

'No, no, may we see, it is amazing'.

And to my surprise this was their choice.

When a painting is in progress I go about tidying up, lighting the fire etc; catching a glimpse of the painting unaware. It is during those unaware moments that the painting can be judged anew as I am no longer so close to it. It is now that the intellect helps. I see that the mountain could be higher, the horizon of the sea lower, the man's hands heavier etc.

In March 2013 when I was walking the Rossbeigh sand dunes, I saw in the distance a neighbour from the Glencar Valley sitting amongst the marram grass on the dunes staring out to sea holding his dog close. I placed a version of this man ascending into the sky and only then realised the subject was Paddy thinking of his death. Each step of that painting was done without much knowledge of the next step, finally dawning on me the full meaning of how this painting came about.

Paddy stopping his farm work and driving to the sea to have a philosophical moment about life and death.

One day recently a witty lady came from Cork and bought a new picture called 'Till midlife crisis due we part'. It was a painting of two people in church, sharing their oath during their wedding ceremony.

'That's just the stage me and my husband are at', she laughed. She later told me: 'that painting did not go down very well with himself'.

It was early morning, a painting was started without getting myself ready for the day, nightdress still on, hair uncombed, when out of the corner of my eye I spotted movement. It was two people slowly walking up the drive with a baby, they were looking left and right and discussing the garden.

Catching sight of me the man rushed up saying:

'Pauline Bewick I must kiss you'.

'Excuse me I am not dressed yet'.

'We just want to say hello'.

However that did not stop them. They kept on walking towards the studio, entered the open doors and looked at the start of my new painting.

'I won't hold it up for you because it is just so fresh in my head, it might go away'.

They took no notice of all my hints.

'Darling I think he needs a nappy change. Oh! Move the picture, lay him out on Pauline's table'.

They rolled up the shitty nappy and dropped it into the waste paper basket.

'I think he needs a feed now. Oh! Lie on Pauline's table and feed him'.

She lay down on my table, took out her breast and the baby suckled happily. She then turned over for the baby to empty her other breast. It seemed to take an eternity, with the father asking me was I planning exhibitions or further travels. Finally they packed up their baby bag and left.

When they left my studio the new painting had completely lost its excitement, so turning the sheet over I painted a woman lying like a dog on her side with three babies suckling three breasts like a row of pups; behind, a clothesline full of pink and blue baby clothes, a house with the door open and beside her face a mirror, lipstick; around her neck a chain and cross representing how tied she was to her situation. A good painting, called 'Mother of Three', as a result of my intruders.

I physically feel my mind opening, like sliding doors, for the flow to come out of that cavern of the unknown. It then becomes something I think about and then it becomes something I'm glad to have done. It is amazing what comes out when intellect is out of the way.

When painting scenery, I start way over my left shoulder, drawing the end of the lake, gradually turning my head towards the right, putting down what is in front of me as I go, ending up with the river entering the lake over my right shoulder, so on the flat surface I have, in fact, created a semi-circle.

I jot down in the middle of the night ideas for paintings, inventions, jokes – a solider engaged in war being annoyed by a mosquito biting him.

One was sculpture designs for windmills. I felt that the famous Irish legends would lend themselves to this. While on the Board of the National Gallery of Ireland. along with Loretta Brennan Glucksman, Anthony Cronin and Loughlin Quinn amongst others, I showed Loughlin the windmill idea and he put me in touch with John Redmond of the ESB who took the project very seriously over a cup of tea and cucumber sandwiches.

Sitting in John Redmond's office was a qualified windmill engineer. When he heard my proposal he put his head to one side and said rather sceptically:

'Well it *could* be done!'

I had designed the leader of the windmills in such a way that they too would gather energy, but the engineer commented that it would not be possible for them to collect as much as three-bladed windmills. Mr Redmond looked sternly at his engineer and announced to him:

'You've got a job'.

The recession bundled that idea out the window and I haven't heard anything from it since. Recently Poppy has discovered several artistic sculptural windmills internationally.

Other ideas that I came up with were the ice buster car, the divorce car, the tidal energy dykes and many more. The majority of the paintings are about the sensuality of nature, flowers, fruit, animals and the human body. The body is drawn from the flow of how my body feels, the high-boned hip, the slope of the belly that gravity brings to the earth, the heaviness of the head pushing the cheek into a fold.

It's a puzzle that sometimes my paintings predict something that happens in the future. I went to Cork to buy holy trinkets, medals, plastic holy water bottles and various medallions in order to make a collage of Christ on the Cross; the cross was to be made of hundreds of these shiny medallions. I placed on either side of Christ the two robbers, also on shiny medallion crosses. The scene was set in the desert, Christ's face had a dark swordy look. When this twelve foot high work was finished I sent it to the Royal Hibernian Academy where it was put on exhibition. A few weeks after the work was finished, I was in Cork again. It was 9 September 2011. The poet John Montague rushed up to me saying:

'Have you heard what's happening? The twin towers have been blown up in New York'.

I went to see the horrific scene on a large screen in a pub. It was later I noticed that my Christ looked like Bin Laden, set in the desert, the two crucifixes looked like the twin tower skyscrapers. This work hung in our tall glasshouse, it glowed at night, the holy trinkets were luminous.

On another occasion I was painting New York City, the subject being the Wall Street Crash. I painted a building that happened to look like an aeroplane falling into the Hudson River, which later echoed the reality of a plane crashing into the Hudson.

One morning in the 1970s I was doing a black and white line drawing of a man playing the penny whistle with two little girls dancing a jig on the whistle when, after school, Holly and Poppy announced to my surprise:

'We are going to learn how to play the penny whistle'.

Whenever I travel I pack bound sketchbooks that Paul Curtis of Muckross House makes for me. They go with me to every country, including a bijou box of watercolours, my favourite sable hair and duck quill paintbrush, along with a Mont Blanc broad-nibbed pen which I fill with FW Indian ink to Mont Blanc disapproval! I never use the inks that they provide as it runs when in contact with water.

These sketchbooks get filled one after the other, they help to absorb the character of each place. If I am there long enough, as I was in the South Seas, it helps to understand their culture, superstitions and traditions. It meant a lot that the islanders would gather around, chat, tell stories and would paint along with me. I liked the sense that we were participating and I was not just a visitor intruding on their lives.

Everything is intertwined, a spider eating a fly, a lion killing a cub to procreate again, the selfishness, chaos and order of the world. All that puzzlement I put into one subject, like a philosopher in the desert, a heron plucking a tadpole from a pool, or ants in line scuttling through their lives.

When a painting is going well it is all consuming, it makes me deeply involved and happy. I am surprised at how dependent I am on producing a good painting. When I experience a dry period, a block, my attempts are dead and without inspiration, without spark, without any depth. I realise then I am trying too hard, the intellect starts coming in, 'the sliding doors' have not opened, they are being forced.

All through our marriage, during these dried up periods Pat tries to comfort me:

'You always come out of it. Just wait'.

'I find that hard to believe'.

I am blessed to have married Pat as he has never analysed me or the strange subjects that have flowed out of me; when a couple is making love he has never asked 'who's that?' or why is a woman covered in frog spawn? Pat told me of his teacher in Baggot Street Hospital, the famous Professor Synge. He had discovered that the artist Paul Henry was colour blind. Synge wisely felt that if he informed Paul Henry about his colour blindness he might have tried to alter his mainly blue pallet of colours.

Have I found my art changing over the years? In many ways I feel it's the same, but when I look back and compare works I can see that there has been a very slow and gradual change, from a flat linear style to a fuller rounder style, expressing the same subjects of relationships, beauty and cruelty. The colours are getting stronger, the canvases bigger and I have extended my studio space. Everything is mushrooming along.

A question often asked is what would I say to young artists? Express your day-to-day loves, hates, worries, problems in your picture; don't bother about anybody else's – express your own emotions and out of that comes you and your style. If you've something that's really heartfelt to say it will resonate with the viewer as true.

In return for a work of art I was lent a beautiful big apartment in Paris set in a courtyard across the River Seine to the Tuileries Garden. It was there I really got into pastel painting. I use pastels to express the view outside me. The paintings are not as emotional as the ones I have been talking about. When Regine and I went to Paris to paint, the first thing we did on arrival was to visit an art shop, 100 metres down from the apartment on the side of the Seine. There before our eyes was a feast of colours of Union pastel sticks made of finely ground pigments. We started buying just a few and after a short while we ran down to get more, more and more.

The paintings that followed were of the Tuileries Garden, the River Seine, the Louvre and the distant Eiffel Tower. This joy of pastel painting has been with me for years since.

I invented this way, using three-metre high fine canvasses I stretch the primed side of the canvas to the back and the unprimed side to the front. The fine tooth of the raw canvass holds onto the powdery pigment – this is the freest way to paint that I have ever experienced. I stand on the ground, pastel in my hand, reach to the top of the canvas and swish down, creating without pause the trunk of the magnolia tree. When the painting is finished I spray it first with pastel fixative, then I make a mixture of museum quality PVA matt finish varnish and water, spraying it on the pastel from a gardener's bottle. This has to be done five or six times until the pastel is thoroughly covered in diluted PVA. Then the final undiluted coat of PVA can be applied with a fine broad soft varnish brush. The whole work now is rendered impervious and has no need for a covering of glass to protect it. This technique was recorded by a Dutch art journalist, Eric Beets, for *Palet* magazine in 2010.

The other mediums that I use are watercolours, oil paints, acrylic inks, charcoal, pencil, Indian ink, ceramic painting in majolica glazing, tapestry weaving, three-dimensional collage work, feathers, false teeth, eye glasses, religious medallions, sweet papers, sawdust, lichen, lace, tree bark etc – even eggs shells which Betty sorted into piles, the green duck eggs, the brown hen eggs and the white and then placed them into bags, hammering them into pieces for me. All of which I spray with museum quality PVA when in place on the work, rendering them permanent.

Betty is a good, natural judge of my paintings. I often ask.

'What's wrong with this painting Betty?'

She carefully looks at it:

'You'd need to put a bit more blue up there. What's that quare thing? You can't tell what it is'.

And sure enough she is right.

Why do so many women and perhaps men keep being drawn to, and falling in love with the wrong person? It happens to them over and over, the pattern continues. This topic is bringing forth practically a full exhibition.

As I go along painting these unsuitable relationships, I am trying to suss out the why. Could it be that early on in life the woman's inner wisdom has been damaged by some event, disabling her clear vision of what's in front? It could be that they think they deserve to be treated badly, simply for being a woman.

I have often thought that the male is deeply envious of a woman being the main creator of life. All he has to do is plant the seed, have a good laugh and go on to plant another seed somewhere else. Women can choose whether they procreate or not. Men basically have no choice, all they have is a seed.

25

OUR OLD AGE

For the last twenty years Pat and I have happily shared life together, going on many walks, gathering mushrooms, looking at nature and birds. One of our favourite walks is along Lickeen river. It shows up each season. Spring – bluebells, primrose and little ducklings; Winter – icicles, flooded rivers and leafless trees.

On one of these winter walks, Pat, Aran and I went up the Lickeen river path. Ben, our golden retriever, no matter how cold the water, would jump in gleefully and collect sticks that we would throw in for him. On this occasion he grabbed by mistake in his jaws a rather large log and started to drift downstream with it, gurgling what I thought was a happy growl. Then Pat said:

'I think he is going under. I think he is drowning'.

At that I took off my long padded winter coat and my nightie which I had on underneath and, completely naked, I jumped into the river to save Ben. He was going towards a rushing waterfall. It had to be me because Aran was too young and Pat was too old. I caught hold of Ben's neck and found that the log was stuck to his teeth. I pulled him and the log to the bank where Aran and Pat dragged him up the side and they wrenched the log from his teeth. I scrambled up the bank and sat on the grass. Then it struck me as I looked down at my wet and naked body:

'What am I doing here?'

'You have just saved Ben'.

'I have just saved Ben?'

My memory had completely gone. Pat told me the circumstance of Ben and the log over and over for about fifteen minutes until my memory slowly dawned back again. I was told later that women over fifty get a condition called sea amnesia when a sudden rush of cold water hits the back of the neck.

What a joy it is to go on walks with Aran as he is so into nature. He jumps from rock to rock peering into the Lickeen river to study the fresh water muscles, small fish, jumping salmon and all the season's flowers and creatures that he would spot on any of our walks. He has made a museum above their turf shed. It is filled with rows of bird feathers, shells, fossils and bones, each labelled. He has now taken to burying such things as a stranded dolphin, an otter and whalebones in the garden so that the bones will be cleaned by various insects and lavas. It doesn't matter that Aran has dyslexia. The Carnegie school read aloud his exam questions. Occasionally he has to write, but says things like:

'Doing my homework is very labrador' (laborious).

He tells me today (17 August 2015) that he has been offered a place in Trinity College, having received 500 points in his Leaving Cert. Pat and his father Conor studied there.

What an unusual human Adam is. When he answers the phone there is a long silence. I ask:

'Is Poppy there?'

He goes, 'aaaaaaaaaaaaaaahh, I don't think soooooooooooooo'.

'Will you go and see?' I ask.

'Aaaaaaaaaaaaaahh, you want me to go and see?'

'Yes'.

'Aaaaaaaaaaaaaaahh, ok'.

He is the absent-minded professor. In all his exams he gets top marks, he knows every country on the globe, he plays the violin beautifully, he will stick his head into computer games for ever and ever if let. He can quote Billy Connolly or any of the stories that I tell him, word for word. In fact I love the way he laughs at my stories, he rolls about the floor from side to side then sits up to listen to more, twitching his nose and smelling his fingers. He is a one-off and I love him; so very different from his brother Aran.

Here are some of the stories that I tell Adam and visiting children. First the Buddha Stories taken out of a small leather case full of tiny figurines. There is the green Buddha, red Buddha, brown Buddha and they all sit about talking to black Elly, the elephant or the headless boatman and they go flying on a goose's back and land in a village of other figurines, of all types, randomly picked out of the little leather case.

I could have an audience of ten or twelve children sitting around as I tell these stories. Chiara and Giada, Holly's girls, particularly enjoy hearing them and ask especially for the famous New York boxer, Rocky Marciano stories. One Christmas I had stitched up a three-foot doll; the face was made of an old t-shirt, buttons for his nose, eyes and mouth, a shrunken sweater for his upper body, with one of Pat's ties around his neck; his legs were stuffed baby leggings. Holly had done the same using Chiara and Giada's shrunken baby clothes to create Blondie, his wife.

Rocky swears, curses and punches.

'Get my lunch, you stupid woman, put it on the table quick ... It's disgusting, throw it away'.

'Ok, Rocky', Blondie squeaks, subserviently.

'Hurry, hurry, hurry', shouts Rocky. 'Take that stinking dinner out of my sight', to which the children roll around with laughter, then they would punch Rocky with gusto.

In June 2009 Pat developed Alzheimer's – disbelief, anger, then slowly acceptance. One has to constantly work at acceptance. Pat's intelligence and wit still show in flashes. It is hard to believe that his memory loss is so bad for such things as where his room is.

'Hey Pat, you are in two pairs of pyjamas', to which he humorously replied with his finger in the air:

'Tricky. Tricky'.

Ever since Pat was young he has come up with funny quips:

'God is everywhere', said the nun. 'Miss, Miss, is he in my inkwell?' making the whole class laugh, after which Pat got a slap from the nun.

Another day I said:

'No one wants to hear you moan and groan, do they?'

'Well they'll miss a few gems then'.

Over a silent dinner I dared to ask Pat:

'Do you think you have had a good life?'

'O yes!', he answered, 'from the very beginning my parents loved me and so did my Nanny Rose and her husband. We've had a marvellous marriage and a wonderful life with Holly and Poppy, not to mention our darling Ben', as he looked down at the dog saying:

'Isn't that right Ben!'

To talk of his long term, which is so clear, Alan Hayes suggested that Pat write a book. He ended up writing two: *Three Friends on a Boat* about a sailing trip with Barry and Philip Castle, then *From Trinity to Treanmanagh*, both were published by Arlen House. Pat delights in his own memories as Lizzy Walsh and Seamus O'Sullivan read them to him and I would recommend that people with Alzheimer's write about their past. It is very therapeutic.

For three years Lizzy, an energetic intellectual came to help every weekend. She would read aloud Bill Bryson etc to him. One day she asked us:

'Can I cook for you?'

That was the beginning of a series of the most delicious gourmet dishes.

Betty, our neighbour, has helped us for the last thirty years. Her daughter Eliza can solve all problems from fixing the Aga, assembling a new gadget, cooking and finding health foods and is also excellent with computer work. Her little daughter Emily comes to play with the box of Buddhas and lies on her stomach on the rug making them talk.

'You know, Pauline, I didn't cry when our neighbour died. I only cry if the hens and dogs die'.

We had a visit from an old friend, he too had developed Alzheimer's. I bristled with pride that Pat was well behaved and so good natured compared to him. He would bitterly shout, 'I am not through yet'.

Insisting on driving he would inevitably get lost on the road.

Is it wrong to feel happy when many are sad?
Should one be active and tackle the bad?
Is it wrong to feel guilty for feeling so good?
Is it wrong to eat plenty when some don't have food?
When others have nothing, not even a sup,
is it wrong to be comfy and pet the wee pup?
Is it right to give up stuff and share things around,
to bend over backwards, help folk off the ground?
Is it right to keep killers alive in a jail?
Is it right to blame women or men when we fail?

'John Piggott is very poorly'.

It wasn't long before we heard he had died, leaving Pat, his twin brother alone. That evening Michael, the postman, arrived at the Piggott's to find out that John had died. He gave an hour helping to get ready for the wake. Many neighbours rallied round, clearing the path, making sandwiches and busily getting the house ready for this sad happening until the middle of the night.

When we were getting Pat Melia ready to say his farewell for the wake, we commented:

'Hey Pat, you forgot to do up your fly'.

To which he answered, 'better than forgetting to open it'.

Maurice Galway, the film director and CEO of Dingle Film Festival, made a significant film called *Fallen Angel*. The monastery monks gave him an old carving of an angel that they were throwing out, filled with woodworm holes on the painted pale colours. In the last scene he set the angel alight and put her out to sea. The mixture of flames and water lapping about the faded angel was moving and symbolic, her inscrutable face stays in one's mind.

Years later Maurice came to discuss making a documentary. We talked for ages in my studio. He told me of a fox that sat beside him in a field. I enjoyed his stories and felt he connected with my work. He was impressed by the gestalt analyst finding the Grey Man within the right side of my body and the Yellow Man on the left side, and so the *Yellow Man Grey Man* documentary was made.

We, the family, went to Italy. Maurice stayed in the garden house and I gave him access to all the Yellow Man Grey Man material; Tony Clare's speech, catalogues, the video that I made with Sean from Glenbeigh who played the part of the Yellow Man covered in yellow powder. Betty and Sean laughed so much as he was getting yellower and yellower.

When we returned from Tuscany, Maurice had a substantial part of the documentary completed.

'I now need you, Pauline, for about a week to film and interview you'.

He had organised a crew of six. The wonderful music was composed by his friend Nico Brown, accompanied by Martin Brunsden. The camera man was Eugene O'Connor, famous for his camera work on the Beatles, Katy Perry etc. They made me feel at ease, it didn't bother me to nip behind a furze bush and have a pee. I found I could think and paint on camera, no need for rehearsals that would spoil the immediacy of it all.

The last scene of this film showed the back view of the Grey Man at dusk waltzing with me wearing a yellow dress. As they waltzed we see the Grey Man has a fox mask. Nico's haunting music carried us to the finishing shots over the lake into the night of the film.

The documentary was premiered to a full house in the Dingle Film Festival. David Norris had a question and answer session, it was funny and lively. Benners Hotel was full to capacity, the party afterwards was a real celebration. RTÉ bought the film and it was aired twice; shown on the big screen in the Irish Film Institute in Dublin and the Galway Film Festival and it was bought by Sky Arts, New Zealand. Wherever it was shown Maurice told me there were lively questions and conversations afterwards.

The TV premiere followed a debate on an upcoming Irish Senate referendum. Declan Lynch in the *Sunday Independent* totally copped on to the Yellow Man philosophy: 'To move from the utter degeneracy of the Seanad debate to the truth and brilliance of Bewick, was to be reminded that, somehow, our civilisation can withstand just about anything that the grey men can do to it'. Referencing my relationship with Pat, he quoted me saying: 'He [Pat] never ever made me change my personality in any way ... mind you that doesn't stop me trying to change his ... I suppose he has a larger understanding of the problems of life ... There may be times when I'm cross with Pat, and I think, *aw*, I wish I had Pat, to tell Pat, how horrible Pat is ...'

There was a frenzy of exhibitions. The first, in Glenbeigh.

'Wouldn't it be great, Pauline, to have an exhibition in the Protestant Church'.

'Brendan Sweeney will give it to us', said Geraldine Murphy, Vera Foley and Francis Joy.

The primroses looked lovely around the gravestones and up the path, the walls were painted and the windows cleaned. Francis Joy used his engineering skills to hang the paintings. They had gone to no end of trouble to make this exhibition a huge success. The local people came and many bought the works. Sean O'Sullivan came in with a friend singing 'I'm the Yellow Man, I'm the Yellow Man' and waltzed together all around the stone-slabbed church floor. What a joy and a good idea this exhibition was.

The next exhibition was at Waterville with Fiona and Paddy Bushe, then Cill Rialaig with Noelle Campbell Sharpe. As well as all of that I was organising an exhibition for my 77th birthday at the Taylor Galleries, Dublin.

Another film was in development, directed by Ronan O'Leary, an eccentric man, his shirt hanging out over his trousers and his long shoelaces undone which wiggled around the floor as he rushed about directing the cameramen filming paintings being hung.

The last painting hanging on the wall and the invitees arrived, amongst them Mary Clayton and Niall MacMonagle with Graham Norton who was to open the exhibition. Graham looked more handsome than on television. He wore a navy-blue velvet dinner jacket with a satin roll collar, a pair of jeans and runners. Niall looked like Graham's brother rather than his teacher; he was the English teacher in Bandon Grammar School where Graham attended. I first met Niall when he contacted me to purchase a painting for the school on the Arts Council scheme in 1983. He chose 'Mother and Daughter Asleep'. It showed the pair all curled up with a kilim blanket over them, the child's toes on the mother's pillow, the mother's toes on the child's pillow. It looked good hanging on the stairwell of the school.

I showed Graham around the exhibition.

'Tell me about that one, "Holly's Life"'.

'It's Holly, our daughter, pregnant with her life of not only her children, the garden, feeding her hens and living in the community in Tuscany'.

Graham listened to each description, the four rooms were now filled with guests including people on the outside steps. John Taylor introduced Graham who gave an incredibly generous and well-researched speech, giving us a huge belly laugh recounting how he dealt with bat shit in his bathroom in West Cork.

Around 8pm the exhibition crowd started to thin out. We walked past the Shelbourne Hotel, past O'Donoghue's pub where The Dubliners used to sing, to the United Arts Club in Fitzwilliam Street where I had organised a dinner party with the help of the lively Sarah Leahy. It was to be for 72 people, the maximum capacity allowed. Each person invited had something to do with the organisation of the exhibition. After dinner the singer Rose Lawless, at Regine Bartsch's suggestion, sang for us. The Arts Club chef cooked delicious delicate salmon. His choice of foods was sophisticated and fresh. The film crew came into the room and continued filming. Rose Lawless, accompanied by Julie Cruickshank on piano, made us all laugh at her words, so original, outrageously witty, along with the sexy movements of her body.

The guests, Mary O'Sullivan (one of my dearest and longest pals), Brendan O'Connor, who sat opposite Graham Norton, Kieran Corrigan, Abdul and Catherine Bulbulia, Nell McCafferty, Maurice Galway, his wife Catherine, Alan Hayes and the Kerry contingent etc, created a great sense of fun filling the room. Suddenly Liam O'Connor, the accordionist who used to travel the world with Riverdance, jumped onto one of the tables, his energy burst like electricity in the room. Everybody clapped and banged their feet, there was a frenzy of angled photography as Liam held the squeeze box at arm's length, defying gravity in his outstretched arms.

It was interesting to see how Graham was inundated with leaflets, CDs and booklets and an enormous book given to him by an artist. Graham commented:

'I could put four legs under this and it would make a great coffee table'.

After midnight, Graham, Niall and Mary took off in their car full of all these pieces. Niall gave Graham a room in their house that led into the garden where his two dogs Bailey and Madge awaited Graham's return.

Fiona Hyde, a beautiful beautician who works in Killorglin, put on a show in Library Place of all my Ann Kerins' clothes made for exhibitions over the years. Amongst the *Seven Ages* Kerry Collection she set out rows of seats and organised Joan to announce each outfit, after which she sang wonderful jazz in a deep voice. The audience looked as glamorous as the models that Fiona had chosen. The make-up was extraordinary, the lipstick black, long plaits were added to their hair and for the Yellow Man coat she got the witty extroverted Dr Cotter to model. He pranced along the platform – in the middle of this he was called on duty and off he went with yellow grease paint on his face. Once again it was being filmed by Ronan O'Leary. Ronan and his crew stayed in the garden house and filmed the locality in order to slot it into his film later. I reckon he will be filming me as I'm lowered into the grave!

Then a strange thing happened. I got a mini stroke.

The morning came for a trip with Regine to Cork.

'My God, Regine, my right leg is as weak as water. I must have slept on it in a strange way'.

We sat into her red classic Mercedes and talked of all our usual subjects – paintings, clothes, how different men are from women, food and face cream.

We parked in the Crawford multi-storey car park. I had completely forgotten that my leg was weak but got a quick reminder when I stepped out of the car. I had to link Regine's arm and we went to have lunch in the Crawford Art Gallery restaurant.

Then we walked over the river to a beautiful old house, up the stairs to a studio full of string instruments. A handsome old man with a white beard noticed I was limping and provided a seat. We proceeded to discuss the violin that I had brought, it had belonged to Harry's sister Minnie. Now Minnie's violin was to be fitted for Adam who is becoming so good. It's amazing to hear him play with such vigour, his mouth moving with the effort.

When our business was done my right leg had got even weaker. Regine decided the best place to go to in Cork was the University Hospital; a phenomenal amount of different doctors tested the strength of both my knees, seeing if I could blow my cheeks out equally, close my eyes equally and stick out my tongue. There was a series of debates as to whether there was a nerve pressing in my back as it didn't appear to be a stroke.

I was put onto a high trolley and wheeled along a darkened corridor where I was to spend the night with a varied collection of patients. The noise from the patients was phenomenal. A handicapped girl kept shouting 'fuck off'. The man behind me coughed so loud I thought he might tumble off his trolley. The woman in front of me gave long lonesome sighs. It wasn't until five in the morning I was wheeled to a ward of four women and one man and there I stayed a week. A young twenty-year-old girl in the bed next to me had a stroke as her left arm was limp. She practiced walking, she wore cool trendy clothes. I observed the woman opposite me. She taught me a lot about family life. Her teenage sons would notice that she was asleep and simply sit beside her bed reading their books, her husband would do the same. They gave off an atmosphere of calm family love. Next to her was a thirty-year-old woman whose stroke had affected her speech and the only word she could say was 'yes', but she put a lot of expression into that one word. Her large family took up every inch of her bed as they sat around her having hours of conversation with just the word 'yes'. The one man in the ward spoke only to the cleaning woman. They shouted to each other a whole stream of banter.

'Ah sure ye men are all too quick to get into the bed and be looked after'.

'Ah you're a hard woman'.

'Ah the women are always right. Even when they're wrong, they are right'.

When I walked across the ward in socks, the cleaner shouted:

'Get your shoes on. This floor is covered in germs'.

The handicapped girl had been moved up to our floor and she continued to shout 'fuck off' to all the nurses. During the week I was wheeled into many clinics and tested with many machines. In one particular waiting room the wall were covered in posters, stating cigarettes can kill, do you have multiple sclerosis, venereal disease, or if you think you are having a stroke, and a sweet little boy of about five said, 'look Daddy, lots of lovely stories ...'

Each visit, Dr O'Connor and his student assistant looked through my sketches and poems.

The CT brain scan's normal,
the lumber spine is worn,
the cholesterol level is far too high,
when three to five's the norm.
The blood count's very normal,
the kidney's normal too,
the liver seems to function well,
and the sugar levels too.
We'll wait for the fine tune MRI,
it's then we'll know the score
and a few more tests will see you through
so off on a trolley you'll go.
Down corridors blue with a dangling shoe

and into a very long spaceship,
do not panic I say to myself,
lie flat and still on this spaceship shelf.
Engine on – off like a bomb,
the rattling noise is shockingly strong.
An awful fear that things will go wrong
so I thought of this MRI wrapping song.
Go, go, go, go, go,
whatever, whatever, whatever,
you're wrong, you're wrong, you're wrong, you're wrong
no never, no never, no never,
you're strong, you're strong, you're strong, you're strong.
Whatever, whatever, whatever,
no, no, no, no.
No never, no never, no never,
go, go, go, go.
Be clever, be clever, be clever,
you're on your own
on a spaceship throne
forever, forever, forever.

THE ALZHEIMER'S ALPHABET

A's for Alzheimer's, Arthritis and Aches
B is for Boyles, Bypass and Breaks
C's for Cystitis, Coughs and Cramps
D for Dementia, Diarrhoea and Damps
E is for Earache, Eyesight and Eczema
F is for Fever, Farting and Fear
G is for Gastritis, Gallstones and Gripe
H for Hepatitis, Hallucination and Hype
I is Incontinence, Insomnia and Itch
J is for Jaundice, Jitters and Jits
K is for Keratosis, Kidney Failure and Krones
L for Lung Cancer, Lupus and Lumps on the Loins
M for Menopause, Meningitis and Mumps
N for Nausea, Neuritis, Nasal Drip and Nits
O for Obscenities, Obituary and Obesity
P is for Piles, Prostrate and Pleurisy

Q is for Queasiness, Quivers and Quits
R is for Ringworm, Rheumatism, Rigor Mortis and Ricketts
S is for Sciatica, Sties and Strepacarpas
T for Thrombosis, TB and Tinnitus
U for Urine, Uterinedyplasia and Ulcers
V is for Vaginitis, Varicose Veins and Vomiting
W is for Weakness, Warts and Wanting
X is for X-perts who can get it all wrong – X-ray
Y is for Yellow Fever, Yelling and Yuck
Z for Zimmerframe, Zero and Zucked

Spring comes again. Out of the ground comes new life, stiff with vigour and youth. The sun shines into Pat's loft bedroom. Each morning I go upstairs to join him, we have breakfast in bed, listen to the news and I sometimes sunbathe at the end of his bed with the doors open to the McGillicuddy Reeks. Pat enjoys this moment of the day and needs to be told what is happening for the rest of the day. I still limp and have a weak right leg. Dr O'Connor said expect two years or more to heal.

Five months after my stroke and we are in Tuscany. It is June 2013. Pat wanders around, puzzled but happy, looking at the vegetables and herbs that Holly and Luca grow, then chooses a place to sit under an olive tree. Luca has turned Barry's pigsty into a studio apartment. I had helped them to buy it when Barry died. Holly and Luca rent out part of the building to tourists. This time there was a family from Canada, two little girls around the age of 10. They were delighted with a basket of eggs that Luca had given them from all the hens. He had placed purple flowers around the pastel-coloured eggs. The two little girls walked from the hens looking with sentimental faces at their gift, Luca following looking equally sentimental. We were told later when their mother cracked open the first egg a chicken dropped out into the pancake mix. The poor chicken, the poor girls, what a shock they will never forget it. When Holly came back from the shops she shouted:

'Luca, *per que non vista le croche su uvo* / did you not see the hatching eggs had crosses on them?'

We closed the doors on Tuscany for a trip to the island of Elba where we were to meet Pat's relatives. We had booked into a hotel that overlooks a tiny beach full of umbrellas and little paddle boats. Everybody looked after Pat, his greatest wish was to go out in a boat. It was only a plastic paddle boat but Pat insisted that somebody had to be the captain. Luca was chosen to be Captain. Pat was right, that paddle boat did need a leader or we would have got tangled in various ropes and buoys. Even though Pat's back is rounded with age he slid down the plastic side of the boat and happily swam in the seas off Elba. Our meals were a huge affair of about 18 of us.

One day when we exited the dining room of the hotel, Pat thought we were on a ship and said:

'How lovely! A ship should have pots of flowers along its deck. I am going into the cabin now for a rest'.

Way back in 1992 when I returned from the South Seas having lived like a Maori, opera was the furthest thing from my mind. It seemed histrionic and unreal having lived with the islanders of Aitutaki, crab hunting, sleeping under the moon and the Southern Cross. So instead of meeting up with the Royal Opera House people in London I put my synopsis of the opera into the bottom drawer. Until one evening when driving back from Dublin I heard Ethna Tinney on Lyric FM talking of the composers Alma and Gustav Mahler that reignited an interest once more in the opera. I took the synopsis out of the bottom drawer for Ethna. She was fired with enthusiasm and so the process started. In 2013 it was performed. Having gone through stages and many title changes the composer that Ethna got to write the music was Raymond Deane and the libretto was by his friend Gavin Kostick. The two of them took many months before they announced they were finished.

The RTÉ Symphony Orchestra rehearsed the opera conducted by Fergus Sheil. Raymond Deane sat alone and aloof in the middle of the stalls and I sat in a high-up box sketching and listening. I felt that the music was over dramatic and needed a softness, such as a Viennese waltz to contrast the drama of Raymond's composition. He nodded without words when I said this. I felt cut off from the whole project. However to my delight Fergus asked me to write a piece for the programme on how the opera came about. When all was ready for the performance in the National Concert Hall, Poppy and I travelled to Dublin by train. We never let any of our friends know of the performance. We took our seats. The opera was beautifully produced, projecting my artwork on a large screen behind the singers and orchestra and I began to feel included. The conductor's arms lifted, the opera started. Yes, it was a Viennese waltz and it moved along and embraced the audience with its power and magic. I was thrilled to the core.

The director Ronan O'Leary came with his camera and arranged that the Yellow Man doll should be sitting in the audience for the opera. He filmed the doll from behind, the two antennae looked very witty sticking up with the stage in the background. This linked up with Maurice Galway's *Yellow Man Grey Man* film and Ronan's piece on the birthplace of the Yellow Man, filmed in Tuscany.

During the interval it was exciting to meet Raymond, his brother and Gavin. We were buoyed by the creativity of it all. I wished that I had had the confidence to have let my friends know about this magnificent opera, which I hope in time will be performed again.

'You are invited by President Michael D. Higgins and Sabina Higgins to a party of creative people at Áras an Uachtaráin'.

The invitation stated not to arrive more than ten minutes early or ten minutes late. The crisp weather iced my face as I walked from Dawson Street and picked up a taxi, driving through the Phoenix Park to the big main gates. There was a shuttle bus and many cars. We were in fact all too early. The gate man invited me and four other guests into the gate hut as the taxis had to go. A shuttle bus eventually came and filled up with long-haired men and women with skull caps and arty capes. There was the artists Brian Bourke and his wife Jay, Mary Coughlan, singers, comedians, poets and writers, a queue of laughing confident people. Sabina and Michael D. opened their arms with a warm hug and kiss for all of us.

'Your book is in our reception room for all to look at', he said.

There were rows of trays laden with wines and water. A girl with pitch-black hair, tied in a tight bun, was a singer who had been the subject of a series of paintings by Brian Bourke.

The party went on until well after twelve. One of the musicians was fed up that he hadn't brought his drums as one after another got up and improvised a piece of music, poetry, a song or a piece on the penny whistle.

'Come, said Mary Alice, their daughter, 'to the kitchen and we will find something to do as a drum'.

Out they came with wooden spoons and a great big saucepan. The crack was mighty. I was so proud that the President of Ireland and his wife twirled us around the floor and stayed up with us without pomp and ceremony.

Throughout the party there was a serious-looking soldier who kept her eye on the President and his wife. The rest of the staff were laughing and tapping their feet but not her – she had the important security job of minding the President and his wife at this huge party.

The flow of paintings for my 80th birthday exhibition taking place on 4 September 2015 is really exciting. I can't fully understand myself yet, I'm letting it flow. It is later that the meaning of a painting will dawn on me but while it's being done it comes from some unknown area – a dark hole in the back of my head. If I intellectualise it will actually close the doors on that unknown dark area.

Some years ago my lovely friend, Jackie Dutton, came to visit me as I was to do a portrait of her. She would read aloud while posing; the book was called *Women who Run with the Wolves* by Clarisa Pinkola Estes. The first legend that Estes analysed was the Bluebeard legend.

That story has stayed somewhere in the back of my head since Jackie read it to me. Bluebeard was a charismatic rich lord with a long flowing blue-black beard, a quiet mysterious man. He owned a castle and had many servants and horses. The youngest of three sisters fell in love with Bluebeard. The two older sisters tried to warn her against Bluebeard but she was captivated by his charm, riches and good looks. Shortly after their marriage he told her he was going away for a short trip, saying to her that she could have a party and the cooks could throw a banquet for her. She could use the horses and do anything she wanted. Then he handed her a bunch of keys, one of which he warned:

'You must not use this key'.

After he left the three sisters ran from door to door throughout the castle using each of the keys, and when they came to the forbidden key the young bride could not resist opening the door. To all their horror the room was full of bones, corpses and blood. Try as she may to clean the key they could not stop it from bleeding. On

Bluebeard's return he noticed that the special key was blood stained. He became enraged and proceeded to try and murder her. There is many a key that we don't or can't open to the one we love. Many a mystery lies within but the wisest wants to know what the key is hiding, in my opinion. I enjoy asking my friends what they would do if they were handed the bunch of keys. Some of the answers were:

'I would not dream of opening the door. My husband knows what I should or should not see'.

'Sure, of course I'd open the door. I wouldn't be able to resist'.

Two male friends said, 'I would bore a hole through the wall and not use the key or I would ask one of the staff to open the door'.

Poppy said if her husband could not explain the key, she would not want to live with him.

Added to the Bluebeard legend, Conor gave me a copy of *National Geographic* with an article on the wild men of Europe who dressed themselves in amazing disguises, covering up the person within. The antics that these men get away with are done anonymously as they are in heavy disguise.

My paintings depict smitten brides with these hidden men.

The latest media I've tried is drawing with light – as depicted on the cover of this book. It was Veronica Nicholson's idea that she should photograph me in the darkened studio. She gave me a small bright torch which I held in my right hand. It was such a pleasure to dance, creating this image. It was supposed to be the Yellow Man but it turned out more like a cat. Picasso once painted with light. He tried everything, I love that.

It is summer 2015; life is busy with painting for my 80th birthday exhibition on 4 September 2015 and finishing writing this book. I continue to recover from my stroke, though still have weakness and dizzy spells. I am healthy and sometimes think I could live for another 80 years. I'm like a young woman pulled back by an old woman. I can't wait for this exhibition and book to be done so I can start something new.

Pat is still baffled with Alzheimer's, but thankfully has wonderful support in our house from the caring and intelligent Seamus, Eliza and Betty. Last month, the whole family stayed with Holly, Luca, Chiara and Giada in our beautiful Tuscan place, loving the heat, the fruits and the neighbours. Pat was able to swim, reminding us of all his earlier vitality. Over there I took a break from the writing of this book, yet got excited to create some new illustrations to add to ones from my sketchbooks.

In July, Ben, our golden retriever, struggled to walk out the door to where he would normally piss; the grass turning green after his antibiotics. He panted all night long for 2 nights. The vet examined him and judging by the x-rays said the outlook was poor. Seamus drove Pat, Ben and I to the veterinary hospital where the compassionate vet didn't take Ben out of the car, but shaved a patch off his left leg and injected him; his head dropped into death immediately. At home Adam, Aran and Poppy dug a four-foot deep grave by the magnolia tree. Hopefully the tree will enjoy living off Ben now.

I have had a full and interesting life so far, despite not having had a father in my life and never feeling the need for one, whether it was Corbett Bewick or the 19 year old. But this summer, along with my sister Hazel's daughter Julia, we decided to take a DNA test to see who I came from. We spat a yucky spit into a bottle and so far the results say my mother Harry is distantly related to Meryl Streep! I'll look forward to sharing the news when all the results are in one day. Life goes on in the beautiful now.

County Kerry
18 August 2015

ACKNOWLEDGEMENTS

Publisher Alan Hayes suggested that I write my life story; he inspired me to have a go but stressed that the book be written by me and in my own voice. Since I have dyslexia I asked my very good and witty friend and neighbour, Helena Golden, to work with me typing my words. Francis Joy and Fiona McCormack also helped. We had a ball.

I don't look back – the odd time little replays (like a smell that brings to mind the steps of a house in the village of Gaiole-in-Chianti or the taste of mango brings back the South Seas) might flow to mind, odd insignificant past moments and memories. In fact pondering in the past seems a sad thing to do. It's to live in the moment, the now. So while working on this book I closed my eyes and felt the past become the present as I told my story.

The first words of this book started on a sunny flower-laden flat roof of an apartment in the pretty village of Puerto de Mogán in the Gran Canaries. It was our friends Marie Claire Stacey and Sylvia Harvey who suggested that we mix work with fun in the sun. During our stay we would take off on an adventure out to sea or in a jeep to see the island. This book was written during wonderful trips around the Canaries and in Kerry.

Thanks to Pat Melia for his long-term memory and one-liners. ('Are those your own teeth, Pat?' 'I sincerely hope so'). To Veronica Nicholson, photographer; Conor Mulvihill; Poppy Mulvihill; Holly Melia.

Yoga at Mogan